THE
BREAKTHROUGH
IMPERATIVE

How the Best Managers
Get Outstanding Results

Mark Gottfredson and Steve Schaubert
BAIN & COMPANY, INC.

WITH JOHN CASE AND KATH TSAKALAKIS

Collins
An Imprint of HarperCollinsPublishers

FIRST EDITION

Designed by Kris Tobiassen

Library of Congress Cataloging-in-Publication Data

Gottfredson, Mark.
   The breakthrough imperative : how the best managers get outstanding results /
by Mark Gottfredson and Steve Schaubert with John Case and Kath Tsakalakis.—1st ed.
      p.   cm.
   Includes bibliographical references.
   ISBN 978-0-06-135814-2
   1. Organizational effectiveness.   2. Management.   3. Success in business.
I. Schaubert, Steve.   II. Title.
   HD58.9.G68 2008
   658.4'09—dc22   2007037658

08   09   10   11   12   DIX/RRD   10   9   8   7   6   5   4   3   2   1

We dedicate this book to the clients we have each served for more than twenty-five years—men and women who applied their unique managerial styles and skills with insight, courage, and commitment.

—MARK GOTTFREDSON
AND STEVE SCHAUBERT

Acknowledgments

WE HAVE BEEN HUMBLED AND INSPIRED BY THE PROCESS OF BUILD-
ing this book. Our initial idea—to codify the fundamentals of dramatic
performance improvement and tell the stories of top managers who have
put those fundamentals to work with resounding results—seemed straightforward enough.

But the process of analyzing a broad set of company results to identify
top organizations and their managers became a revelation. Clearly, today's
general managers in all types of organizations are up against increasingly
formidable odds when they tackle a turnaround or attempt to transform
operations. Customer needs are changing faster than ever before. Globalization and geopolitics have added risk and complexity to basic decisions,
such as where to procure raw materials, assemble product, and recruit talent. Emerging economies are fostering new competitors with cost positions that are challenging organizations worldwide to remain competitive.
And the general manager has less time than ever before to make his or her
mark—about three years. In this context, the organizations that rose to the
top, and the managers who powered them, are even greater heroes than
we initially believed. So first and foremost, we thank those we interviewed
for sharing their journeys. Your stories are an invaluable guide to us and to
others.

We also want to thank another set of heroes: our colleagues at Bain &
Company who have probed and studied many of the fundamentals that
have become a top manager's "four laws." A special thanks to Chris Zook,

Bain author of three growth strategy books—*Profit from the Core*; *Beyond the Core*; and *Unstoppable*—for his careful review of our own efforts and helpful suggestions. His insights on costs, customers, and the quest for profitable growth inform aspects of all of our laws. We also thank Vijay Vishwanath, the father of "High Road, Low Road" thinking on market share and brand strategy, first captured in the 1997 *Harvard Business Review* article "Your Brand's Best Strategy." This thinking informs our second law. Rob Markey has given us extremely valuable input on the intricacies of customer segmentation strategies and tactics, and we are grateful for his contributions.

We thank our chairman Orit Gadiesh and former colleague Jim Gilbert for their work elucidating Bain's thinking on profit pools, which appeared in two *Harvard Business Review* articles in 1998 and underpins our third law. Thanks to Keith Aspinall, a coauthor of the 2005 *Harvard Business Review* feature "Innovation vs. Complexity," the basis of our fourth law. And to Paul Rogers and Marcia Blenko, authors of the *Harvard Business Review* feature "Who Has the D?" for their thinking on stripping the complexity out of organizational processes and decision making.

Loyalty guru and Bain fellow Fred Reichheld's metric for, and approach to, creating advocates among customers—the Net Promoter® Score—forms an important part of diagnosing your company's point of departure, the topic of chapter 6. And colleagues Todd Senturia, Lori Flees, and Manny Maceda have dedicated significant energy codifying our approach to change management, which appears in chapter 8.

Jeff Bradach and Nan Stone, our confreres at the Bridgespan Group, Bain's sister consultancy to nonprofits, helped us identify relevant organizations to study in the nonprofit sector.

Truly, we stand on the shoulders of giants.

Also, special thanks to our team of researchers and editors who captured the findings and stories. In particular, we thank researchers Tony Horsley, Genia Jacques, Eric Lee, and research director Kath Tsakalakis, all of whom supported the project throughout its development (in some cases, for several years). Working alongside them for significant stretches were Blake Apel, Riccardo Bertocco, Erin Billman, Adam Burgh, Melissa Burke, Angela Chou, Simoina Dargan, Emilia Fallas, Stephen Garrison,

Michael Heinrich, Wren Kabir, Angeliki Kasi, Brandon Luna, Maggie McArthur, Jesse Stuckey, Molly Tapias, Ben Tseng, Eric Weiner, and Chris Wolfe. Thank you all.

We also thank our editorial team, including our agent, David Miller, who guided our book proposal and found it a good home, and John Case, whose writing brought both the laws and the stories to life. Bain's publisher Katie Smith Milway guided the manuscript's development with our publisher HarperCollins; our core team at HarperCollins, including editor Ethan Friedman and marketing director Angie Lee, gave us good counsel along the way. Bain's quality control team shouldered the critical task of checking every fact and quote, and we thank managing editor Elaine Cummings, manuscript editors Maggie Locher and Jitendra Pant, fact checker Cassidy Healzer, editorial assistants Samantha Peck and Megan Miller, and the Bain Capability Center.

In addition, Bain's marketing partner, Wendy Miller, and her entire marketing group have been invaluable allies.

Finally, we thank our executive assistants, Irene Faustino, Allison Ramsey, and Nancy Taylor, for their tireless help, scheduling the many CEO interviews and helping with our travel. They put up with us day in and day out, in the best of times and the worst of times.

Contents

THE
BREAKTHROUGH
IMPERATIVE

ONE

The Two Keys to Breakthrough Results

You only have to do a very few things right . . . so long as you don't do too many things wrong.

—WARREN BUFFETT

GARY DICAMILLO TOOK OVER POLAROID CORPORATION IN 1995. It was his first job as CEO, but he was hardly inexperienced. He had gone to Harvard Business School and built a successful career. Before coming to Polaroid he was a high-ranking executive at Black & Decker, charged with turning around the company's power tool division. Though trained as a chemical engineer, he described himself as a "consumer products guy." The press portrayed him as smart, likable, and decisive.

Polaroid's board knew that the company faced some strategic challenges. Its signature instant cameras weren't the big hit that they had once been. Digital photography was coming down the pike fast, threatening traditional film-based cameras. But the right CEO with the right strategy, the board believed, could turn things around and lead the company into a profitable digital future. After all, Polaroid had been conducting intensive research and development on digital imaging for nearly fifteen years. Its image-sensor technology and image-compression algorithms were highly advanced, and were protected by several key patents. It even had a professional-grade digital camera, the PDC-2000, ready for production. When the camera came out in March 1996, it won rave reviews from analysts and photography experts.

But though Polaroid seemed to know where its future lay, it wasn't able to get there. The reason is clear in hindsight: though the company had great R&D, it didn't have the other capabilities required to execute a winning digital strategy. Five years later, Polaroid's business was a shambles, and the company filed for the protection of bankruptcy court. Its digital cameras were doing poorly in the marketplace. Its instant camera and film sales were continuing to decline. Polaroid was eventually acquired by a Midwestern holding company, Petters Group Worldwide, which owns a variety of consumer brands.

IN LATE 2002, WARREN KNOWLTON TOOK OVER A COMPANY CALLED Morgan Crucible, a 150-year-old UK-based manufacturer of carbon, ceramics, and other industrial components. Like DiCamillo, Knowlton was assuming the role of CEO for the first time. And he, too, was an experienced executive. He had spent twenty years with Owens Corning and five with Pilkington, the big international glass manufacturer.

Morgan in late 2002 was in far worse shape than Polaroid in 1995. Sales had declined for three straight years. Profits had vanished. Debt was high, and pension liabilities were three times the company's market capitalization. The banks were growing nervous. So were shareholders: Morgan's stock price had declined 90 percent between 1997 and 2002.

And yet, only three and a half years later, Knowlton had executed a transformation. By mid-2006, Morgan's continuing businesses had registered 5 to 6 percent revenue growth for three straight years. Operating margins were more than three times what they had been when Knowlton arrived. The company had paid down its debt and secured its pension fund. The share price had risen more than tenfold, and analysts were once more issuing "buy" recommendations.

ONE COMPANY THAT SHOULD HAVE SUCCEEDED BUT DIDN'T. Another that seemed destined for failure but turned itself around. Two smart, experienced, and capable leaders. What accounts for the difference?

We will try to answer that question in this book, and not just for Polaroid and Morgan Crucible. Rather, we want to use these two companies and many others to dissect the challenge of improving an organization's performance. We want to highlight the lessons learned by leaders who have run the management gauntlet, who have learned to achieve results for their companies as they rose through the ranks. We hope to distill the best of their insights and experience for other CEOs, especially those new to the job, and for every up-and-coming general manager who may aspire to the corner office.

Our aim is not to convey new strategies; rather, it is to articulate a short list of business fundamentals that are essential to performance improvement, and then show how to apply them. Staying focused on the fundamentals takes enormous discipline. Whenever new leaders take over the reins of a business unit or indeed any kind of organization, they face a daunting list of tasks. They find they must spend time with other managers in the company, with key customers and suppliers, and with the company's financiers. They must simultaneously look to the future and run the day-to-day business. If the company is public, the new general manager will feel the pressure of reporting quarterly results. If it's a private company, a division of a corporation, or a nonprofit, the pressure will still be there—it will just come from investors, bosses, or donors, who will expect answers about cash flow and covenants and forecasts. Knowing what to do and in what sequence can become an overwhelming challenge, particularly since everything initially appears so urgent.

Today the pressure on managers is more intense than ever. The average price-to-earnings ratio on Wall Street and other global exchanges has generally been climbing for thirty years. Companies find that they must deliver increasing levels of growth and profitability or leave themselves vulnerable to takeover. Top executives facing this clamor for performance naturally expect quick results from everybody under them. Managers throughout the organization "have to perform or perish," said CEO John A. Challenger of the outplacement firm Challenger, Gray & Christmas, which tracks managerial tenure. "If you don't produce immediate results, you just don't have much room to move."[1]

One sign of the increased pressure is that nobody gets much time to show what he or she can do. Between 1999 and 2006 the average tenure of departing chief executive officers in the United States declined from about ten years to just over eight.[2] The distribution is bimodal: about 20 percent of CEOs have very long tenures (the average is twenty-three years for this segment), and about 40 percent last an average of less than two years. (In 2006, median tenure of departing CEOs was five and a half years, well below the average.) And it isn't just CEOs who face this kind of time bind: the job tenure of chief financial officers, chief operating officers, chief marketing officers, and division general managers is even shorter than that of CEOs, and now stands at around three years, on average. *BusinessWeek* in early 2007 wrote about several high-level managers whose tenures lasted less than a year. "The brutal reality," said the magazine, "is that executives have less time than ever to prove their worth."[3]

So there is the challenge: nearly every CEO and general manager today is expected by his or her stakeholders to achieve new breakthroughs in performance. Those who don't make visible progress toward that goal within the first year or two may find themselves looking for another job. It is precisely because of this growing breakthrough imperative that general managers today need to get off to a fast start. They don't have time for mistakes, or for going back and redoing what they should have done right in the first place.

Despite the intensity of these pressures, despite the high expectations and short time frames, a number of CEOs and general managers turn in truly exceptional results.

Warren Knowlton is one example, but there are plenty of others. Three years after Bill McDermott came on board as the new CEO of SAP Americas and Asia Pacific Japan, the division had more than doubled its core business, adding seventeen points of share in the market for integrated business software. Under chief executive Idris Jala, Malaysia Airlines went from near-insolvency to profitability in less than a year. When Kathleen Ligocki took over Ford of Mexico, the division was expected to lose $89 million in the year she arrived. At the end of the year it had *made* $200 million—a turnaround of nearly $300 million compared to what had been projected. In the world of private equity, John Chidsey and his team reversed a long decline in Burger King's fortunes, while Gerald (Jerry) Storch launched a promising turnaround at Toys "R" Us. Comparable achievements can be found in the nonprofit world. Wendy Kopp of Teach For America, for instance, created an ambitious growth plan that took the organization from 4,000 applicants a year to 18,000, and from 1,000 teachers to 5,000, while simultaneously putting it on a firm financial footing. Great managers in any organization "want to chart [its] destiny," says Ligocki, "and somehow have the strength to perform under the pressure that it takes to do that."

Accomplishments like these raise a whole series of questions. Can outstanding performance really be traced to one great manager and the team he or she assembles? If so, what makes those people successful? What do they know that others don't? Can other managers learn their secrets?

Much has been written about what makes great leaders, and we agree that a successful general manager must have the attributes and skills of a great leader. But by the time people get to be general managers, they have necessarily exhibited leadership abilities and a talent for running organizations. They have beaten out dozens of competitors, risen through the ranks, taken on more and more responsibility. And yet many still don't succeed. So leadership attributes, while necessary, are not sufficient to explain managers' relative performance.

Similarly, much has been written about the attributes of "great" or "excellent" companies. But our concern is different. We wanted to study how general managers can achieve breakthrough results as they tackle the task of running any business. It may be easier if they find themselves in companies that regularly and consistently outperform the competition. But we want to help them meet the challenge even if they find themselves in average or underperforming organizations.

UNCOVERING THE KEYS TO SUCCESS

In a nutshell, what we found is that successful general managers seem to rely on two keys to success. One is that they have a deep understanding of the fundamental laws of business. Because of that, they see things others don't, do things others won't even consider, and avoid the mistakes that can trap even the best leaders. The other key is that they identify and follow a clear path to performance improvement, based on an assessment of their organization's full potential. They know how to use the fundamentals to diagnose their starting point accurately, craft a realistic and compelling set of objectives, and map out a trajectory from one to the other. Neither one—understanding the fundamentals nor following the path—is enough by itself. It is the combination that enables strong execution and leads to success.

To uncover these keys to success, we drew partly on our combined fifty-plus years of consulting experience. We have seen and worked with many great managers over the years. We have also seen how companies can get themselves into trouble.

In addition, we drew on extensive research into corporate performance, both our own research and that of our colleagues at Bain & Company.

One set of studies, for instance, was originally conducted by our partner Chris Zook, author of a trilogy of books titled *Profit from the Core*, *Beyond the Core*, and *Unstoppable*.[4] Zook compiled a database tracking the performance of 1,804 public companies in the G8 economies over ten years. His three books help companies understand when to focus on their core business, when to look for adjacencies to expand the core, and when the core must be redefined.

We used the latest version of Zook's database to focus on a different set of concerns, namely the role of individual managers in improving a company's performance. First, we took the 202 companies in the database that maintained profitable growth of at least 5.5 percent a year over the ten-year period ending in 2005, a group Zook had labeled "sustained-value creators." (See appendix 1 for the exact criteria that put a company into this elite category.) Next, we examined the tenure of the 413 CEOs leading these companies during this period, and we compared the stock

FIGURE 1.1

Analysis of Company Stock Price Performance During CEO Tenure

Porsche Outperformed the Broader Country Index by
8 to 1 During CEO Dr. Wiedeking's Tenure

Source: Bloomberg; "Can this man turn Porsche around?" by Tan Bah Bah, *The Straits Times*, May 15, 1994; company Web site

performance under each leader with a broader index. Figure 1.1 illustrates the approach, using Porsche as an example. From the beginning of Dr. Wendelin Wiedeking's tenure in mid-1993 until December 2005, Porsche outperformed the CDAX index in Germany by a factor of eight.

Overall, we found that for the first six months of a CEO's tenure, these companies' average stock performance tracked the relevant index almost exactly: the ratio was about 1.1 to 1. Performance then crept up steadily, but not until nearly six years after the CEO took office was the company outperforming the index by an average of 2 to 1. It took the full average tenure of nine years for these companies to outperform by 3 to 1, as shown in figure 1.2.

So we knew that one individual could make a big difference over time. But how could general managers get better results more quickly? What specific practices make some more successful in just two or three years than peers with equally stellar track records and leadership attributes?

To answer these questions, we turned from study to experience. We

FIGURE 1.2

Under a New CEO, Sustained-Value Performance Increases With Tenure

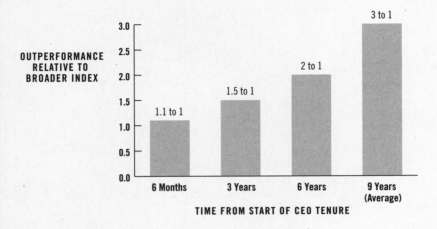

Source: Bain analysis, research on CEO tenures

interviewed more than forty leaders from industry and the nonprofit sector, most of whom had held multiple general-manager positions en route to CEO. Many were people we or our colleagues had come to know in the course of our work. Many others came from our search for successful general managers. We spoke with leaders from companies as diverse as Northrop Grumman Ship Systems, Burger King, the Australian telephone company Telstra, and the Vienna-based plastics company Borealis. We interviewed people who had turned in exceptional performance in the past, such as Paul Fulton—the man who introduced L'eggs pantyhose, one of the blockbuster consumer products of all time. We talked with leaders of business units, such as Ligocki, and of nonprofit organizations, including Teach For America's Kopp and Jim Yong Kim of Partners In Health, the pathbreaking international organization cofounded by Paul Farmer. We interviewed the mayor of Providence, Rhode Island, who has done much to turn around that city's government in a short period of time. We also studied (through public sources) the success of several dozen other managers, and we have included some of their stories here. The stock-price performance of the CEOs we feature outperformed relevant indices on average by 5 to 1, substantially more than the baseline of the sustained-value creators.

All of this study revealed a striking commonality in successful general managers' approach to their task. Like engineers designing a mission to Mars, they understand and apply the basic laws that govern what they do. Using those basics, they map out where they are starting from, where they are going, and how they plan to get there. And then they actually do it.

FOUR LAWS

Let's continue the Mars analogy for just a moment, because it will help you understand exactly what you will learn from this book. Engineers designing a mission to Mars need to know many different things, and they need to have many different skills. But if the mission is to succeed, they all must know and apply the basics. They must understand the laws of gravitation and of motion. They must understand the laws of rocket propulsion. They must understand the principles that allow remote communication with, and control of, a spacecraft.

So it is with business. Business may not be rocket science, but it is complex. You and your competitors have an infinite number of moves and countermoves at your disposal, and it's always hard to see out beyond the next few moves. And not just that—to implement your moves, you must somehow lead an entire organization, often involving tens or hundreds of thousands of people, in the direction you have mapped out. Depending on your situation and your industry, you are likely to need expert knowledge of sales and marketing, of operations management, of information technology, of financial techniques, and of many other specialized skills. At times you will need breakthrough ideas and new, cutting-edge tools—ideas and tools that you can find in any number of books and articles. But if you don't understand and master the fundamentals, that more advanced knowledge won't help you much. You'd resemble a would-be rocket scientist aiming at Mars without taking into account that the planet is in motion.

The more we considered our research and experience, and the more we pressure-tested our hypotheses in interviews, the more we came to be-

lieve that four laws provide most of the fundamental knowledge necessary to guide a successful manager's initial diagnosis and path to success. Why four laws rather than three or five or six? The tests we used
were these: when we encountered a success—particularly a success that
couldn't be explained by a breakthrough product or some other source
of good fortune—did the responsible manager seem to be applying all
four laws diligently? Did interviewees say they aimed to apply the laws?
Was there some other reason for success that these four fundamentals couldn't account for? When we encountered underperformance,
could it be chalked up to a misunderstanding of one or more laws, or else
a failure to apply the laws aggressively using the simple path-to-success
model? In short, did the four laws explain most of the results we were
investigating?

Like any human endeavor, business has iconoclastic situations, the exceptions that prove the rule. But the rules we developed were robust and
predictive. In our interviews, nearly every case of superior performance
that we encountered reflected a manager's deep knowledge of these four
laws and the development of a path to success guided by them. Further-
more, most cases of underperformance could be traced to a manager's failure to understand one or more of the laws, or to apply them accurately and
aggressively. Other important fundamentals were certainly mentioned,
but not with the same frequency as the four we chose. We conducted an
in-depth analysis of a randomly selected group of 225 CEOs who left their
companies in 2006. Eighty-five of this group left or were fired for underperformance. (The others retired, went through a planned transition, or
left for other reasons, such as ethics violations.) Of the eighty-five, we
found that 91 percent of the cases could be traced back to a failure to heed
one or more of the four laws (see appendix 1). Knowing the laws and their
ramifications seemed to be the hallmark of a great manager.

In calling these laws the fundamentals, we don't intend to imply a halo
effect—that managers and companies that uphold them never stumble.[5]
Nor do we mean to imply that everybody already knows them and just
needs a reminder. In fact, while some of the concepts have been around
for a while, they are frequently misunderstood and misused. Managers
forget them. Business schools may give them only cursory attention. This

is surprising to us. It would be like a soccer coach not running fundamental footwork and passing drills. Indeed, though they are experienced businesspeople, our clients often find that the four laws provide much or most of the insight they need to clarify their options and help them make their toughest decisions.

Here is a brief summary of the four laws, along with some questions to test your own mastery of the fundamentals relating to your business.

Law 1: Costs and Prices Always Decline

Some MBA students (not all) learn the tool known as the experience curve, a downward-sloping curve that shows the relationship between accumulated experience in an industry and the long-term decline in costs and prices (expressed in constant dollars). The experience curve takes a commonsense observation—the more often a task is done, the less it should cost to do it—and gives it mathematical expression, hence predictive power. But even those who learn the tool in the classroom seldom apply it rigorously in their businesses. And many managers have an incomplete understanding of the nuanced competitive economics that define their business, so they set targets based on the wrong curve.

The experience curve works in almost all situations. If a company doesn't obey it, at least one of its competitors invariably does; the competitor can therefore lower its prices and attract customers from others. The experience curve is the general principle that makes sense of such familiar ideas as Moore's Law (the notion that the number of transistors on a chip doubles roughly every two years) and Clayton Christensen's concept of disruptive innovation. The experience curve also helps to explain some of the most dramatic economic developments of the last few decades. Japanese auto makers, for example, could not compete with U.S. companies at first. But they aggressively managed to the experience curve, pushing down costs and raising levels of performance over time. Their cost-and-performance curves crossed those of America's Big Three around 1972, and Detroit has never caught up.

Great managers apply the experience curve correctly. Do you know what the prices of your major products or services are likely to be five years from now? Do you know how your own cost trends compare with the price curve—and how your competitors' cost trends compare? Is there a price umbrella in your industry—and if so, might it collapse? When? What are the potential ramifications for your company?

Law 2: Competitive Position Determines Your Options

Managers have to make choices about which levers to pull to improve performance. But too many do so in a vacuum. Performance-improvement strategies are successful when they reflect a company's position in the market and rely on specific insights as to which actions can improve it in the eyes of the company's customers.

One of the most powerful ways to chart your own and your competitors' positions in a market is to map where you fall on a simple chart. The chart shows return on assets or another measure of economic performance against relative market share—your share divided by the share of your largest competitor if you are not the leader, or by the share of the number-two company if you are number one. Plot these two indicators against each other and you find that companies line up in a handful of typical positions, each with its own opportunities and vulnerabilities (we will discuss this chart in detail in chapter 3). Among other things, this chart shows how market leaders usually earn disproportionate returns, and what you have to do if you are not a market leader. Jack Welch began his term as CEO of General Electric by slashing costs—that's when he was known as "Neutron Jack"—and thus driving every business down to where it should be on the experience curve. Then he developed his famous strategy that GE should be number one or number two in every business in which it competed. These two approaches together accounted for much of GE's extraordinary success under Welch.

Great managers know where they fall on the chart and what it implies for their performance-improvement options. Do you know your relative market share for each of your major businesses? Do you understand the inherent possibilities and constraints that your competitive position creates? Do you know how to improve your position using both customer insight and market power and influence (a concept central to Zook's book

Profit from the Core)? Do you know your competitors' market positions, and are you therefore able to assess the likely strategies that they will follow? How could their actions disadvantage you, and how can you disadvantage them?

Law 3: Customers and Profit Pools Don't Stand Still

Who are your competitors, really? Dell obviously competes with Hewlett-Packard, Lenovo/IBM, and Gateway in personal computers and accessories, and it is a leader in that market. But look at the entire value chain in this business and you get a different perspective. Much of the profit in this chain flows to chip suppliers such as Intel and Advanced Micro Devices (AMD), and to software suppliers, such as Microsoft. Intel and Microsoft may be Dell's partners, but they also compete for profits in the overall industry. We call the analysis of the total profit made by you, your competitors, and other players in the value chain "profit-pool analysis." Aggressive general managers constantly try to protect existing pools and take over or create new profit pools. So, of course, do their competitors.

The challenge in this kind of competition is that the profit pool is always shifting. A primary reason is that customers' preferences and behaviors are always changing, either because they grow dissatisfied with what they are currently buying, or because an innovative company learns how to offer them better value. If you were to map your industry's profit pool ten years ago, say, and compare it with a similar map today, the comparison would almost certainly show dramatic changes in the distribution of profits by competitor. A profit-pool map five or ten years from now probably won't look much like today's, either. The maps would also help to explain the reasons behind the changes. Profit pools shift, but they don't shift randomly. They shift in predictable directions as customers' tastes and behaviors change, and as other forces in the marketplace (or outside of it) exert their influence. What's more, a company's share of the profit pool is seldom exactly proportional to its share of revenue in the value chain. This counterintuitive notion has powerful implications for how you compete for profits.

Great managers anticipate profit-pool shifts and plan their strategies and tactics accordingly. Do you know your share of the relevant profit pool and the shares of your key competitors, suppliers, and customers? Have you rigorously identified shifts in your industry's profit pools during the past several years and likely future shifts? Can you identify the factors that are leading customers to change their preferences and behaviors? Have you planned a series of actions to take advantage of these changes and capture a larger share of the relevant pools for your organization?

Law 4: Simplicity Gets Results

Hal Sperlich is a legend in automotive circles: he led product teams that created both the original Ford Mustang and the first minivan for Chrysler. Both were runaway hits with car buyers, generating billions of dollars in profit for their makers. The key insight of Sperlich and his team was that if you build products that stand out on just three dimensions, your products need only be competitive on all the other dimensions. The insight came from observing that customers who were asked why they bought a particular vehicle could seldom remember more than three criteria, even immediately after making the purchase decision. Find the right three things for the customers you're aiming at, make your vehicle a unique and innovative standout along those dimensions, and you have a winner.

Sperlich's insight applies to individual products; it also applies to product lines, processes, and the organization itself. Human beings can't effectively focus on more than three or four things at once. A company with too many products and options drives up costs and confuses its customers. A simple "Model T" analysis—creating a picture of costs and revenues as if you made just one standard product, then adding options back in one at a time—can reveal where the incremental costs of more products or more-complex processes outweigh the benefits. An organization with too many layers of management will probably be unable to take quick action, even when the need for action is obvious. A diagram of managerial spans, layers, and decision making can show exactly where an organization may be too complex for its own good.

Great managers keep it simple. Do you know how the number of products or services you offer compares to competitors? Do you understand the full systemic costs of product and process complexity in your organization and how it affects your revenues? How many layers are there between the CEO and the lowest-level employee? Can most people in your company or organization describe your critical action initiatives during a six-floor elevator ride?

THESE FOUR LAWS AREN'T PRESCRIPTIONS. THEY ARE DESCRIPtions of the way business works. They provide the context and constraints in which managers must operate. Managers can't afford to ignore them; if they do, they will lose customers. Knowing the laws and all their many implications is the first step on the road to making yourself a great manager.

These laws depend on, and reflect, a fundamental fact of business, which is that if you don't have any customers you don't have any business. The laws are powerful precisely because each one describes how to meet your customers' needs in ways that are superior to your competition. Driving your costs and prices down the experience curve enables you to provide greater value to your customers as measured by cost, quality, or features. An attempt to change your market position will succeed if and only if you can persuade customers to vote for your product more often with their checkbooks. Your profit pools will shift most often because customers move their business to those who provide greater value. And as we shall see, simplification entails great risk unless you understand your customers intimately.

So customers and their needs are tightly woven into everything we have to say in this book. This is a central theme because customers are your ultimate boss. They will judge all that you do, and they will make their decisions accordingly. Great managers know that everything begins and ends with an understanding of customer needs and perspectives on value.

THE PATH TO SUCCESS

A theoretical physicist might understand all the laws necessary to build a spacecraft to Mars, yet have no idea how to construct one. Great managers must not only know the laws, they must be able to put them to work. They must organize a team that includes everyone necessary to make the mission succeed. They must create performance-improvement plans based on the laws and get the organization to implement them, all in a relatively short time.

This is where our simple path to success comes in. The easiest way to understand the path is to break it down into its component parts.

New CEOs or general managers always inherit an organization that is headed in a particular direction. It has strengths and weaknesses, and it faces threats and opportunities. The existing condition of the company as determined by the four laws is the *point of departure*. Diagnosing the point of departure is the new manager's first and most urgent task: it should set his or her agenda for the first 100 days or so. This is the first place the laws prove their worth. In effect, they define what the new manager needs to know in this process. Where are the company's prices and costs headed, for example? What is its competitive position in each major product line and customer segment? We will show you how to conduct a *"full-potential performance-improvement diagnostic process"* that compares your company's position against competitors and against its own best practices, both current and historical. (In the book we will often shorten this mouthful to "full-potential diagnostic" or simply "the diagnostic.") This kind of robust data-based diagnosis allows you to assess the *true potential* of your business. It lays the groundwork for better performance by showing where the company stands on the four critical dimensions.

New managers presumably also have a set of objectives in mind, usually derived from the expectations of their stakeholders. These are the goals that they want to accomplish in the time they have. The goals might include boosting the organization's growth, increasing customer satisfaction, beating the competition, and increasing profitability or shareholder value. Whatever the goals may be, they define the manager's *point of arrival.* Developing and honing the point of arrival, then building consensus around it, is his or her next job. The point of arrival has to be big, ambitious, and inspiring—a set of objectives that get people fired up and eager for the fray. Yet it must also be specific, realistic, and attainable. It must be a set of objectives that can be rigorously tracked and monitored. The four laws help frame a point of arrival that meets these criteria, and help show how to reach it.

Finally, managers will also be devising a set of actions and initiatives that they hope will bring the company from the point of departure to the point of arrival. This *road to results* spells out the small number of critical action imperatives that will drive the organization forward and the metrics by which it will track its progress, all of it informed by the original performance-improvement diagnosis. Time after time, successful general managers told us that their organizations could act effectively and aggressively on only three to five major change initiatives at the same time. Figure 1.3 shows the process great managers follow in applying the four laws to diagnose their point of departure, set a point of arrival, and identify a handful of the most critical initiatives on the road to results to get there. It's a process we will detail in chapters 6, 7, and 8.

We will also look at all the possibilities for failure in this scenario. If the manager gets the point of departure wrong—if he misdiagnoses the situation he inherits—he is likely not to do everything he needs to do and will thus miss his point of arrival. If the manager gets the point of departure right but posits a point of arrival that is too timid, the result will at best be what we call "satisfactory underperformance." It may satisfy some people's expectations, but it will fall short of the organization's full potential. If the point of arrival is unrealistically ambitious given the real point of departure, the result will fall short of everybody's expectations. It's much the same if the manager gets both "points" right but can't map out a focused, effective road to results that matches her likely job tenure. In either case, she will most likely be replaced for not delivering the performance that the boss or the board expects.

So there are several routes to failure but at least one clear approach to getting each step right. *Great managers can succeed by applying the laws to*

FIGURE 1.3

Going from Point of Departure to Point of Arrival

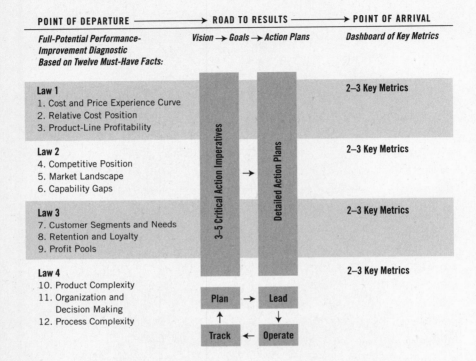

POINT OF DEPARTURE ⟶	ROAD TO RESULTS ⟶	POINT OF ARRIVAL
Full-Potential Performance-Improvement Diagnostic Based on Twelve Must-Have Facts:	*Vision → Goals → Action Plans*	*Dashboard of Key Metrics*

Law 1
1. Cost and Price Experience Curve
2. Relative Cost Position
3. Product-Line Profitability

Law 2
4. Competitive Position
5. Market Landscape
6. Capability Gaps

Law 3
7. Customer Segments and Needs
8. Retention and Loyalty
9. Profit Pools

Law 4
10. Product Complexity
11. Organization and Decision Making
12. Process Complexity

3–5 Critical Action Imperatives

Detailed Action Plans

2–3 Key Metrics

2–3 Key Metrics

2–3 Key Metrics

2–3 Key Metrics

Plan → Lead
↑   ↓
Track ← Operate

each of the steps, focusing on the insights they gather, and acting accordingly. The laws provide the tools for diagnosing the point of departure: an understanding of the company's relative strengths, relative weaknesses, capabilities, and challenges. They enable the manager to develop a point of arrival that is at once aspirational and achievable. And they provide guidelines for the plan, targets, and interim metrics that will enable the company to reach its point of arrival in a time frame that matches the general manager's likely tenure. In effect, they create that simple path to success—simple in concept, anyway, though admittedly complex in practice (see figure 1.4). As we'll see in the chapters that follow, Warren Knowlton at Morgan Crucible was able to develop and follow such a path. The leaders of Polaroid, unfortunately, were not.

FIGURE 1.4

The Four Laws—and How to Pick Up Speed on the Road to Results

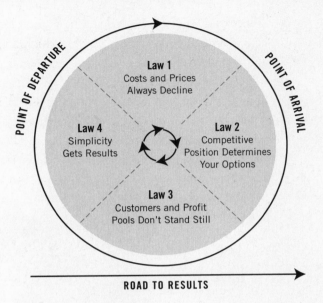

READING THIS BOOK AND APPLYING ITS PRINCIPLES WILL NOT tell you everything you need to know to be successful. Nor will it provide all the latest tools and techniques you might ultimately require. You will still need superb leadership skills. You will have to counter your competitors' moves, and you will need to be vigilant in tracking your customers' ever-changing needs. And there will always be room for proprietary insights, breakthrough thinking, and innovative products. But we believe this book will dramatically increase your chances of success. Great managers, like great athletes, don't win all the time. But because they are well grounded in the fundamentals—because they train, study, and practice—they can do things that others can't. So they outperform their competitors more often than not. Great athletes, like great managers, have to know and do a lot of other things as well as the basics. But Tiger Woods or David Beckham wouldn't have achieved all they did unless they had mastered the basics first.

Mike White, the head of PepsiCo International, is one general manager who is well grounded in the four laws we have outlined; he says he has used them consistently during his career as a general manager. When we asked him for advice, he told us, "You know, what you really need to do with this book is create something that lays out the fundamental principles of business. The biggest challenge I have is that often new general managers, many of them trained at the best business schools, lack a holistic, strategic perspective. They come up with ideas without understanding the principles that will create success. They just lack the framework. If we can create that framework for them, we can dramatically improve our ability to move forward and succeed." This book is designed to do exactly that.

The simple path to success guided by the four laws represents the basics of great management. Get them right and you are laying the foundation for success.

TWO

First Law: Costs and Prices Always Decline

The only source of knowledge is experience.

—ALBERT EINSTEIN

THE FIRST LAW IS POWERFUL. IT EXPLAINS A GOOD DEAL ABOUT the business world, such as why the U.S. steel industry lost so much market share to the Japanese, how Emerson Electric has managed to stay at or near the top of its markets for so many years, why some CEOs regularly claim (and actually seem to believe) that their competitors are colluding or "dumping" goods, how Southwest Airlines makes money in a business that everybody else thinks is one of the worst around, why Polaroid never succeeded in digital photography despite a sizable technological lead, and why your chief competitors may be widening the gap between their companies and yours even as we speak.

Then, too, the first law helps us understand what's likely to happen in energy-related industries; why milk bottles, microprocessors, and mobile phone services are all so much cheaper than they used to be; and how a tire company was able to make itself a market leader in the commercial-roofing business in a remarkably short time.

All this from a fundamental law of business that has been known for a while, yet in recent years has been underappreciated, misunderstood, or simply ignored. The foundation of the law is called the "experience curve." Knowing what the experience curve is and how to use it can often make the difference between leading a business to success and leading it into a quagmire.

UNDERSTANDING THE EXPERIENCE CURVE

The immediate ancestor of the experience curve is the learning curve, an idea that pretty much makes sense to everybody. If you're an experienced pastry cook, the first cake you baked in your life took a lot longer to prepare than the ninety-first, and it probably wasn't as good. If you're a golfer, you undoubtedly found it harder to drive your ball straight down the fairway on your first outing than you do now. One of the perils of the computer age, at least for those of us who never took a typing class, is that we have all had to learn to use a keyboard. But sure enough: our typing speed and accuracy both increase with time, thanks to the learning curve.

Quantifying the Learning Curve: The Paper Airplane Test

In business, we have to imagine that factory managers from the dawn of the industrial revolution noticed that there was a learning curve for every combination of tasks they asked their employees to perform. The first person to study the curve systematically in an industrial setting was the commander of the Wright-Patterson Air Force Base in Ohio. Beginning in 1925, he observed that the labor time required to assemble an airplane declined over time—and more than that, it declined *in a predictable manner.* Subsequent studies found that the fourth plane took only 80 percent as much time as the second, the eighth only 80 percent as much as the fourth, and so on. Every time cumulative production doubled, the time required for assembly was only 80 percent of what it had been. Later investigations found a similar relationship in all kinds of aircraft manufacture—fighters, bombers, and transport planes.[1]

There is an instructive hands-on exercise that we use in training our new employees to help them understand this dynamic. The exercise helps everyone "get" the learning curve at a gut level, and maybe begin to see why it engendered such a useful management tool.

Here's the drill: the objective is to create as many paper airplanes as possible in thirty seconds. The airplane will be deemed successful if it flies more than five feet when thrown. We'll assume that labor cost is $8 for the thirty seconds, and that the materials cost is 50 cents per airplane.

If you actually get a group of people to do several iterations of this exercise, you will get something like the results in table 2.1.

TABLE 2.1

Results of Paper Airplane Exercise

TRIAL NUMBER	SUCCESSFUL FLIGHTS*	COST PER AIRPLANE	ACCUMULATED EXPERIENCE
1	2.1	$4.31	2.1
2	3.3	$2.92	5.4
3	4.8	$2.17	10.2

*Data shown is average result from eight different training groups

Note a couple of things about these results: one is that labor costs are decreasing, just as the learning curve would predict. The other is that quality is *increasing*—there are more successful flights in each successive trial. The builders are learning what makes an airplane successful. They are learning how to do their jobs better as well as faster.

If we chart the cost per successful airplane against accumulated experience on an ordinary linear scale graph, the curve looks like this (see fig-

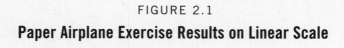

FIGURE 2.1

Paper Airplane Exercise Results on Linear Scale

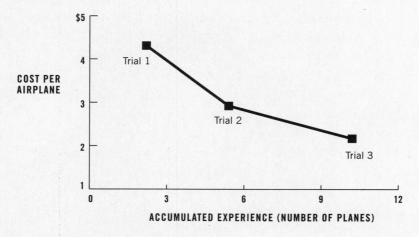

ure 2.1). The graph reflects the fact that, although the *percentage* improvement in costs remains about the same each time production doubles, the *absolute* cost improvement diminishes. So the curve soon flattens out.

But now let's note the fact that this graph is driven by exponents—namely, that recurrent doubling of production. An exponential curve can be represented by a logarithmic scale on both axes. (We won't go into the math here; those who are interested can find it in appendix 2.) Converting the graph to a log scale changes the shape: now the curve becomes a straight line (see figure 2.2).

In effect, the conversion to logs gets rid of the diminishing change in absolute costs and focuses attention squarely on the constant decline in percentage costs. What we will call the slope of the line—in this case, 74 percent—indicates how much of the cost is left after production doubles.[2] To put it the other way around, every doubling in accumulated experience results in a 26 percent decrease in unit costs. The lower the slope, the steeper the curve, and the more costs drop with each doubling of experience. A 50 percent slope, for example, would be unusually steep, since every doubling of experience would cut costs in half.

And here's where we're headed with this: that straight line can be ex-

FIGURE 2.2

Paper Airplane Exercise Results on Log Scale

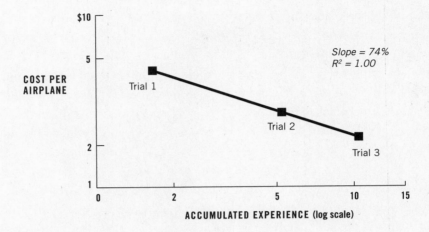

tended out indefinitely into the future, thus showing the likely cost after every doubling of accumulated experience.

You may question this conclusion, thinking (correctly) that at some point you will reach the physical limitations of your fingers and progress will then stop. But if you found it worthwhile to continue building paper airplanes, you might figure out how to design the planes differently, use different materials, or automate the process. Such innovations wouldn't have the same limitations, and you would be likely to improve them over time. These kinds of innovations can continue indefinitely.

You can make this projection for paper airplanes, real airplanes, or—as we shall see in a moment—nearly every other industry. If you know how long it takes for an industry or a company to double its accumulated experience, you can predict with a high degree of accuracy what its costs ought to be in any given year.

From Learning Curve to Experience Curve

For years, most people in the business world never heard of the Wright-Patterson findings, nor did they try an exercise like that just described. But in 1966, a consultant named Bruce D. Henderson had an insight that would transform the learning curve into a tool no business could afford to ignore.

Henderson was familiar with the learning-curve studies, and he understood that production employees learned to do their jobs faster and more efficiently over time, just as the curve suggested. But surely everyone else in the company was also learning. Purchasing managers would learn how to buy better, cheaper raw materials and parts. Salespeople would learn how to sell more effectively. Accountants, human-resources managers, R&D specialists, marketers, even senior executives—all had learning curves of their own. All should be learning to work more efficiently, and the cost of their services per unit produced should be dropping.

In an entire industry, moreover, the principles of the learning curve would apply throughout the value chain. Producers of capital equipment, parts suppliers, and service companies would all learn to do their jobs smarter and more efficiently as they accumulated experience in producing their goods and services. As customers become more knowledgeable and sophisticated, selling costs and customer-service costs would also decline. All of these factors would combine to lower the final cost of that industry's goods over time as experience accumulated.

As researchers studied the behavior of costs in a variety of industries, they found that costs do indeed decline over time in a highly predictable fashion. Each time the accumulated experience of an industry doubled, costs (corrected for the effects of inflation) typically dropped about 25 percent. Soon the phenomenon had a new name: the *experience curve*. It also had a powerful corollary. Individual companies in an industry would accumulate experience at different rates depending on changes in their market share. Those that were growing the fastest, and were therefore doubling their own experience more rapidly than others, would be coming down the curve at the quickest pace. Their costs would be dropping more rapidly than those of their competitors, and their profits would be growing more rapidly as well. To be sure, there was nothing automatic about the curve: managers had to learn to manage their costs along it. But if one company failed to do so, a competitor almost certainly would, which meant that the curve would ultimately reflect costs and prices in the entire industry.

Like many good management insights, the experience curve fell out of fashion for a while. Some consultants went on to newer ideas. Some executives decided that it didn't apply to their industry. Some management theorists struggled to see how it applied to specific businesses and situations, while others simply never learned about it. What we know now, after forty years of study and experience, is that the experience curve is a rich, nuanced concept, and one of the most powerful implements in any general manager's tool kit.

Characteristics of the Experience Curve

The experience curve can be found today in virtually every industry. Here, for example, is the curve for brokerage services (see figure 2.3).

FIGURE 2.3

Experience Curve for Price of Brokerage Services

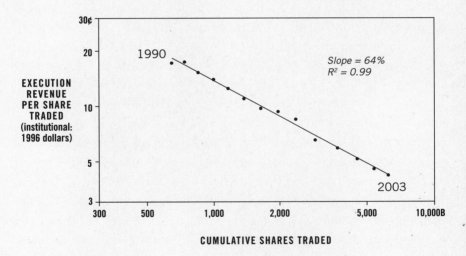

CUMULATIVE SHARES TRADED

Note: Listed and NASDAQ shares
Sources: NYSE, NASDAQ, SIA Databank, Banc of America Securities

Here is the curve for butter (see figure 2.4), which shows considerably more volatility around the downward trend line (due to declining government price supports and fluctuations in production and inventory).

FIGURE 2.4

Experience Curve for Butter[3]

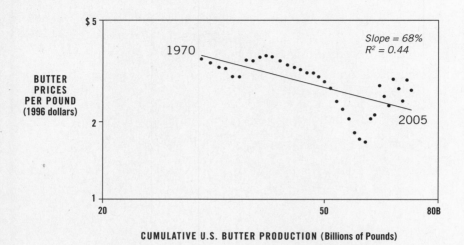

CUMULATIVE U.S. BUTTER PRODUCTION (Billions of Pounds)

Sources: U.S. Bureau of Labor Statistics; USDA National Agricultural Statistics Services; Albert Mann Library at Cornell University

Table 2.2 shows a sample of other industries, along with the slope that applies to each one. In each case, the underlying prices were expressed in constant dollars, meaning that they were corrected for inflation. (We address some special situations in appendix 2.)

The experience curve in any industry reflects a wide variety of cost-reducing efforts. The learning curve for individuals makes intuitive sense, and it can be demonstrated in practice. The experience curve is partly the result of everyone in an industry or a value chain learning to do their jobs better and more efficiently.

But many other factors also contribute to continuing cost declines. Companies grow, and so enjoy greater economies of scale. They introduce new, more efficient technologies. They substitute lower-cost materials or procedures. They organize the production or distribution process more efficiently. Take Wal-Mart as an example. In its earlier years, the company invested heavily in cost-minimizing measures such as large-scale distribu-

TABLE 2.2

Experience Curve Slopes for Sample of Industries

	INDUSTRY	DATES	EXPERIENCE CURVE SLOPE
RELATIVELY STEEP SLOPES	Microprocessors	1980–2005	60%
	LCDs	1997–2003	60%
	Brokerages	1990–2003	64%
	Wireless Services	1991–1995	66%
RELATIVELY MODERATE SLOPES	VCRs	1993–2004	71%
	Airlines	1988–2003	75%
	Crushed Stone	1940–2004	75%
	Mobile Phone Services	1994–2000	76%
	Personal Computers	1988–2004	77%
	DVD Players/Recorders	1997–2005	78%
RELATIVELY FLAT SLOPES	Cable Set-Top Boxes	1998–2003	80%
	Cars	1968–2004	81%
	Milk Bottles	1990–2004	81%
	Plastics	1987–2004	81%
	Color TVs	1955–2005	83%
	DVDs	1997–2002	85%

tion facilities and state-of-the-art store information systems. Those investments helped Wal-Mart drive down its nonpurchasing costs per dollar of fixed assets year after year. More recently, the company has been focusing on its purchasing costs. In 2002, it established a global procurement group, which at this writing involves 1,600 employees in twenty-three countries. Separate teams in this group undertake tasks such as identifying world-class suppliers, developing new products, simplifying supply-chain processes, and assuring quality. Wal-Mart's teams expect year-after-year price reductions, and will turn to private-label goods or alternative suppliers if name-brand vendors don't meet price targets. (Buyers are compensated partly on their success in winning price reductions.) Across categories, the teams work to achieve supply-chain efficiencies through tactics such as bulk packaging and automatic replenishment systems. Since Wal-Mart is the single biggest customer for many suppliers, the suppliers have an incentive to work cooperatively with buyers and to manage their own costs down the experience curve.

Astute nonprofit organizations make as much use of the experience curve as for-profit companies. "We are much better at starting treatment projects for TB or HIV on the ground than we have ever been," says Jim Yong Kim, a cofounder of the Boston-based organization Partners In Health (PIH). "Every time we do it, we're more efficient and use resources much more effectively." When Kim, Paul Farmer, and their colleagues at PIH's Peruvian partner, Socios En Salud, began their first program attacking multi–drug-resistant tuberculosis in Peru, the cost for just the medicines was roughly $25,000 per patient. By 2006, the organization had been able to cut the per-patient cost of medicines to as little as $1,500. Elisabeth Babcock, former executive director of the Lynn Community Health Center in Lynn, Massachusetts, found the health center in receivership when she took the job. When she left, it had significant operating surpluses; had built a new main facility and launched a number of new satellite clinics; and was the largest provider of health care in the city. One key to its financial success was growing its programs to lower its costs. For example, Babcock established a new health maintenance organization (HMO) specially designed for the elderly. Because the HMO learned to emphasize preventive and in-home care, thereby keeping many patients out of costly nursing homes, its per-capita operating costs declined over time. Because it was closely tied to community agencies, its selling costs declined as well. "Because we partnered with a senior social service agency in the ownership of the HMO, they shared in the success of the program and made appropriate referrals. They became our sales force," says Babcock.

Note that the experience curve doesn't depend on people working harder. There's a limit, after all, on how hard people can work, so cost reductions derived from "sweating" the workers soon peter out (or backfire, as employees seek out more agreeable workplaces). The experience curve does depend on people working smarter—on learning new techniques, using new technologies, and so on. Productivity gains from these sources can continue indefinitely. The experience curve is the result of the dynamics of a competitive marketplace. It is the effect of companies' purposeful, continuous actions to manage the costs of serving their customers more effectively over time. In chapter 1 we described how business fundamentals can be harnessed to diagnose current performance, set targets for future performance, and form initiatives to achieve them. The law of the experience curve specifically helps you understand how to manage your costs to maintain prices that retain customers. In chapter 6 and appendix 3 we will review some of the cost-management techniques that many companies have found to be especially effective.

Experience curve slopes cluster within a narrow range. In most industries, data points relating to costs and prices can be fit to curves that look quite a lot like the simple one we constructed for paper airplanes. Moreover, the percentage change in costs and prices for every doubling of accumulated experience usually falls within a remarkably narrow band. Recently, Bain researchers created experience curves for seventy-three different products and services, ranging from technology products and telecommunications services to airline seats and financial services. The slopes of the curves ranged from 49 percent to 99 percent, but the vast majority clustered in the range between 69 percent and 81 percent. Remember that the lower the percent, the steeper the slope, and the more costs (in constant dollars) decline with each doubling of accumulated experience.

It may seem odd that the slope curves cluster so closely. A dynamic young industry such as PCs is at 77 percent, while a mature business like milk bottles is at 81 percent, only four points higher. But in younger industries, prices drop faster in a given amount of time because accumulated experience is doubling and redoubling rapidly. In mature industries, it may take years for accumulated experience to double, so the percentage price change in each year is less.

Prices follow costs. It also shouldn't be surprising that prices—in general, on average, and over time—follow costs downward. Companies operate in a competitive marketplace. If one company sets its prices too far above costs, others (including new entrants) will undercut those prices and take market share. If prices in an industry fail to decrease commensurate with the curve, customers will begin finding substitutes.

To be sure, an industry's prices in any given year can fluctuate for a variety of reasons, so the experience curve may not appear to be "working" all the time. A bottleneck in supply can push prices up, while a sudden dropoff in demand can push them down. And customers may not be able to—or may not choose to—switch to a substitute immediately. The first discount brokerages, for example, were far cheaper than traditional full-service brokerages, but many investors preferred to stick with the tried-and-true full-service houses. Only over time, thanks to mass television advertising and growing sophistication among investors, did discount brokerages become popular. At that point they pushed down the price of all brokerage services.

But the experience curve does work. In the long run, average prices always follow average costs, so the experience curves for prices and those for costs run more or less parallel.

Quality improves as costs decline. Note one other fact as well. Lowering costs does not depend on lowering quality. Quite the contrary: just as with paper airplanes, the quality of a company's or an industry's output tends to rise even as costs and prices decline. We have all seen this firsthand with the new products created in the last few decades: today's personal computers, DVD players, digital cameras, cell phones, GPS devices, handheld PDA devices, and so on are far better than those of a decade ago, even as prices have continued to decline. But the same phenomenon is visible in mature industries. For example, the left-hand side of figure 2.5 shows the cost experience curve for polyester filaments. The right-hand side charts a quality index for the filaments, measuring such factors as color, tensile strength, evenness of denier (thickness and thinness), and the crystalline structure of the polyester fibers.

"Quality," to be sure, is a slippery concept. It sometimes refers to improvement in an identical product—a more durable umbrella, for instance (or polyester filament). And it sometimes refers to the addition of features that essentially transform the product into something quite different from what it was (think of today's PC versus the original Apple II). We'll take up

FIGURE 2.5

Cost of Polyester Declined Over 13 Years While Quality Increased

Disguised Company Data

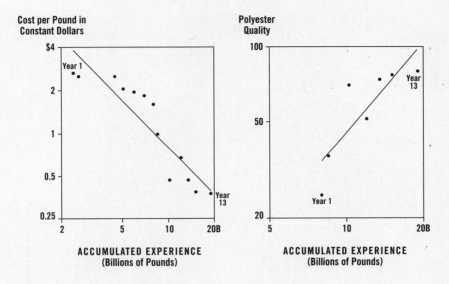

these complications in a moment. Right now we simply want to dispel the idea that lower costs mean lower quality.

Market Leaders Are Experience Curve Leaders

The experience curve describes the likely behavior of an industry's costs and prices. It provides general managers with the information they need to *manage* costs and prices downward according to the first law. In the real world, of course, some general managers will choose—and will learn how—to manage costs and prices according to the curve, while others won't. But for those who do, the value of leadership can be considerable.

Consider, for example, a graph of an industry's experience curve. Often the four largest competitors in an industry line up as shown in figure 2.6.

Because it's a competitive marketplace, at any point in time there is an industry price. The largest competitor, A, farthest down the curve,

FIGURE 2.6

Relative Profitability

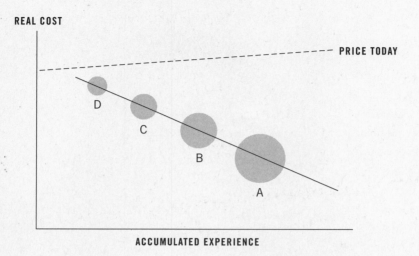

enjoys the lowest overall costs and therefore the highest margins. (We're assuming it has managed its costs aggressively.) Competitor A also frequently commands a price premium relative to other competitors, based on brand, product, or a superior reputation. Competitor A is thus much more profitable and can reinvest more than the others in research and development, marketing, quality, or anything else—it has the resources to continue to gain market share, lower its costs, and improve its products even more. If it does so successfully, it can move down the experience curve faster because its accumulated experience grows faster than that of competitors. The others are followers, trying to catch up but rarely succeeding.

If this picture is right, Competitor A essentially determines whether Competitor D gets to stay in business. Without some kind of innovation or disruptive strategy, D itself may not have much control over whether it succeeds or fails. Not to put too fine a point on it, if you run D, your business performance and your bonus probably depend more on what A decides to do than on anything *you* might do. This is not an enviable situation for any general manager.

There are two things to remember about this picture. First, market leaders typically do outperform their competitors, as we will see in the following chapter. The gravitational pull of market leadership, so to speak, is strong. Competitor A has enormous advantages, and followers have significant disadvantages. In our studies of companies' performance over a ten-year period, we have consistently found that close followers overtake leaders less than 5 percent of the time. In fact, one study suggested that four out of five market leaders that are twice the size of their largest competitors earn returns greater than their cost of capital, while only one in five followers less than one-third the size of their largest competitor is able to accomplish the same feat.

But second, the picture isn't fixed for all time. In certain circumstances, with the right performance-improvement strategy and execution, B, C, and D or another competitor entirely can challenge A for leadership. There are many examples of companies that have developed the right approaches, and that have unseated leaders. We will return to this subject in chapter 3, highlighting the ways that followers can challenge leaders.

Of course, the most common key to success is to *reduce your costs and prices relentlessly and systematically*, using the curve as your guide. This is what most market leaders do—and those that don't are likely to lose their leadership position to a more aggressive competitor.

Who are these cost leaders? A familiar example is Southwest Airlines. Southwest has always built its business model around keeping costs low, and it hasn't let up in recent years. It has invested heavily in Internet-based reservation systems, airport self-service kiosks, and other labor-saving technologies. It has asked its employees to come up with productivity-enhancing suggestions—one team, for instance, observed Indianapolis 500 pit crews to get ideas on how to reduce aircraft turnaround times. Southwest highlights the fact that scale alone is not sufficient to drive costs down; it must be accompanied by accumulated experience in key business drivers. Southwest is not the largest U.S. airline, but it has had far more experience than its larger rivals in one critical area, flying point-to-point routes. It has thus been able to increase its routes and its revenue without a corresponding increase in staffing levels and costs. Its inflation-adjusted cost per seat-mile, the standard measure of productivity in the airline industry, declined from 1986 to 2005 with a slope of 81 percent, compared to 95 percent or more for some of its competitors with larger overall scale. Thanks to continuing cost reductions, Southwest has been consistently profitable almost since its inception—a record unparalleled in an industry known for its red ink. (The airline's costs have risen in recent years because of the rising price of jet fuel, but they are still lower than those of most of its competitors.)

A less familiar but equally dramatic example of managing to the experience curve, and the one that shows best what such management really entails, is the St. Louis–based company Emerson Electric. A manufacturer of technology products and systems for industrial, commercial, and consumer markets, Emerson has less public visibility than a Wal-Mart or a Southwest Airlines, even though it is a global corporation with some $20 billion in (2006) revenues. But it is extraordinarily well known to investors, as befits a company whose earnings and dividends grew at more than 10 percent a year on average from 1956 to 2000. It's also well known to students of management.

Emerson's secret weapon is a rigorous, meticulous, and thoroughgoing approach to goal setting, planning, and execution—a "management process," as the company terms it. "The management process helps us develop superior strategies at all levels of the company," wrote Charles F. Knight, Emerson's CEO from 1973 to 2000, "and keeps us on track as we execute them with discipline and intensity."[4]

Nowhere was Emerson's management process more visible—and more etched into the company's DNA—than in its approach to managing costs. In the 1960s and 1970s, Knight wrote, cost reduction was a "religion" at Emerson. Division presidents presented their cost-improvement goals to headquarters at the beginning of the fiscal year, then reported actual results monthly. Cost-reduction teams in each plant competed with teams in other plants to achieve or beat their targets. In the 1980s, Emerson learned that competitors from Brazil and other low-cost countries were offering better prices to its customers. Quickly the company developed a "best-cost producer" strategy: "We stopped using ourselves as a benchmark and focused instead on the best-in-class competitors, wherever they happened to be," wrote Knight. As a result of this global benchmarking, Emerson opened state-of-the-art plants in Mexico and gradually moved some of its production there. Costs continued to decline.

In the 1990s, Emerson's margins were once again under attack by competitors, and again the company mounted an offensive. It developed a "containment" program for the costs of both hourly and salaried personnel; the program was designed to reduce the unit cost of both. Under this program, it searched out other low-cost areas, such as Eastern Europe, for plant locations. It reduced annual wage increases, instead substituting lump-sum payments. It expanded the use of temporary employees and redesigned medical plans to increase employee co-pays. "Despite these tough actions," said Knight, "our [employee] opinion survey scores actually went up, a testament to the tremendous strength of our communication policies and our people's understanding of the challenges we faced."

The company also embarked on a massive effort to reduce the cost of materials. It created a centralized procurement organization and consolidated its list of suppliers. It developed a multiyear strategic plan for each commodity it bought. It developed a corporation-wide "material information network" and began to use Internet-based reverse auctions. By the early 2000s, it had saved more than $100 million in materials costs alone. Meanwhile, it had introduced a company-wide lean-manufacturing and Six Sigma initiative that improved productivity an average of about 25 percent and increased inventory turnover 32 percent. Costs continued to drop. Emerson was able to maintain its margins despite brutal competition and severe pricing pressure.[5] Despite difficult years between 2001 and 2003, it is back on track at this writing: both sales and earnings have been rising steadily since then, and in 2006 hit records.

Throughout, two relatively simple tools have helped support Emerson's cost-management discipline. The first is the company's "profit waterfall"— a technique for decomposing the cost structure of a business, plant, or product into its components. Emerson's ability to track individual cost components, and then to challenge divisions to pull every possible lever for improvement, has long been a hallmark of its approach. The second is the strategic planning process itself. Every year, Emerson challenges its businesses to project their product costs three to five years out, with appropriate (inflation-adjusted) reductions. It expects the leadership team of each business to know exactly where 80 percent of the reductions will come from in the first year. The percentages are lower for the second and third years, but the teams know they will have to fill in the gaps quickly. They will have to review their new point of departure each subsequent year, reassess their point of arrival, and adjust initiatives to get there.

Note that Emerson had its down years. Other cost leaders have had occasional difficulties as well and probably will continue to do so—often because management at the time doesn't focus on the four laws as aggressively as previous managements. Tight cost management is not sufficient for success, but it is certainly necessary, especially in the global cost-competitive environment most businesses face today.

MANAGING TO THE EXPERIENCE CURVE

The experience curve is a tool for the general manager. It is not enough to just observe how Southwest or Emerson cut costs; the real issue is how the company or business unit that *you* run can cut its costs. That's where the experience curve comes in. It enables you to understand *what* you have to do, *how* you can do it, and *how fast* you have to do it.

Create Curves for Your Company and Your Competitors

Part of the job of creating experience curves for your company and its competitors is simply to gather data and perform the analysis. That can be difficult enough; we describe the technical procedures in appendix 2. But the process will allow you to understand your situation so that you can take the necessary actions to get your costs where they need to be. At times, however, companies get off track by gathering the wrong data or misinterpreting the numbers. Here are four things to be sure you get right:

Use the right unit of value—what your customer is really buying. If you were to plot a curve of the inflation-adjusted price of automobile tires from 1960 to 1980, you would find it trending upward. A tire buyer paid almost 50 percent more in real terms at the end of that period than at the beginning—and a higher net price for a differentiated product is, indeed, the mark of a successful incremental innovation, a concept we'll explore more in chapter 3.[6] An observer in 1980 might have scrutinized this data and concluded that the experience curve wasn't working and so wasn't relevant to managers in the tire industry.

But is a car owner really buying just a tire? Nobody hangs a tire in the living room above the fireplace. What car owners really want is a ride on a set of tires. When they buy a tire they are really buying a certain number of *tire-miles*. And the fact is, tires in 1980 lasted a lot longer than tires in 1960—they gave the buyer more tire-miles, and they improved gas mileage as well. If you plot the real price of a tire-mile during that twenty-year period taking those factors into account, you find that it declined, just as the experience curve would predict. The slope of the curve was about 83 percent.

So it is with many products and services: customers don't necessarily want the product or service, they want the benefits that the product or service provides. Take energy. The price of petroleum, though it fluctuates dramatically with short-term variations in supply and demand, has been slowly but steadily rising over the last sixty years.[7] Improvements in the technology of exploration, drilling, and recovery—the added value provided by the industry—have all made it significantly less expensive to drill a given well: the cost per foot has declined steeply. But that decline has not been sufficient to overcome the fact that oil is a dwindling resource, and that new oil fields (in deep water, for instance) are much more costly to work than those that were discovered years ago. At any rate, businesses and consumers don't want oil, they want energy. They want British thermal units (BTUs) of heat and cooling, lumens of light, kilowatt-hours of power, and miles driven or flown. Nearly every other energy source, from coal to solar power, has been coming down predictable experience curves. So has the price of electricity generation, most of which (in the United States and many other countries) comes from coal. As substitutes continue down the curve, and as oil continues to increase, customers will turn to other energy sources. (We discuss special cases such as depleting natural resources in greater detail in appendix 2.)

For some industries, identifying the right unit of value can be tricky. Take software, for example. Customers who buy software are generally looking for ways to save time and increase productivity. So the unit of value might be based on the benefits customers get per dollar spent. An example is money-management software such as Quicken. People buy it because they can spend less time writing checks, and because they can get added value such as budget reports and tax-related data with a few keystrokes.

So the value provided by a given piece of software can be difficult to measure precisely. Even so, there is no question that software companies should be improving their products, reducing their costs, and constantly increasing the value to the customer. On the cost side, a software manager might have to look at measures of productivity and measures that show the value of features to the customer. Each component should be coming down the experience curve.

Ultimately, to get the unit of value right, look at what you are selling through the eyes of the customer. That's the right basis for your experience curve.

Account for feature and quality improvements, and for changes in product mix. The tire a typical car owner bought in 1970 was of a type of construction known as bias-ply. The tire the same car owner bought in 2000 was a radial.[8] Radial tires not only delivered more tire-miles, they also delivered other benefits. They had fewer flats. They provided better gas mileage. Many drivers felt they gave a more comfortable ride. So it is with many products, from personal computers to machine tools: they improve over time, and customers buy models with more capabilities or features. The prices customers paid last year may not be directly comparable to what they paid in 1990 or 1980, because they were buying a different combination of benefits. For many of the products and services we studied, customers' expectations are more and more directed both at the price of goods and services and at the value or features they receive. They have come to expect improvements in both.

Usually this distinction isn't so important for analytical purposes, because prices decline anyway. Tires, for instance, declined in price after 1980, and the price of a tire-mile declined even more precipitously than it had in the earlier period. And we all know about PCs, cell phones, and other electronic gadgets—prices have been dropping rapidly.

Sometimes, however, a product's price increases precisely because it is delivering so many more benefits to its customers. The prime example of this phenomenon is automobiles. Over the last several decades, the inflation-adjusted price of a new car has increased about 1.2 percent a year (still less than the average real annual increase in disposable personal income). But cars have undergone substantial changes in product and feature quality. Today's automobiles are uniformly better built than cars were in 1980. They are safer. They last longer, require less maintenance, and break down less frequently. They get more miles to the gallon for the same level of horsepower, and they emit considerably less air pollution. When they do need service, built-in diagnostic computers often are able to tell the mechanic exactly what is wrong. Moreover, the typical new car looks and feels quite different from its 1980 counterpart. It is far more likely to have all-wheel drive, power windows, keyless entry, power seats, heated seats, air conditioning, cruise control, multispeed wipers, automatic rain sensors, and other amenities. It may also have devices that weren't available back then, such as airbags, antilock brakes, a CD player, a satellite radio, a cell-phone port, collision-avoidance sensors, and a global positioning system (GPS) device. Some of these improvements, such as pollution reduction, were mandated by government regulations. Most came from companies pursuing technological innovation and managing their costs down the experience curve, so that more and more car buyers could afford the improvements. A curve showing the purchase price of a car per year of ownership and adjusted for equipment that was not on cars in 1980 declines with a slope of 81 percent.

If inflation-adjusted prices seem to be rising in your industry, look again. Has your product or service changed as dramatically as the automobile? Have customers been steadily upgrading to more expensive combinations of goods and services? If so, don't be misled into thinking that the experience curve doesn't apply; its effects are just masked by the changes in quality and features.[9] Of course, rising prices may also indicate that managers in your industry are asleep at the wheel, as the U.S. auto industry was from roughly 1950 to 1970. That was a time when the U.S. manufacturers operated as an oligopoly and did not manage their costs to an experience curve. Unfortunately for them, automakers such as Toyota and

Honda were aggressively managing down that 72 percent curve. The Japanese companies started with a higher cost position after World War II, but gradually were able to overtake U.S. automakers.

Get the business definition right. Not all of your competitors are in exactly the same combination of businesses as you, so they may be moving down the experience curve at a different rate. When PepsiCo entered the bottled-water business, for instance, it could capitalize on its decades of experience in packaging and marketing beverages, and on the scale and experience it could immediately bring to bear. Incumbent bottled-water producers would have made a serious mistake to conclude that they enjoyed lower costs than PepsiCo simply because they had been in water longer.

This kind of situation crops up in many industries. At one point, Outboard Marine Corp. (OMC) was the largest producer of outboard motors; it had twice the market share of its nearest competitor, Yamaha. OMC was moving down the experience curve, but it did not appear to be managing its costs relative to Yamaha. This, too, was a big mistake, because although OMC was the larger producer in outboards, Yamaha—which also made motors for motorcycles, lawn mowers, and other applications—was far larger in small gasoline engines. The experience it gained from making these other motors enabled it to invest in new product technologies: it could produce outboards at lower cost, and with greater fuel efficiency and reliability. Soon Yamaha's costs were lower than OMC's, its products more advanced, and OMC was in trouble. (OMC entered bankruptcy in 2000.)

Business definition issues are precisely the kinds of obstacles that have tripped up even the most thoughtful theorists. For example, some have looked at an industry such as handbags and raised the question: how can niche producers like Gucci be profitable even though they are not the largest or lowest-cost producers? In appendix 2, we highlight a number of situations where critics have argued that the experience curve is not useful. We show in each case how the experience curve is relevant, and how a focus on reducing costs according to a correctly defined experience curve is critical to all businesses.

Look at the entire industry. In a correctly defined business, compiling both price and cost experience curves for your own company and its competitors should shed light on the overall state of affairs in the industry. Compare three archetypal situations (see figure 2.7):

FIGURE 2.7

Experience Curve Price and Cost

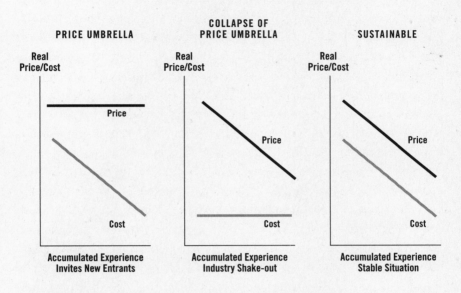

In the first situation, industry-wide costs have been declining while prices have held steady. This is a situation that invites new entrants. If you're an incumbent player, you may be feeling pretty good, because you are probably enjoying healthy margins. But the days of living high on the hog may be numbered.

In the second situation, costs have been holding steady while prices have been declining. That's a recipe for an industry shake-out. If you're in the business, you may already have been feeling the pinch. The experience curve shows why.

The third situation is relatively stable: prices and costs are declining in parallel. That's the equilibrium state toward which industries will tend to move over the long run.

Examine and Manage *Every* Major Cost Element

Any seasoned manager knows how to cut some costs; he or she has probably had a lot of practice in recent years. But even veteran executives occasionally fall into the trap of thinking that some costs are beyond their control. What if hourly labor costs are determined by the terms of a union contract? What if the company has invested heavily in in-house production facilities, only to find that it can't compete with outside vendors? Cost structures like these take time to change, but managing to the experience curve means examining every single cost element, including labor and procurement costs, and attacking them all with equal vigor. Indeed, it often entails a different way of thinking about the business. All costs must be seen as variable in the long run. As one CEO told us: "The world is moving too quickly for old distinctions and definitions to apply."

Focus on productivity. Managers in autos, steel, and other old-line manufacturing industries often have a ready scapegoat for their companies' failure in the past to reduce costs commensurate with the experience curve. Union-negotiated contracts, they say, forced wages and benefits up every year. The contracts made it difficult to reduce headcount, to reorganize production systems, even to alter job descriptions. Executives of the so-called legacy airlines sometimes offer the same reason for their companies' poor profit performance.

It's true that these companies allowed their labor costs to rise beyond competitive levels. But nowhere is it written that unionization has to lead to this result. Japanese auto and steel workers are heavily unionized and enjoy wages comparable with those of American workers, yet their employers have lower costs than U.S. producers. Southwest Airlines employees are also heavily unionized, and receive overall compensation in line with (and in some cases better than) industry averages. In all these cases the unions realized that their own and their members' well-being depended on the economic health of their employers, and so were willing to tie wage gains to gains in productivity or profitability. They were willing to put their shoulders to the wheel—to figure out how the companies could reduce costs every year, make the production of goods or services more efficient, and grow. Today, the results are visible for all to see. Carl Kuwitzky, president of the Southwest Airlines Pilots Association (SWAPA), was recently quoted as saying, "We look forward to continuing the positive working relationship we have with our Company in order to provide excellent service for our passengers, encourage the team spirit we have with our fellow employee groups and assure growth for the Company and in turn our pilot group."[10] Such a sentiment would have been hard to find among union leaders at other airlines in the recent past.

"The lesson for a new CEO," says Warren Knowlton of Morgan Crucible, "is that he or she must find ways to create this type of win-win. You have to start by understanding what is important to your customer and to your people from the very beginning."

Analyze your suppliers' experience curves. Sourcing of goods and services is much more important strategically today than it was in the past. Most companies these days buy a large fraction of the materials, components, and services that they use in their business, and they are likely to be revisiting the make/buy decision regularly for those that they do not already outsource. Many companies are developing partnerships with suppliers that provide them with capabilities they cannot easily develop on their own.[11] The experience curve—different for every industry and for every company within that industry—should inform all such decisions. If you are not yet outsourcing a particular item, is your internal production a significant portion of overall production of that item? Can you come down the experience curve faster than a potential supplier? Is there a specialized producer or service provider—UPS in logistics, for example—that has developed capabilities far beyond your own, and that will come down the curve faster? For goods and services that you do outsource, where are your vendors on the experience curve, and are you choosing them according to that criterion? Would you rather buy from a small supplier that gives a lowball bid in hopes of ramping up volume, or from a large supplier that will come down the experience curve more quickly? Are you taking actions that will help your suppliers lower their own costs and therefore ultimately benefit you? In chapter 6, we'll examine how some companies answer these questions.

Make/buy decisions can be costly to change, because companies often have big investments in in-house production facilities. But getting those decisions wrong can have dire consequences. Look at Polaroid. The conventional wisdom about Polaroid is that it somehow missed the impending revolution in digital photography. But that is wrong. The company's extensive research and development in the field had allowed it to bring out the professional-grade camera called the PDC-2000 in 1996, when the market was still young. Seeing that camera's apparent success, new CEO Gary DiCamillo asked the company's Consumer Imaging division to come up with a plan for a digital camera priced for consumers. He knew that two-megapixel cameras were already selling for $1,200, so he set an aggressive target for his product-development staff: a three-megapixel model that could be sold for $800. But the market moved faster than Polaroid could. Before the company could produce that camera, competitive models with even more functionality were selling for half the price. Instead of bringing out its own product, Polaroid ended up selling a Chinese-made camera under the Polaroid brand.

Polaroid's leadership team knew photography, and they knew instant photography better than anybody. Its in-house research-and-development teams could boast a proud history of pathbreaking products. But the rules were different in digital. No longer could Polaroid (or anybody else) sell cameras at low margins and make up the difference by selling or processing film. No longer would the relevant experience curve be that of photography—companies in digital photography were now on the consumer-electronics curve. In consumer electronics, growth rates were high for many different products, and prices were dropping rapidly because accumulated experience was doubling so quickly. No longer could Polaroid (or any other company) expect to manufacture all of a camera's components itself. Chip makers, battery manufacturers, software developers—all would be on experience curves of their own, producing better and cheaper components faster than any integrated manufacturer could. So long as it relied only on in-house product development for most of its components—the very capability that had led to past successes—Polaroid would always be behind the curve.

Set future price and cost targets according to the experience curve— and expect competitors to do the same. If your costs are higher than your competitors' costs, you might be tempted to use your competitors as a benchmark and aim to equal their costs. That may have been what Polaroid was trying to do. The company underestimated the speed with which competitors would be managing down experience curves of their own. By the time it got to where it wanted to be, its competitors' costs were lower still.

Ignoring this lesson can lead general managers to conclude that their competitors are colluding, dumping goods, or otherwise acting irrationally. Take the famous case of Allis-Chalmers, a big old-line industrial company then based in Milwaukee. In 1946, Allis was a relatively new entrant in the business of manufacturing steam turbines for generating electricity. Company executives carefully studied the industry leaders, Westinghouse and General Electric. They concluded that the two companies were producing turbines that cost about $330 per megawatt of electricity. Allis-Chalmers set its cost target at just that: about $330 per megawatt. By 1963 the company had moved down its experience curve to just that point.[12]

All along, however, General Electric and Westinghouse had been undercutting Allis's prices. The Milwaukee company's leaders were outraged; they concluded that the companies must be colluding to divvy up the market and drive Allis out of the business. They complained to the Federal Trade Commission that GE and Westinghouse were fixing prices ("predatory pricing"), with just such an aim in mind. They didn't believe their competitors could be making money at those prices.

Of course, nothing of the kind was occurring. GE and Westinghouse had simply been moving down their own experience curves, and every year were gaining a cost advantage over the latecomer. By 1963, when Allis had reached a cost level of $330 per megawatt, GE's and Westinghouse's costs were far lower. Allis-Chalmers lost its case and exited the steam-turbine business soon thereafter.

Incidentally, remember that the experience curve governs not just cost and price but quality and features. It wouldn't have done Polaroid any good to come out with a three-megapixel model for $400 if competitors were offering a four-megapixel model at the same price.

Watch for Cost and Price Umbrellas

You will want to look carefully at any cost umbrellas that may have been permitted by your own temporary price umbrellas. You may also be able to exploit price umbrellas left by the competition.

Where do these umbrellas come from? The first law says, in effect, if you don't manage costs and prices down the experience curve, someone else will, and you will lose your position in the market. But some companies seem to forget this law. Now and then a whole industry will ignore it, and will pay the price.

An example is the American steel industry. For many years it was dominated by a few very large companies. It faced little or no international competition. Companies were actually able to raise prices every year. From 1965 until 1979, indeed, steel prices increased almost 30 percent for every doubling of accumulated experience, and the resulting experience curve actually sloped upward (see figure 2.8). The industry had erected a price umbrella. Prices were higher than they would have been if the companies had been managing to the experience curve.

FIGURE 2.8

Steel Experience Curve

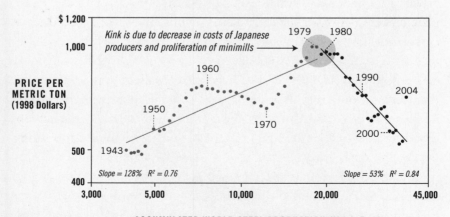

ACCUMULATED WORLD STEEL PRODUCTION (Metric Tons)

Source: U.S. Geological Survey

The price umbrella had two sorts of effects, both utterly predictable.

Price umbrellas attract new competition. In 1960, Japanese steel-makers faced costs about 15 percent higher than those of American companies. But the Japanese were managing their costs aggressively, and were bringing them down an experience curve with a slope of 72 percent. Soon the American market began looking attractive. By 1985 the Japanese companies' costs were about 30 percent less than those of U.S. companies, and they could price their steel accordingly. That's why Japanese competitors were able to make significant inroads in the U.S. steel market. Steel, of course, wasn't the only industry where the Japanese gained market share. Indeed, the Japanese Ministry of International Trade and Industry may have targeted precisely those U.S. industries—such as autos, steel, and consumer electronics—that had not managed to experience curves in the period after World War II.

Meanwhile, a company known as Nuclear Corp. of America decided that steel was an attractive industry to get into. It broke ground for its first steel minimill in 1968. (Minimills, which are smaller than the integrated mills that make steel from iron ore, use electric-arc furnaces to make new steel out of scrap.) It began production in 1969, and it changed its name to Nucor in 1972.[13] Nucor could have enjoyed a comfortable existence at the margins of the steel industry, operating under the price umbrella established by its giant competitors. Instead it grabbed the opportunity that the price umbrella created. The company's first minimills could produce low-end products such as rebar (the steel bars used to reinforce concrete) far more cheaply than the big integrated companies, so Nucor was able to gain a sizable fraction of those markets. As its earnings grew, it reinvested them aggressively, both in building new mills and in moving up-market into higher-value steel. It also learned other ways to boost productivity, thereby pushing costs down. It invested in new technologies. It created a performance-based pay system that allowed its workers (who were not unionized) to earn as much as or more than their counterparts in unionized companies—but only as they pushed production levels higher and higher. Nucor thus created a virtuous cycle of lower costs, higher returns, greater reinvestment, more new products, better quality, more market share, still lower costs, and so on. It grew rapidly, and in 2006 was number

177 on *Fortune* magazine's list of the 500 largest companies in the United States—only nineteen places behind venerable U.S. Steel.

After 1979, competition from the Japanese (and other overseas producers) and from minimills forced steel prices downward rapidly: the experience curve from 1980 to the early 2000s shows a steep slope of 53 percent. Some old-line U.S. producers sought the protection of bankruptcy court. Others reorganized and restructured their businesses, and were then able to compete in the new marketplace. The price umbrella had collapsed, and the experience curve was once more the driving force in the industry.

Nucor and other minimill companies illustrate another danger of the experience curve for incumbents. Successful new entrants in an industry don't reinvent the wheel: they draw on the industry's accumulated experience to date. So they can start at close to the same experience point as incumbents, using much of the existing learning about technologies, processes, materials, and best practices. If they then grow faster, they come down the experience curve more rapidly, and so will gain share quickly. Southwest Airlines and JetBlue are examples of this phenomenon.

Price umbrellas encourage customers to find alternatives. Steel cans began to replace glass bottles for beer and soft drinks back in the 1930s. Though their initial cost was higher, cans provided cost advantages elsewhere in the value chain. They were unbreakable. They were lighter and more easily stacked than bottles. Trucks could carry 400 cases of cans as compared with only 200 cases of bottles. By the 1960s, steel cans were the container of choice for most beverage makers.

But then, with steel prices rising, beverage companies began casting about for alternatives. One was at hand: aluminum cans, which had been developed in 1959. As steel prices increased, aluminum prices decreased. (The experience curve for aluminum between 1943 and 2004 has a slope of 87 percent.) The companies soon realized that aluminum had other advantages as well. It was lighter. It was recyclable. It had greater thermal conductivity than steel, so drinks cooled faster in the refrigerator. Soon the companies were switching to aluminum in droves—and the steel industry had lost a set of customers.

Industry-wide price umbrellas of this sort are rare in today's world of global competition. But individual companies often erect price umbrellas of their own. A company may have a proprietary product, or it may have come up with an innovation that competitors have not yet copied. It may be a market leader, and its executives may decide that they can raise prices with impunity. But the effects are the same: price umbrellas invite competition, and they encourage substitutes. Costs and prices are going to decline. The only question is who will force the issue, and with what product or technology.

The Experience Curve's Threat—and Opportunity

Two more anecdotes about the power of the experience curve before we move on to the next law. They show just how fast the experience curve can undermine a company that ignores it—and how great the reward can be to a company that exploits it.

The price of skepticism . . . In the early 1990s, we observed a company that made tape cassettes, videotapes, and 3½-inch floppy disks. Examining this company's tape business, we found that many competitors were exiting the industry. Because the industry was mature, it took a long time for accumulated experience to double, so prices weren't dropping rapidly. The company could compete effectively in these markets. The 3½-inch floppies were another matter entirely. An experience curve for the floppies showed that annual cost and price reductions were precipitous.

The company's chief executive, a believer (like many people) in the high quality of German engineering, had bought some machine tools in Germany for making floppies. The tools would allow him to manufacture at so many cents a disk. He could have made money if he got them working by February of that year. If the machines came on line in May, the price would be below his initial cost of production, and he would never catch up to it. Unfortunately, the supplier couldn't get the machines to him until May, so he should have pursued other avenues. But he decided to go ahead anyway, spending (and ultimately losing) millions of dollars.

. . . and the rewards to the believer. With astute use of the experience curve, your company can take on and beat even a well-entrenched competitor. One of the best examples of this lesson took place some years

ago, when Firestone took over a large fraction of the commercial roofing business.

Most architects designing flat-roofed commercial buildings today specify a roof made of ethylene propylene diene monomer, known to the trade as EPDM and to casual observers as rubber roofing. It's the most frequently used material on these buildings because, for most applications, it has the cheapest overall cost and the best performance. But it wasn't always so. A couple of decades ago, EPDM had only about 5 percent of the market. Its performance was better than asphalt and other competitive materials. But it was expensive: a square foot of installed roof cost 25 percent more than a square foot of asphalt. The market leader in EPDM was Carlisle (now Carlisle SynTec), which had a profitable business in this market niche.

Firestone, the big tire company, was in the EPDM business as well. A leader in polymer technology, the company had extensive experience with EPDM and related compounds, but in roofing it was a distant follower to Carlisle. So its executives asked the question: should it try to expand the business and take on its well-entrenched competitor? Firestone realized that its current capacity to manufacture EPDM would always put it at a cost disadvantage relative to Carlisle.

But Firestone saw something that Carlisle did not. At sufficient scale, the overall economics of EPDM roofing in certain large segments of the market were superior to asphalt, so the material could become a preferable substitute. The trick would be to bring down manufacturing and installation costs, and the key to that trick was the experience curve. So the company made a bold decision. Quietly, it invested nearly $60 million to build a plant capable of supplying the entire country—the company's largest capital expenditure in ten years. Its managers charted what the price would have to be to get enough volume to run the plant at full capacity; they also determined that if they were able to come down the experience curve at an 80 percent slope, the business could be profitable at that price. Then they priced Firestone's EPDM at that level, even though they knew they still had to come down the experience curve. Along the way the company pursued other cost-reduction measures, such as figuring out how to bypass distributors and sell directly to contractors who were installing large jobs.

It also differentiated itself from competitors through a skilled salesforce, a knowledgeable technical staff, and a warranty program.

Firestone had targeted a price level that Carlisle couldn't match without quick, aggressive action. But Carlisle—worried about protecting its profits—was slow to respond. It hadn't managed its own costs particularly aggressively, and its executives didn't see how Firestone could possibly make any money—ever—at the prices it was charging. For nearly a year, Carlisle didn't cut its own prices.

Soon Firestone was overtaking Carlisle and other competitors. "A devastating price war has gripped the market," reported the trade magazine *Rubber & Plastics News* in 1983, "leaving many producers and marketers fighting for survival . . . Before the little guys got their business established, Firestone came in and started pounding away . . . Firestone is getting all the big jobs. Period. And they're doing it on price." By 1986 Firestone had captured the majority of all growth in the business; its sales had swelled to nearly 1.4 billion square feet from near-zero only four years earlier. And it could make money in this business because it was the cost leader, the company that was coming down the experience curve faster than any other.

THE FIRST LAW IS POWERFUL, AND THOSE WHO KNOW HOW TO take advantage of it can be great managers and lead successful businesses. It is a strong predictor of success or failure. But its implications go deeper, and indeed lead us directly into the second law. Your competitive position dictates how quickly you can come down the experience curve and reduce prices relative to competitors. Your performance along the curve, in turn, will materially define your starting position. In fact, where you are in a competitive marketplace largely dictates what your options for action will be. But the experience curve does not *determine* what will happen. Many great general managers have been able to improve their performance in ways that beat the odds. We will turn now to the second law, and to those strategies for improvement.

IMPLICATIONS FOR THE GENERAL MANAGER

- Determine what unit of value your customers are really buying and all the competitive alternatives they are considering.

- Construct accurate cost and price experience curves for your industry, your company, and each of your competitors.

- Act to ensure that every component of your costs is declining so that they are where they should be on the experience curve. Set annual budgets and targets based on the cost position necessary to remain on the curve. Choose your suppliers carefully, based on their cost position and experience-curve performance; manage the costs you incur from them based on experience-curve expectations, and draw up your contracts accordingly. Look for opportunities to help your suppliers manage their own costs down appropriate experience curves.

- Assume that your future prices will be determined by the experience curve. Plan and budget accordingly.

- Watch for price umbrellas. Capitalize on them where you can, but be prepared for them to collapse.

THREE

Second Law: Competitive Position Determines Your Options

Never interrupt your enemy when he is making a mistake.

—NAPOLEON

IN THE 1980s, NIELSEN MEDIA RESEARCH, THE MARKET LEADER IN the television-ratings business, found itself under sharp attack from competitors on two fronts. Nielsen fought back. When the dust cleared, Nielsen was still on top. It remains there today.

The experience curve, taken to its logical extension, implies that as long as a leader maintains its focus, followers will never catch up. They won't have sufficient funds to invest in overtaking the leader. So maybe we could chalk up Nielsen's success simply to the power of market leadership. But then how do we explain challengers' victories? In 1994, the Super Nintendo Entertainment System was far and away the leader in the videogame-console business, with a market share twice that of its nearest competitor. Sony Computer Entertainment Inc. (SCEI) attacked, and in only a few years had displaced Nintendo from the number one slot.

In many cases, the battle seesaws as management teams and strategies change. Before 1985, Tesco was the leader in grocery retailing in the UK. From 1985 to 1994, Sainsbury's took over the top ranking. But Tesco counterattacked, and at this writing owns a market share substantially larger than Sainsbury's or anybody else's. And though SCEI took over leadership of the videogame market, Nintendo has been coming back fast as we write.

And then there are seemingly anomalous situations—companies that are far from market leadership, yet consistently seem to turn in above-average performance. The Whole Foods Market chain, for example, held a tiny 1 percent share of U.S. supermarket sales in 2006, far behind Wal-Mart (14 percent), Kroger (9 percent), Safeway (6 percent), and others. It was usually a follower in any given locality as well. Yet Whole Foods's gross margin was a full six percentage points higher than the average for conventional supermarkets, and its EBITDA (earnings before interest, taxes, depreciation, and amortization) was nearly double.

So followers occasionally overtake leaders. Leaders occasionally fall back into the pack. Companies that are not the largest in their industry, and that may not enjoy the lowest costs, nevertheless earn higher returns than might be expected.

How can we explain all these facts?

Let's begin with some basics. A primary objective of any business is to earn attractive and sustainable returns. Broadly speaking, a company can follow three paths to this goal. The most common is to achieve outright market leadership. Well-managed market leaders will generally stay on top of their industries, just as the experience curve would predict. They will drive down costs and prices. They have the opportunity to invest more in product and service innovation and in maintaining their brands, and they will continue to earn outsized returns. A second path is to focus primarily on product differentiation through innovation and branding. Customers who value innovative, prestigious, or unusually high-quality products are often willing to pay a premium. A trusted brand may connote higher quality, reliability, status, or some other attribute valued by a customer, and so may carry a higher price. A third path is to cultivate customer retention and loyalty. Loyalty economics—the fact that loyal customers lower a company's customer-acquisition costs and are likely to spend more with a company over time—is the most important driver of returns in these cases.

These three improvement strategies aren't mutually exclusive. Often one reinforces another. But the categorization is useful for analytic purposes, in part because the effectiveness of each strategy depends on the dynamics of particular industries. Cost differentiation based on scale and accumulated experience tends to dominate industries with high fixed costs as well as industries that are early in their life cycle and are rapidly coming down an experience curve. Brand building tends to work well in consumer-products industries, because certain segments of consumers are frequently willing to pay extra for the benefits conferred by a trusted or prestigious brand. Customer-loyalty strategies are often the most powerful driver of profitability in the credit-card industry, because the cost of acquiring a customer in this business is so high and because the "share of wallet" a company earns tends to increase significantly the longer a highly satisfied customer stays.

So the central driver of attractive, sustainable returns depends not only on your competitive position within an industry but also on the economics of the industry in which you compete. However, it is extremely rare to find any competitive situation where the lowest-cost position or high market share isn't critical to sustaining a company's strategy. Cost leadership might not fully drive the economics of your business—but a good cost position in any industry can give you the flexibility to outinvest your competitors, to innovate, and to drive customer loyalty.

Cost leadership aside, not every improvement strategy is available to every company. You must not only understand what drives your business, you must also know where you stand in the marketplace vis-à-vis your competitors. In this chapter, we will show you how to map your competitive position so that you can see the options available to you. We will then explore in greater detail, in both this chapter and the next, how you can apply the various performance-improvement approaches to escape the pull of the first law.

The analysis will also show you some important considerations in crafting a merger-and-acquisition strategy that optimizes the performance of a portfolio of businesses. M&A is always a risky option: most mergers actually destroy value rather than create it.[1] But some companies can create substantial shareholder value by understanding the competitive positions of all the businesses in their portfolio. Dun & Bradstreet, for instance, was able to grow its revenue and earnings about 13 percent a year for a ten-year period mainly by divesting certain kinds of companies and acquiring others, all based on assessing their competitive positions in the way we will describe.

MAPPING YOUR POSITION IN THE MARKETPLACE

In the previous chapter we suggested that you analyze the experience curve for your industry, your competitors, and your own company. That's a good way to begin assessing your competitive position in the marketplace, and it leads to a tool that is even more useful.

Market Leaders Outperform Followers

Let's start where we left off, with the fact that market leaders in general outperform their competitors. Table 3.1, taken from an annual analysis by *Fortune* magazine, shows a sample of leading companies compared with followers in nine different industries. The average ten-year return for the leaders was 267 percent. For the followers, it was 68 percent. A similar relationship holds for price-to-earnings ratios and price-to-book-value ratios. Market leaders are nearly always far more valuable than followers.

Note that the disparity in performance—profits, shareholder returns, and other measures—far outweighs the disparity in revenues. A market leader might sell twice as many units as a follower. But since it is farther down the experience curve and its costs are lower, it might make four times as much profit on each unit sold. Its profits on that line of business

TABLE 3.1

Market Leaders Outperform Their Peers

INDUSTRY	LEADER	TEN-YEAR RETURN (%)	FOLLOWER	TEN-YEAR RETURN (%)
Airlines	AMR	48%	Delta	−96%
Chemicals	Dow Chemical	116%	DuPont	34%
Commercial Banks	Citigroup	381%	Bank of America	211%
Entertainment	Time Warner	992%	Walt Disney	63%
Motor Vehicles	GM	10%	Ford	−10%
Pharmaceuticals	J&J	211%	Pfizer	116%
Food Consumer Products	PepsiCo	159%	Sara Lee	34%
Household & Personal Products	Procter & Gamble	184%	Kimberly-Clark	79%
Petroleum Refining	Exxon Mobil	305%	Chevron	184%

AVERAGE OF LEADERS: 267%   AVERAGE OF FOLLOWERS: 68%

Source: *Fortune,* April 30, 2007. Note: while we do not believe that *Fortune* chose exactly the right peer comparison in every case, our own research (reported in this chapter) bears out the overall conclusion.

will thus be eight times those of the follower. In effect, it is capturing most of the "profit pool" in that industry—an idea we will return to in chapter 4. That is the true power of market leadership.

The relationship between market share and performance turns out to hold up across the board: on average, a larger share translates to superior returns. How do we know? A database called Profit Impact of Market Strategy, or PIMS, has tracked the results of more than 3,000 "strategic experiences" for more than forty years. PIMS data support two broad conclusions.

One is that the greater the market share, the greater the return. Strong market leaders in the PIMS database earned an average 28 percent return on investment (ROI). The ROI for more distant followers was 17 percent.[2]

A second conclusion may be less obvious: market share *relative to competitors* correlates with greater return. Regardless of absolute market share, PIMS companies ranking number one in the markets they chose to compete in averaged 28 percent ROI, while number-two competitors earned 21 percent, and number-three competitors earned 17 percent.

Market share relative to competitors, it turns out, is a more powerful predictor of business performance than absolute market share. But what we need in order to assess this relationship isn't just an ordinal series—who's number one, who's number two, and so on—it's a measure of *how much* one company's market share differs from another's. This is the metric that we call "relative market share," or RMS.

Your Company's RMS—and What It Means

To calculate your company's RMS, simply follow these rules:

- If you're a market leader, divide your market share by the share of your closest competitor. If you have 30 percent of the market and the follower has 20 percent, your RMS is 1.5.

- If you're a market follower, divide your market share by the share of the market leader. If you have 20 percent and the leader has 30 percent, your RMS is 0.67.

In one study, we and our colleagues analyzed the relative market position and economic performance of 185 large companies in thirty-three industries. Companies with an RMS of less than 0.3 had returns that were 8.2 percent below their cost of capital on average. Companies with an RMS between 0.6 and 1.2 earned an average of 2.3 percent above the cost of capital, while leaders with an RMS of 2.0 or greater earned 13.4 percent above the cost of capital (see figure 3.1).[3] This study also revealed that only about 20 percent of companies with an RMS less than 0.6 earned more than their cost of capital. Conversely, for companies with RMS above 1.2, only about 20 percent did *not* earn more than their cost of capital. Leadership not only provides higher average returns, it also increases the probability that companies will achieve those returns.

Market leadership is also a more potent factor influencing financial returns than which industry you happen to be in. Another study we and our colleagues conducted—this one of 2,000 companies in the Compustat

FIGURE 3.1
Higher Returns from Leadership

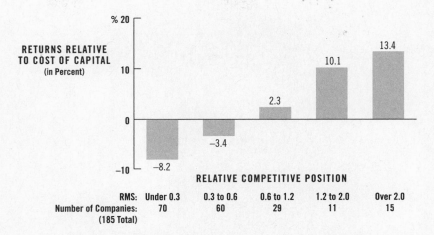

RETURNS RELATIVE
TO COST OF CAPITAL
(in Percent)

RELATIVE COMPETITIVE POSITION

RMS:	Under 0.3	0.3 to 0.6	0.6 to 1.2	1.2 to 2.0	Over 2.0
Number of Companies:	70	60	29	11	15

(185 Total)

Note: 33 industries/185 companies studied in detail by Bain & Company teams, including analytical determination of business definition. Numbers shown in the figure differ from the results of the PIMS database quoted earlier because figure 3.1 shows return on assets minus cost of capital, while the PIMS study measured returns on invested capital.

database—found that only about 17 percent of the variation in company performance could be attributed to differences from one industry to another.[4] All the rest was attributable to a company's position *within* its industry. In other words, market leaders in slow-growth industries, on average, outperform market followers in high-growth industries.

The studies also illustrate our point about *why* market leaders earn disproportionate returns. In one cross-industry survey using the PIMS database, the number-one company was able to charge prices 2.6 percent higher on average than low-ranked competitors could charge, perhaps because it had a better-known brand, noticeably better product, or a better reputation. Its costs were 6 percent lower, thanks to its position on the experience curve. Those seemingly small differences added up to profits for the leading company that were nearly three times as great, on average, as the profits of the lowest-ranked competitor.

The ROA/RMS graph. Now let's plot a different chart, comparing RMS and economic return (usually return on assets or ROA) for all the competitors in an industry. In a correctly defined business, the relative market

FIGURE 3.2

ROA/RMS Chart

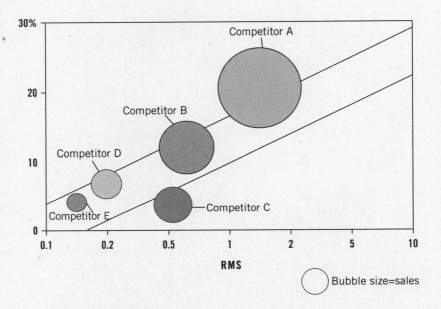

share and the relative long-term profitability of well-managed companies will tend to line up in more or less linear fashion, as seen in figure 3.2. You will notice on the figure that we have drawn two lines designed to capture a reasonable amount of variation, thus making a band. There is nothing magic about the width of the band; it simply helps highlight the general slope and the relationship between profitability and market share for leaders and followers. (The slope of the band, however, is not arbitrary: it is related to the slope of the industry experience curve.) Though we generally prefer ROA as a measure of economic performance, you can use other measures when appropriate. Whatever the measure, relative market share will usually correlate highly with long-term returns. If it does not, the analysis provided in this chapter will show you how to explain the differences. Departures from the band may be short-term aberrations, or they may be evidence of important differences in business models or performance-improvement strategies employed by your competitors. So they're essential to an understanding of what's going on in the marketplace.

As with the experience curve, one essential element is to get the business definition right, to ensure that all the right competitors (and only the right competitors) are included. Companies share a business definition when they share many of the same costs, customers, and capabilities. Shared *costs* refers primarily to costs incurred in serving a company's market segments. A commercial real-estate brokerage, for instance, doesn't have the same cost structure as a residential real-estate brokerage. Shared *customers* refers both to market segments and to how a buying decision is made. Paper-clip manufacturers and computer makers both sell to businesses, but the purchase decision is made by different people in the organization according to different criteria. So the paper-clip company and the computer company don't really have shared customers.

Shared *capabilities*, finally, refers to what a company can do. United Rentals, for example, has become the largest equipment-rental company in North America through an aggressive acquisition strategy. Even though the company's units cater to four different types of customers (construction, industrial, traffic, and homeowners), its best-in-class capabilities in ensuring equipment availability and otherwise managing its assets apply equally well to all four segments. So the appropriate business definition is "equipment rental" rather than, say, "construction equipment rental," and it made sense for United to acquire businesses in all four segments.

Geography is the other critical criterion in determining appropriate business definition. The relevant competitors of a hair salon are local, because the market for that kind of personal services is local. The relevant competitors of a nationwide trucking company are all the other truckers that operate nationwide, while the relevant competitors of an electronics-components manufacturer might be anywhere in the world. Depending on your business, your competitive battleground might be a mile in diameter or it might encompass the globe. Companies that operate outside your competitive battleground aren't—for the moment, at least—your true competitors.

What the experience curve was to the first law, the ROA/RMS graph is to this second one. It is your map of the marketplace and your competi-

FIGURE 3.3

Semiconductor Foundries (2004)

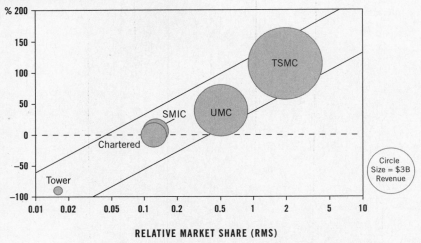

Note: ROIC calculated as net income/capital expediture and is shown in reported currency.

The top two are Taiwan Semiconductor Manufacturing Co. (TSMC) and United Microelectronics Corp. (UMC), also based in Taiwan. Semiconductor Manufacturing International Corp. (SMIC) is based in Shanghai; Chartered Semiconductor Manufacturing is in Singapore; and Tower Semiconductor is a smaller Israeli company.

Source: Company 10Ks

tors, the tool that allows you to assess your position and therefore determine the options available to you to increase your odds of success.

Chart Your Position on the ROA/RMS Graph

On average, most companies are in the band. Figure 3.3, for example, shows the graph for semiconductor "foundries"—the companies that do contract manufacturing of custom computer chips typically designed elsewhere. We have compiled ROA/RMS graphs for industries as diverse as electronics retailing, soft drinks, equipment rental, and many others over a period of years, and they all look remarkably similar.

But on many such charts, not every company falls within the band. Averages can be misleading, and the most instructive examples for a manager are those where companies do not fall in the band. There are plenty of businesses where performance seems to be driven by factors other than RMS, as we suggested earlier. In the rest of this chapter, we'll discuss all of these variations, along with strategies you can use to better your position on the chart.

Overall, there are five generic positions a company can occupy on an ROA/RMS chart (see figure 3.4):

1. In-band leaders

2. Overperformers (leaders or followers)

3. In-band followers

4. Below-band leaders (high RMS but below-average returns)

5. Distant or below-band followers (low RMS and below-average returns)

The ROA/RMS graph reflects the challenge that faces followers. In our study of sustained-value creators (see chapter 1), we looked at the perfor-

FIGURE 3.4

Five Broad Areas

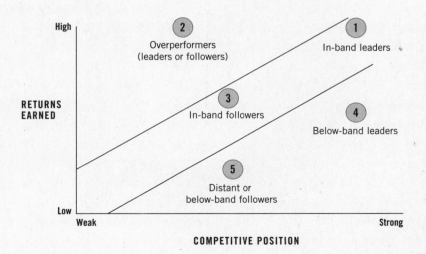

mance of close followers as well as leaders. Over the ten years from 1996 to 2006, about 35 percent of these followers declined in position to become distant followers or else exited the business, while about 40 percent stayed in roughly the same position. Only about 20 percent were able to achieve parity with the leader, and less than 5 percent took over the leadership position. But followers don't have to abandon hope. In this chapter, we will show some of the methods followers have used to challenge—and outcompete—leaders.

Why would a company fall outside the band? There are a number of reasons, as we'll see in a moment. Some represent opportunities for you, but others represent danger signs and potential vulnerabilities. Some relate to choice of strategies or an ability to meet customer needs better than the competition; others reflect a failure to manage to the experience curve. Often an outside-the-band position is temporary. Over time, the company will be pushed by competitive forces back into the band or will be driven out of business. But some innovative or very aggressive companies—the overperformers in the chart—are able to keep themselves above the band for extended periods. You can use some of the overperformers' strategies to improve your position regardless of where you currently fall in the band. Most often, these come from developing proprietary insights into customers' needs and behaviors.

Your position on the graph reveals much about your capabilities. It shows how you have managed your prices, costs, and your relationship with your customers, all as compared with competitors. It shows whether you have some combination of capabilities that can place you above the band—or whether, by contrast, you lack the capabilities even to be in the band. It determines what your options are and what resources you will have at your disposal. Though you can follow some improvement strategies regardless of where you are in the band, others depend on your position. Your competitors' positions will determine many of their options as well. Using the graph, you can predict what they are most likely to do, and you can assess what you must do. For all these reasons, one of the most critical diagnoses a newly appointed general manager can make is to understand her company's position on the band and the likely direction of movement if she does no more than preserve the status quo.

UNDERSTANDING YOUR OPTIONS
FOR PERFORMANCE IMPROVEMENT

So the first task is to diagnose where you are and where your competitors are. The second task is to know *why* you and your competitors occupy the positions you do. The final task in this context is to decide on the options available to you and on the implications for action. We'll discuss these tasks for each of the five generic positions on the chart, since each position has its own characteristics, drivers, and possibilities (see table 3.2). We'll also recount some stories about companies that found themselves in each position, and what they did to maintain or change it.

1. In-Band Leaders: Stay the Course, Aggressively

In this situation, the market leader is where it ought to be. Its costs and prices are in line with the experience curve. It has a high market share and high, stable returns. It generates plenty of cash that it can reinvest in the business. Because of all that, a market leader is usually the leader in quality, service, and technology as well. Some companies, such as General Electric, are leaders in several industries at once. Others, such as Apple with the iPod/iTunes combination, are leaders in only one of their lines of business.

For most, the chief strategic imperative is to reinvest to gain still more market share. More share is most valuable to the leader: not only is it more profitable, it also widens the experience-curve gap between the leader and its competitors. Frequently, it is less costly for the leader to acquire share than for a follower.

Because of its financial returns, the leader is in a good position to set and then *raise* industry standards of excellence in products, service, quality, and innovation. That's one way it can protect and extend its position. It also may be able to expand into adjacent markets, thereby enlarging the profit pools to which it can gain access (as we will discuss in more detail in the following chapter). When Wal-Mart moved into groceries, it could bring to bear all its well-earned expertise in sourcing and retail operations, and so could outperform most of its competitors in that market as

TABLE 3.2

Your Performance-Improvement Options

MARKET POSITION	TYPICAL CHARACTERISTICS	EXAMPLE ACTIONS
1. In-band leaders: *stay the course, aggressively*	– Has high market share, with high, stable returns – Generates plenty of cash to outinvest competitors on quality, service, technology, and innovation	– Reinvest to gain share, continue to cut costs, widening profit gap with competitors – Raise industry standards of excellence in products, service, quality, and innovation – Exploit close-in adjacent businesses
2. Overperformers: *invest to maintain position*	– Operates under a price umbrella (in danger of collapsing), charging a premium, with disproportionate returns or – Has unique innovations and capabilities, e.g., a drug under patent, unusually high customer loyalty, or a breakthrough product like the iPod – Takes the "high road" in differentiating products from competitors or serves customers better	–Reduce costs to prepare for price umbrella to collapse – If distant follower, consider opportunistic sale/merger at current high price for business – Market the innovation effectively to prospective customers by segment and increase loyalty – Set prices to maximize earnings, but continue aggressive cost management – Invest in building brand, detailed segmentation plans, improving products and services, trading up customers to new premium products – Manage costs aggressively down the experience curve
3. In-band followers: *innovate and improve*	– Is a solid number-two or number-three player, rarely the cost leader, with acceptable though fluctuating profitability	– Invest aggressively: innovate, cut costs, improve customer loyalty – Acquire underperformer to increase scale and market share – Closely monitor potential missteps by leader
4. Below-band leaders: *diagnose the reason, invest for leadership*	– May be coasting on past performance, not managing costs well, suffering from quality problems or lack of innovation – Or may be investing to gain share	– Diagnose the reasons for underperformance and invest in the right actions, e.g., improving relative cost position, reducing "price leakage" (ad hoc discounting, markdowns, allowances that reduce actual prices below expected), increasing customer focus, etc.
5. Distant or below-band followers: *up or out*	– Has low market share and below-average earnings, may be caused by many factors (e.g., not managing costs as well as competitors, not keeping customers through poor service, etc.)	– Merge with a larger competitor – Differentiate for and win niche segments, then defend and expand – Pursue very aggressive performance-improvement actions – Use the band to make M&A decisions and manage a portfolio for higher returns

well. A leader almost always has some capabilities that it can leverage to continue to drive market power and influence. As Chris Zook has shown, these capabilities can be based on a better understanding of customers (discussed later); they can also be based on channel, on product cost or innovation, and on access to capital (the market leader outinvests the competition). Gillette, for example, has continually invested in break-through innovations such as the multiblade razor. It has introduced incremental product improvements (blade lubricant strips, for example), and it has moved aggressively into adjacent markets (women's razors, disposables). It has also relentlessly pursued operational efficiency, reinvesting the proceeds in brand building and product development. Between 2000 and 2004, its sales grew at a compound annual rate of 7.8 percent, even though it already commanded a strong leadership share of the market.

But sometimes a market leader comes under attack, usually because it has let its costs rise beyond where they should be or because it has grown complacent in dealing with customers. In fact, the biggest single danger for market leaders is falling into what we call "satisfactory underperformance." Executives begin to think "We are the biggest and most profitable company in the business—isn't that good enough?" The fact is, "good enough" may not be good enough when compared with where you ought to be. You ought to have a solid leadership position not only in market share but in cost, quality, and customer loyalty. If you don't achieve your full potential, you are underperforming. You are also vulnerable to attack.

One company that highlights this kind of vulnerability—and also the power of a market leader to respond—is Nielsen Media Research. Nielsen was an in-band leader, but it was not operating at full potential. It came under severe attack on two fronts. A competitor was introducing new technology, potentially changing the dynamics of the business. The company's own lack of attention to costs and customers had weakened its position. But it was able to marshal the resources of a market leader to counterattack on both fronts, and thanks to its forceful response it was able to recover. One of the virtues of leadership is that it provides many advantages, even to a company that has temporarily let down its guard.

Nielsen fights back. The Nielsen ratings of national television shows are well known today, just as they have been for half a century; you can find selected ratings for the United States every Wednesday in *USA Today*. Nielsen Media Research, once a division of ACNielsen and now owned by a privately held firm called The Nielsen Company, is the organization that provides these ratings. It has long been the unquestioned leader in its industry.

Back in 1984, though, Nielsen Media Research president Jim Lyons found himself with a huge, two-front battle on his hands.

Until that time, Nielsen had always had a commanding lead in the market for national television ratings. It relied both on diaries kept by survey participants and on meters attached to participants' sets. But these "passive" meters recorded only whether the television was on and what channel it was tuned to. Now a UK company, AGB, had come up with a new technology that many in the industry thought was better. Dubbed Peoplemeters, AGB's devices allowed individual viewers in survey homes to record when they were actually watching a show. AGB's system would thus be able to provide the demographic information that advertisers craved. If networks wanted to claim that a show was popular among women between eighteen and thirty-four, they would now have the data to prove it. Nielsen had no comparable technology in the works. AGB also promised to provide its service at 70 percent of what Nielsen was then charging.

The prospect of this new technology was so enticing to customers that the major U.S. networks were helping to fund AGB's tests. Customers loved the idea that Nielsen, which they thought had become unresponsive, would finally face some competition. They loved the idea that they would get a better, more accurate product, a product that would allow them to sell more targeted advertising at a premium. And they particularly loved the prospect of getting all that information for a lower price.

Nielsen was also a leader in the local television-ratings business, although in that business it had always had stiff competition. Traditionally, local ratings of shows depended exclusively on diaries; Nielsen and its chief competitor, Arbitron, had only just begun to wire up survey households with passive meters. In the days when survey respondents only filled out diaries, television stations often subscribed to both Nielsen and Arbitron. The diaries were unreliable, and the stations figured they needed all the information they could get. With meters now supplementing diaries, most stations decided they needed only one provider. So the race was on to get meters into people's homes, locality by locality, and to win the resulting business. But Nielsen took longer than Arbitron to install meters, and its costs were higher. At one point, Arbitron had won seven straight competitions.

So Nielsen, while it was still positioned in the industry as an in-band leader, had in fact established a kind of price umbrella. It had been lax in managing its costs and had failed to come down the experience curve. It had been indifferent to its customers' needs to the point where the customers were actually funding potential competitors. Faced with the new competition, Nielsen executives didn't respond effectively at first. They wrote white papers, for instance, on why AGB's Peoplemeters wouldn't work.

Finally, however, Lyons and his team conducted a full-potential performance-improvement diagnostic of their company's situation. On the local front, said Lyons, "we realized that our product was overdesigned, and that our processes for metering a market were unwieldy. Arbitron would continue to win the competitive battles unless we did something about our costs and lead times." On the national front, they realized how dissatisfied their customers were, and that those customers in fact would be glad to have another competitor in the marketplace. They could see that AGB was likely to win significant market share, provided it could raise the capital required for a nationwide rollout of its Peoplemeters.

Next, Nielsen took quick, effective action on both fronts.

Locally, the company launched what was known as "Project Civic"—a reference to the popular Honda model that met customers' needs at a very low cost and price point. ("Our product is a Cadillac," said Lyons, "and what our customers want is a Civic.") It slashed expenses relentlessly, reducing costs 32 percent on a one-time basis and ongoing costs 16 percent. It cut installation time by 47 percent. The reductions enabled Nielsen to offer prices and installation times that Arbitron couldn't match. Nielsen also moved up the timing for rolling out metered markets.

Nationally, the company invested heavily in creating its own Peoplemeters. It announced an aggressive roll-out plan; indeed, it began installing them in its markets as fast as it could manufacture them. Thanks to its greater resources, it was quickly able to overtake AGB in installations. It also promoted its Peoplemeters heavily, and the ensuing publicity made it difficult for AGB to secure the financing it needed for expansion. Soon Nielsen was maintaining its aggressive installation schedule while AGB, short of funds, had to postpone installing its own devices. "I never thought taking on Nielsen would be quite the challenge it is," AGB's president told the *New York Times*. The *Times* itself commented, "This could be called a David and Goliath story, except that in such a story David wins."[5]

The results were everything Lyons and the company might have hoped for. Nielsen's local division, its costs and lead times down, won the vast majority of new local-station business and ultimately forced Arbitron out of the market for local television ratings. Its national division had the first working national Peoplemeter sample and effectively discouraged AGB from completing its planned assault. In 1988, AGB halted its operations in the U.S. market. For Nielsen, it was a success story that lasts to this day—the company remains far and away the dominant player in the television-ratings industry.[6]

The story shows what a market leader can accomplish when it diagnoses its position accurately and takes fast, coordinated action to achieve its full-potential performance. In both cases, Nielsen was able to lower its costs, move quickly, and take advantage of its greater experience and scale to outperform its competitor. It solidified its position in the upper part of the band. The story also shows just how difficult it can be for followers to overturn a leader's position once the leader awakens to the threat of competition.

2. Overperformers: Invest to Maintain Position

Overperformers are in an apparently contradictory position: they are not necessarily market leaders, but they earn the kind of returns that market leaders earn. How do we explain this? There are at least three possibilities:

Price umbrella (in danger of collapsing). One situation that can account for a company being in the overperformer category is a price umbrella. Price umbrellas are great as long as they last: you can charge a premium price, earn disproportionate returns, and outinvest your in-band competitors. Trouble is, price umbrellas don't last indefinitely. If they did, the American steel industry would still be thriving on the same basis that it always did.

Blockbuster recently discovered how easily price umbrellas can collapse, in this case because of the emergence of a new technology. Blockbuster was dominant in the video-rental market, with several thousand stores and a market share of 45 percent. But it had created a price umbrella, particularly because its widely despised late fees significantly raised the average price its customers paid. As use of the Internet spread, upstarts in many different industries were trying to use the new technology to take on incumbents. Thanks to the price umbrella, video rental turned out to be one of the better bets. Netflix, the Internet-based upstart, was able to offer online subscribers four DVDs at a time, with unlimited exchanges and no late fees, all for $19.95 a month. Blockbuster had its own subscription model, but it was for in-store rental only and was priced at $29.95.

Netflix grew rapidly, and Blockbuster was slow to react. It began to incur operating losses, and its stock price plunged. In 2004, Blockbuster finally launched an online rental business, and soon thereafter it eliminated its late fees. But as Adrian Slywotzky notes in his recent book *The Upside*, it may have been too little, too late. Two years later, Blockbuster Online had only a little more than one-quarter as many subscribers as Netflix. Today, says Slywotzky, "other companies—not Blockbuster—are maneuvering to position themselves as the next decade's leaders in entertainment distribution." Netflix, meanwhile, was "moving up the value chain with coproduction and marketing deals for independent movies."[7] (In mid-2007, however, Blockbuster's online service was growing faster than Netflix, thanks partly to a decision to allow subscribers to swap an online rental for a new movie at a Blockbuster store. Netflix was fighting back with price cuts and twenty-four-hour customer-service telephone lines.[8])

The real danger of a price umbrella is that a company's executives will neglect to manage their costs down the experience curve. They may even add costs to "support" the price premium driven by features that are not really valued by the customer. The longer the umbrella continues, the greater this danger—and the greater the chance that someone else will spot the opportunity and figure out how to come in under the umbrella and offer customers a better value proposition. If you find yourself the beneficiary of a price umbrella, analyze exactly what the situation is. A company-only price umbrella like Blockbuster's makes you immediately vulnerable. You need to invest your outsized earnings quickly in reducing costs and prices, in innovating to deliver more value to your customers, or both. Otherwise you may lose market share to a competitor with a new technology, cost structure, or business model. An industry-wide umbrella, like that of the steel industry until the 1960s, presents the threat that someone outside your industry may enter it, or that a current competitor could suddenly decide to break the umbrella. If your cost position is good relative to competitors, you may be able to gain market share even as you invest in reducing your costs still further. If you are a distant follower, you may be better off selling the business while the price is relatively high.

Unique innovations and capabilities. Some innovations are easily copied by competitors. Others are difficult, costly, and time-consuming to copy. A drug under patent is protected from direct competition for roughly twenty years. A breakthrough product such as the iPod and iTunes may have a portion of the market to itself for as much as five years. Any such hard-to-copy innovation can put a company into the overperformer category for a while; this is one of the three generic strategies that help companies escape the experience curve. But companies in this position will always be under attack. Without sustained investment in continuing innovation, they will find it difficult or impossible to keep this advantage for a long period.[9]

Investing effectively in innovation, of course, is always a challenge, and theorists have described a wide range of approaches. Adrian Slywotzky reminds us of the concept of "little box/big box" thinking: rather than simply improve its products (the little box), a company should figure out how to address other, broader customer needs (the big box). Continental AG, for example, deliberately moved from one relatively narrow business (tire manufacturer) to a much broader one (supplier of complete technology systems to auto makers), thereby increasing its share of the automotive value chain.[10] Our colleagues Darrell Rigby and Chris Zook pioneered the idea of "open-market" innovation, in which companies collaborate with vendors, customers, or even competitors to exchange and develop ideas. The big packaging company Tetra Pak, for instance, was attempting to develop a revolutionary paperboard package that would permit sterilization of the food inside; it found a company with expertise in sterilizing hospital equipment to help it with the technological challenge.[11] More recently, Rigby has developed what he calls a Bothbrain™ approach to innovation, through which companies combine imaginative, creative thinking (right brain) with a hard-nosed analysis of customer needs and product economics (left brain). Procter & Gamble, for instance, spends half of its research-and-development funds on long-term projects; its "blue sky" and long-term R&D groups report directly to the CEO and are responsible for coming up with wholly new ideas. Meanwhile, shorter-term innovation is part of every brand manager's job, and innovation metrics (such as speed to market) are a key part of brand managers' bonuses.

Innovation need not be limited to products. A company that develops extensive *process* innovations may put itself in the overperformer category by creating a unique cost structure. The classic example is Dell. Dell's direct-sales, build-to-order business model has never yet been successfully copied. The model has allowed Dell to turn its inventory much faster than competitors (eighty-nine turns a year in 2006, for example, as compared with eighteen for IBM/Lenovo and ten for Hewlett-Packard) and to bring new technology to market faster (about one-third of the average time required by competitors). The company has leveraged that advantage and managed its costs down over time. Between 1995 and 2001, it increased its market share fivefold, improved its RMS from 0.25 to 1.2, and increased return on sales (ROS) from 4.3 percent to 7 percent—the only company in the industry to improve its profitability during that period.

But Dell also illustrates the innovator's potential vulnerability. Since 2005, competitors have been catching up to Dell's efficiency as the supply chain in personal computers has standardized. Moreover, growth in PCs is now coming from two segments—consumers on the one hand and buyers in emerging markets on the other—that prefer the retail channel. These two factors have combined to slow Dell's growth and threaten its margins.

In response, Dell has moved to cut costs further. It also revamped its consumer-product-development efforts, aiming both to make its offerings more appealing and to introduce new models at least twice as frequently as before.[12]

The "high road." A second generic strategy that can place a company in the overperformer category is rigorous customer segmentation and successful differentiation of its products through branding. This is what we call a "high-road strategy," as described by our partners Vijay Vishwanath and Jonathan Mark in a *Harvard Business Review* article in 1997.[13] A word of explanation is in order.

Customers in many markets divide into three rough categories. One category buys largely on price, always looking for the cheapest possible offering. A second category wants higher-quality goods than the bare minimum, additional services, or both, and is willing to pay extra. A third category of customers is loyal to a particular brand, and regularly chooses that brand over its competitors for prestige or other reasons unrelated to the performance of the product. The categories obviously aren't hard and fast. People may choose a given brand precisely because they think it always offers the best quality for the price. Whatever their predilections on that three-part scale, moreover, customers in all the categories are often willing to pay a premium for an innovative offering. Think of the iPod when it first appeared, or Starbucks's fancy coffee drinks.

So companies can, and usually do, attempt to differentiate their offerings from those of competitors. They come out with improved products and services. They offer particular combinations of features and capabilities. They invest in building their brand and try to associate their products or services with status or prestige. Rather than focusing solely on cost leadership—the "low road"—they take the "high road" and try to earn a premium by selling something that is distinctive in the customer's eyes. If companies are successful in this approach, they will land above the band. Porsche, for example, focuses only on premium sports cars and related high-end vehicles—a distinct niche in the auto industry. It enjoys some of the highest operating margins in its business.

The ROA/RMS chart for U.S. wireless telecommunications companies in 2003 illustrates these different strategies (see figure 3.5). Verizon and

FIGURE 3.5
High-Road Wireless Example

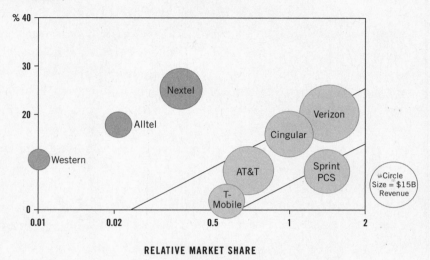

other large competitors were within the band. But Nextel and Alltel, which offered two-way walkie-talkie capabilities as well as regular cell-phone options, were firmly above the band. We will discuss a systematic way of thinking about creating this kind of differentiation in chapter 6.

High-road strategies don't negate the effects of either the experience curve or the ROA/RMS band. Rather, they add an additional variable. In consumer-products industries where brand is important, the prestige or premium conferred by a trusted brand may allow the brand owner to earn higher returns than predicted by the band chart. In financial services and other industries where companies face high upfront customer-acquisition costs, customer loyalty can have similar effects. In credit cards, for instance, customer-acquisition costs are so high that retaining a single customer for one year can generate more profit than bringing in twenty new customers.

But high-road companies face an obvious, and critical, risk. Because they earn outsized returns relative to their market share, they occupy niches that competitors will find highly attractive. So they can expect to be under continual attack. Consider the recent introduction of Stephon Marbury's Starbury One athletic shoes, designed to retail for about $15. Marbury, a star for the New York Knicks basketball team, is trying to break the price umbrella in athletic shoes established by brand-name manufacturers. Time will tell if this attack works; the premium sneaker companies may or may not be able to differentiate their products so that customers will pay up to ten times as much for a similar shoe. In any event, fending off the attackers requires heavy investment on a variety of fronts. High-road companies must invest in building their brand, in improving their products or services so that they really are different from those of competitors, and in trading their customers up to new premium products.

One key to a high-road strategy is segmenting and understanding your customers better than your competitors do, and more skillfully anticipating their future needs and behaviors. Another is to remember the law that costs and prices always decline. Because these companies face heavy expenditures in product innovation, brand maintenance, and other areas, they must manage their costs aggressively down the experience curve. Indeed, in some industries the premium segment can be seen as a business in itself, and a separate ROA/RMS graph can be plotted just for that segment. In this mini-industry, we would again find that market leaders—cost leaders—earn the highest returns.[14] But the slope of the band is steeper than in value-oriented industries, and leaders can win by making it steeper still—that is, making the industry more investment-intensive and thus more difficult for competitors. Look again at the chart in figure 3.5: we haven't drawn it in, but Nextel, Alltel, and Western line up in a band of their own, with higher returns and a steeper slope than the band occupied by their larger competitors.

In summary, all overperformers occupy positions that are hard to maintain. Companies basking under price umbrellas will find that the umbrellas are prone to collapse. Those with unique, hard-to-copy innovations must keep on innovating as competitors catch up. Those pursuing high-road strategies can sustain their position only if they focus on the right parts of the market and invest to keep those customers satisfied—not always an easy task, since competitors are always out gunning for those high-margin segments.

3. In-Band Followers: Innovate and Improve

The classic follower in the public's mind was always Avis, which for years proudly advertised its number-two position in the rental-car business and did its best to convince travelers that since it was number two, it had to try harder. Plenty of other perennial followers are familiar as well: Target (follower to Wal-Mart), General Mills (Kellogg), Burger King (McDonald's), and Advanced Micro Devices (Intel). In-band followers typically occupy a solid number-two or number-three position. They are rarely the cost leader. Their market share is by definition neither particularly high nor particularly low. Their profits are usually acceptable, though not outstanding. Earnings in many cases fluctuate over the course of a business cycle more than they do for the leaders.

If your company is in a follower position, you face certain characteristic threats and opportunities. One threat is that an aggressive leader will continue to drive its own costs down, set ever-higher standards of excellence, and expand its market share at your expense. A second threat is that a more-distant follower will leapfrog you and and push you farther down the band. The opportunities, of course, are to solidify your own position and even to move up the band into the number-one spot, leapfrogging a leader that has grown complacent.

How to take advantage of that opportunity? One way is to avoid direct head-to-head competition with the leader—to find a segment, in other words, that the leader isn't dominating. Target and Lowe's both grew by positioning themselves slightly differently from Wal-Mart and Home Depot. The two followers' stores were more appealing, their products slightly more upscale. They appealed to shoppers who wanted good value but who also wanted a higher level of service and amenities than the leaders provided, and who were willing to pay slightly higher prices. The strategy allowed both to inch upwards on the band.

But sometimes followers choose to attack the leader head on. Consider two stories and the lessons they teach us.

Sony takes over number one. Sony Corp. established its videogame subsidiary, Sony Computer Entertainment Inc. (SCEI) in 1993, and plunged into the burgeoning game industry. The market leader at the time, Nintendo, was almost synonymous with videogames—as in, "Let's go to my house and play Nintendo." In 1994, the Super Nintendo Entertainment System enjoyed a 2.0 RMS. SCEI's early forays into the market, by contrast, were distinctly unsuccessful. In 1994, its RMS was only 0.19, its return on sales a doleful −5 percent.[15]

But SCEI decided to attack rather than retreat. It analyzed Nintendo's and other competitors' strategies, looking for weak spots. It sought out software developers to learn their frustrations. Then it invested in building a game-changing product.

The new PlayStation videogame platform would be built around high-quality, rapid-response three-dimensional graphics. That by itself required a series of other innovations: a custom-designed 32-bit integrated circuit, an algorithm for 3-D image processing, and a low-cost, high-capacity storage medium so that the games could contain all the necessary detail and background music. All of these had to be provided in high volume at low cost. To minimize long-term costs, SCEI built the game functions into customized circuit boards, using chips produced by LSI (one of the most experienced companies in consumer electronics) rather than using general-purpose microprocessors. That allowed it to capture full experience-curve benefits on the circuit boards as volume grew, and to reduce the number of parts required for each machine over time. For memory, it used standard, PC-compatible dynamic random access memory (DRAM) chips. That made it possible for SCEI to capture the benefits of PC-driven cost declines in these chips.

SCEI partnered with third-party game developers who were eager to produce arcade-level games for the home market and had found it difficult to do so with Nintendo. It designed the PlayStation architecture to evolve with future technology upgrades, so that it could capitalize on evolution in chip production (increasing wafer size, for example). And it relied on CD-ROMs as its primary game medium. CD-ROMs, much cheaper and faster to produce than the traditional game medium of mask ROM, enabled the company to respond rapidly to changes in demand. Finally, SCEI put in place a direct-distribution model that cut costs and allowed it to track sales in real time.

All these moves added up to an enormous competitive advantage. SCEI's powerful graphics were more appealing, even though users felt they sometimes took longer to load. The company was driving its costs down the experience curve. It could produce to order and resupply hit titles promptly. Nintendo and other competitors such as Sega, by contrast, produced mask ROMs in bulk, based on forecast sales. If a game turned out to be a hit, the manufacturers needed a couple of months to resupply the stores. If a game bombed, wholesalers and retailers had to dump their inventory on the market at big discounts.

In the seven-year period from 1994 to 2001, PlayStation kept gaining market share, and eventually replaced Nintendo as the dominant gaming console. By 2001, its RMS was 3.5, its ROS 8.3 percent. Sega withdrew from home videogames to focus on software and arcade games. Nintendo began focusing on its portable-game segment in order to increase its return on sales. SCEI, the market follower, had become the market leader.

There's a postscript to this story. By 2007, Nintendo seemed to be coming back fast: its new product, Nintendo Wii, was taking "the lead in buzz and sales over another new console, the Sony PlayStation 3," according to a newspaper report.[16] That may turn out to be another example of how leadership can change hands when a follower develops and executes aggressive strategies.

Tesco counterattacks. The British retail chain Tesco is the largest retailer in Britain and the fourth largest in the world. Founded in 1919 by Jack Cohen in London's East End, the company was incorporated as Tesco Stores in 1932. (The name came from the initials of Cohen's tea supplier and partner, T. E. Stockwell, and the first two letters of Cohen.) It grew rapidly, and in the 1970s and early 1980s was the market leader in British grocery retailing. But the market was consolidating in those years, and Sainsbury's was able to take over the number-one slot with a strategy that offered consumers a better combination of quality and value. Suddenly Tesco was a market follower.

Like Sony, Tesco went on the offensive. Led by CEO Ian McLauren and then by his successor, Terry Leahy, the company focused first on improving its operations and then on moving into larger stores that were outside of town centers. That enabled it to expand its selling space dramatically: square footage more than doubled between 1994 and 2004. (Sainsbury's space increased only about 50 percent.) Then it focused on innovation. It led the market in developing customer loyalty, for instance, through the use of the Tesco Clubcard, now with thirteen million members. It expanded home-delivery service. Unlike Sainsbury's, which traditionally catered to middle- to upper-class customers, Tesco successfully appealed to all income segments with a clearly marked good-better-best delineation of its wares. It created a variety of stores, ranging from giant "Tesco Extra" hypermarkets (which carry the broadest range of Tesco's products, food and nonfood alike) to "Tesco Express" convenience stores and "One Stop" ministores. It also pursued a strategy of acquisition in adjacent markets, expanding into homewares, entertainment, clothing, fuel, telecommunications, and financial services, and it was first to use the Internet as a major sales channel. It expanded internationally, developed its supply chain, and continued to drive down costs.

Thanks to these moves, Tesco passed Sainsbury's in market share in the mid-1990s. Today it has left Sainsbury's well behind; in January 2007, its RMS was 2.0. Its earnings performance is even more dramatic: from 2001 to 2005 Tesco maintained an EBIT (earnings before interest and taxes) margin of roughly 5 percent, while Sainsbury's plunged from just above 4 percent to about 2 percent.

BOTH THESE EXAMPLES SUGGEST THAT IT'S POSSIBLE FOR A FOL-lower to become a leader. But it isn't easy, and it doesn't occur frequently, as we noted earlier. The leader must be relatively complacent. The follower must invest aggressively and astutely to outperform the leader on a variety of fronts. It can develop a series of innovations, like Sony Computer Entertainment—and it must hope that the innovations will meet the customer's needs better than the incumbent can. It can pursue cost improvement and customer loyalty, like Tesco—and it must hope that the leader won't respond quickly along the same lines. Alternatively, a follower may want to acquire an underperformer in order to increase scale and market share. Even then, it is likely to have a tough time taking on an alert and aggressive leader.

4. Below-Band Leaders: Diagnose the Reason, Invest for Leadership

Below-band leaders have a high market share, but they are not earning the returns that their share of the market should give them. Why not?

One possibility is that they are coasting on past market-leading performance. They probably aren't managing their costs effectively. They may be suffering from quality problems or lack of innovation. They may be experiencing "price leakage"—ad hoc discounting, markdowns, allowances, and other measures that lower actual realized prices below expected prices. They may be missing important revenue opportunities. General Motors is the poster child for companies in this situation. GM's costs are still high despite years of cutbacks, and it has been forced to discount its vehicles just to move them off dealers' lots. GM as we write is losing its market-leading position to Toyota, which already enjoys far higher returns. Ford and Chrysler face similar challenges. (Toyota, by comparison, is fearful of complacency, according to reports in the press. In the United States, it has mounted "its most far-reaching initiative in 50 years of doing business here," including a complete reexamination of "product planning, customer service, sales and marketing, and even the car dealers the company doesn't directly own." It is also retraining all of its U.S. factory workers.[17])

But below-band companies in this situation aren't beyond help. Some, as we will see in a moment, can recover themselves in a remarkably short period of time and make dramatic improvements in both performance and competitive position.

A second possibility is that they know exactly what they are doing: they are investing to gain share, temporarily depressing earnings. In effect, a drama is playing out. Will the investments pay off and move the company upward, allowing it both to gain share and increase returns? Will the below-band follower somehow be able to outmaneuver the in-band leader?

We'll look at examples that illustrate both of these possibilities.

Morgan Crucible turns itself around. Morgan Crucible, a materials-engineering company based in the UK, is considerably older than General

Motors, though it found itself in a similar position. Founded in 1856, by 1872 it was the largest manufacturer of crucibles in the world. (Crucibles are vessels for holding molten metals.) Over time the company diversified extensively, and by the late twentieth century was making magnetic devices, carbon brushes, a wide variety of specialty and thermal ceramics products, and many other industrial goods. It had pursued an aggressive acquisitions policy and expanded internationally. At the turn of the twenty-first century, it included nine separate units encompassing nearly 200 different businesses in eighty countries.

But Morgan by then was significantly underperforming on many dimensions. Revenues declined at an 8.5 percent annual rate from 2000 to 2002. Earnings turned negative, and the company's debt-to-equity ratio rose sharply. In 2002, the stock price was only 10 percent of what it had been five years earlier. Warren Knowlton, brought in by the board at the end of 2002 to turn the company around, found huge pension liabilities, unsustainable debt levels, and banking covenants that were close to being breached. He found a culture with little accountability, cost control, or commercial awareness, and no real performance standards. The company was "a turgid, lumbering dinosaur," as one observer put it, "incapable of change."

Knowlton, a veteran of turnarounds at Pilkington Group and Owens Corning, created ROA/RMS charts for all of Morgan's businesses. The company as a whole was a below-band leader. Many of its businesses were in the same position. But some were distant followers, and others were in-band leaders, although still suffering from historic underinvestment and therefore in potential danger. Knowlton set about reorganizing the company based on this information. The followers would be grown or divested. The below-band leaders would be improved, and the in-band leaders supported with new investments.

Knowlton sold off several business units and consolidated those that remained into just three divisions, leaders in their markets. He moved quickly on other fronts as well. He cut overhead substantially within the business units and reduced corporate headcount by more than 60 percent. He closed the company's centralized R&D facility and located R&D staff in the business units to get these capabilities closer to the customers. He reduced total employment costs as a percent of sales from 39.3 percent in 2002 to 33.8 percent in 2006. He also turned around the company's culture, instituting rigorous performance standards and accountability. One symbolic step: closing the company's cafeteria. "We work over lunch," he told his staff.

All these moves worked. By early 2006, the company was not just healthy but financially strong: it had no debt, a secure pension fund, operating margins up to 10.6 percent (from 3.4 percent when Knowlton arrived), a positive cash position, and a share price nearly ten times higher. It had moved from a below-band leader to an in-band leader, and the company's financial performance reflected its new position. (We will explore other aspects of the Morgan Crucible story in chapter 6.)

H-E-B takes on Wal-Mart. H-E-B's name comes from Howard E. Butt, who took over the family's Texas grocery business in 1919. A grocery chain with $12.4 billion in (2006) revenue and 300-plus stores in Texas and Mexico, H-E-B was ranked number eleven on *Forbes* magazine's 2006 list of America's largest private companies. But H-E-B is small compared with the biggest operator of supermarkets in America: Wal-Mart Stores. And Wal-Mart was bent on expanding into Texas, just as it was doing all over the United States. With an average of 20 percent lower prices and 22 percent lower costs than the typical supermarket, Wal-Mart was a potentially devastating competitor.

But Charles Butt, youngest son of Howard and CEO of H-E-B, understood an important fact about the grocery business: it is primarily a local market, not a national one. Wal-Mart and other national grocery chains might be stronger nationally, but H-E-B owned 65 percent of the market in southern Texas, more than 80 percent in some localities. With that as a foundation, it could fight Wal-Mart.

So Butt and his team began investing. They added stores. They reformatted existing stores to serve customers better—for example, they increased the size of produce departments and focused on maintaining freshness, thereby out-executing Wal-Mart in an area of prime importance to the most attractive segments of shoppers. They developed a rigorous analytic approach to pricing, segmenting the products they carried based on demand elasticity and competition from Wal-Mart, then pricing accordingly. They extracted every possible nickel of savings from their supply chain and from overhead, based on detailed analysis of best practices around the world and among their own stores.

The result? H-E-B appeared to be below the band once it began investing; its earnings undoubtedly suffered. But thanks to the investment, it actually grew its market share between 1995 and 2003, despite Wal-Mart's entrance into Texas markets. In Austin, Wal-Mart captured 8 percent—but H-E-B increased its own share by five percentage points to 61 percent of the market. In San Antonio, Wal-Mart got 12 percent of the market, while H-E-B increased its share by fourteen points to 69 percent. H-E-B not only gained market share, its returns grew to be commensurate with its leadership position—*all while the company was competing against Wal-Mart.* Those that lost market share were distant followers, such as Randalls, Albertson's, and Handy Andy. None had the regional share enjoyed by H-E-B, and so none was able to attack Wal-Mart effectively. This illustrates the strategic peril faced by distant followers, especially when giants collide.

5. Distant or Below-Band Followers: Up or Out

Plenty of companies, unfortunately, find themselves in the lower left-hand corner of the chart, either below the band or just barely on it. They hold a low market share, and their earnings are below average. They are in the position of Competitor D, mentioned in chapter 2: their fate depends more on what their higher-ranking competitors do than on what they themselves do. It's not a pleasant situation for a general manager. The business is almost always falling short of expectations, and the general manager is almost always in the doghouse.

Many factors can explain why companies might end up in this position. They might not have managed their costs or prices as well as their competitors. They might offer low quality or poor service, and so have difficulty attracting and keeping customers. They might be late entrants to the market, without an investment level high enough to gain a significant share. Remember Ames Department Stores? A distant follower to Wal-Mart, Kmart, and Target in the discount-retailing marketplace, Ames could never catch up; it entered bankruptcy in 2001.

But some companies have been able to escape from such unhappy circumstances. There are three major strategies to follow.

Merge with a larger competitor. Even distant followers often have something to bring to a merger: their own share of the market, product expertise, distribution channels, and so on. If they merge with a stronger partner in the same business, the resulting combination can be formidable, and can enjoy the benefits of market leadership.

That was the strategy pursued by a major floor-covering company we'll call Floorco. In 1988, Floorco had acquired a competitor for $330 million. The business seemed to be doing well at the time of acquisition, but its performance rapidly deteriorated. By 1993 its revenue was flat. It had built up $90 million in losses over a three-year period. The combined company was still number two in its market, but its RMS was only 0.5, and its negative earnings placed it well below the band. It was in danger of becoming an ever-more-distant follower to the market leader.

Floorco's newly appointed CEO commissioned a thorough evaluation of the situation and saw that the business could be improved significantly. Under his direction, executives consolidated production of individual product lines and reconfigured the largest plant around a simplified set of products. They invested $20 million in new manufacturing technology. They focused the division's sales and marketing strategy on just two distribution channels, and they eliminated two management layers. They implemented best practices in retail centers, aligning managers' incentives with store profitability and asset management.

But the CEO also realized that all these improvements would only put his company back in the band. It would still be well behind the leader, and its profitability would not measure up to corporate expectations. The newly improved company, however, offered the CEO an opportunity to reshape the industry: if he could merge it with the leader, that new company would have a very strong RMS of 4.5. Synergies would provide some

$30 million in annual cost savings, while the one-time costs of the combination would be considerably less.

Once completed, the merger created a strong market leader. The company's value to its corporate parent increased by $340 million. Its return on sales improved from −10 percent to 18 percent—a 28 percentage point improvement. The new company was firmly back in the band, at the upper right, and with a much stronger strategic position and sustainable profitability.

SMALL COMPANIES AND NONPROFITS, WHICH ARE OFTEN CON-signed to being distant followers, can also use the merger strategy effectively to enlarge their presence in the marketplace. In Boston, for instance, Crittenton and The Women's Union were both old, well-established non-profit agencies serving different populations of women. Crittenton, which began in 1824 as a facility to house and care for unwed mothers, had developed a strong program of research and service delivery for under-privileged and at-risk women. But it lacked a diversified funding base. The Women's Union, founded in 1877 to provide education and skills training for immigrant women and other newcomers to the city, had an illustrious history of advocacy and service, along with cash in the bank (as a result of the 2004 sale of its headquarters building), but it lacked focus. And both organizations needed a succession plan, as their leaders were retiring.

Thanks to a timely encounter between board members, they found one in the same person: Elisabeth Babcock, former director of the Lynn Community Health Center (chapter 2), who signed on expressly to lead a merger. With a sharpened focus on helping low-income women and their families achieve economic self-sufficiency, the newly named Crittenton Women's Union has channeled its research and advocacy into sequenced delivery of housing, education, and job training to move families from dependency to independence. Meanwhile, the larger scale of the organization has lowered service-delivery costs (in one year turning a $500,000 operating loss into a $200,000-plus operating surplus) and raised visibility in the community, including among potential donors.

More and more nonprofit leaders, indeed, are finding that scale and market share, traditionally the priorities of the business sector, are important to their mission. "Organizations need to be larger in order to have clout," said Bill Walczak, director of the Codman Square Health Center in Boston's Dorchester neighborhood. As we wrote this book, Walczak and colleagues were looking at the advantages and disadvantages of a merger between Codman Square and Dorchester House, another community health center of roughly similar size. The proposed merger would create a $40 million organization with 550 staff, the second-largest community health center in New England. The benefits would include increased visibility among donors and clients, sizable economies of scale in overhead costs and facilities, greater negotiating power, and greater ability to launch related services—all the advantages of a larger RMS.

Win small segments, then defend and expand. Most markets—even the biggest—have many niches, and it's often the case that the leaders ignore some of the smaller ones. That presents distant followers with a prime opportunity. If they can win and defend small segments, they can use that as a foundation for growth.

One of the best-known names in the automobile industry—Honda— relied on just such a strategy.

Not many people remember Honda's early years. Founded in 1948, it grew to become Japan's largest motorcycle manufacturer. It then brought its small, user-friendly motorcycles to the United States, where the industry had traditionally been dominated by big machines aimed at hard-core bikers, and it trumpeted the little bikes' appeal to everyday citizens. ("You meet the nicest people on a Honda," chirped the advertising jingle.) But Honda then wanted to move into automobiles, an industry it didn't know. Its first car, made for the Japanese market in 1962, was dubbed "an enclosed golf cart" by critics and bombed in the market. Seven years later the company tried to enter the U.S. market. It again flopped—its cars were just too small for American tastes.

But Honda was coming down the experience curve fast: it was learning to build cars cheaper, better, and faster than its competitors. Its took only 2.8 years to bring out a new model, as compared with five years for the best U.S. company at the time and three years for Honda's best Japanese competitor. Honda spent 5 percent of sales on research and development, as compared with 4 percent for U.S. manufacturers. It came out with innovations such as the first engine-exhaust technology that passed the Clean Air Act in the United States without the need for a catalytic converter. It focused on overlooked niches: the Civic, introduced in 1973, was a small, high-quality car that got great gas mileage and turned out to be highly popular because of the sudden runup in oil prices in the 1970s. (Automotive mavens remember buyers showing up at Honda dealers to wait for their cars to arrive on the car carrier, then taking delivery of them on the spot.) In 1986 Honda became the first Japanese car company to introduce a luxury division (Acura).

Honda's revenue grew 17 percent a year between 1979 and 1990, compared with 8 percent for Ford and 6 percent for GM. By 1990, the company had become the number-four player in the U.S. market: its RMS was 0.25 and its operating margin 5.2 percent. It continued to improve during the decade: it could build the Accord, for example, for $1,500 less per vehicle than comparable vehicles made by General Motors or Ford. In 2005, Honda's RMS was 0.37 and its ROS 8.8 percent.

The Honda strategy, so to speak, is more common than it might seem. Southwest Airlines began by focusing on a single small niche, intrastate flights in Texas. Wal-Mart Stores began by serving small towns in Arkansas. If the niche is defensible—or if it is too small to interest a market leader—it can serve as the platform for experimentation, capability development, and eventual expansion.

Pursue aggressive performance improvement. At times, a company finds itself in the position of a below-band or distant follower simply because management hasn't taken the steps necessary to improve its performance. It is capable of becoming at least an in-band follower, but it needs aggressive action on multiple fronts. It has to put to work the performance-improvement tool kit that we will describe in chapter 6.

MEMC Electronic Materials is a case in point. Founded in 1959 as Monsanto Electronic Materials Co., MEMC was spun off to new owners in 1989 and taken public in 1995. It grew steadily from the 1960s through the 1980s and explosively during the 1990s, adding facilities in Asia and elsewhere.

But MEMC hit hard times at the end of the 1990s, and by 2000 it was in trouble. Its RMS was weak, and its operating margin of 1.1 percent was the lowest among the five largest producers of silicon wafers. It lagged the industry in productivity benchmarks such as quarterly volume per employee and quarterly revenue per employee. Though it received a record sixty-two patents in 1999, it was spending more than its peers on research and development—and unlike at Honda, where R&D was also high, this was money the company could ill afford. MEMC's capital expenditures over four years had exceeded its earnings, so it was both destroying shareholder value and burning cash.

By early 2001, MEMC's parent corporation, E.ON AG, was eager to sell the company. E.ON had merged with MEMC's previous parent and was under regulatory pressure to divest. What's more, the wafer industry was approaching a historic low, and E.ON wasn't eager to continue pumping money into MEMC. In July, the private-equity firm then known as Texas Pacific Group (today TPG) offered $150 million for the company. By the time the deal was finally done, in September, TPG had negotiated the price down to a token $6. In return for its pocket-money offer, TPG would get all of MEMC's equity. It would be owed $936 million by MEMC, and it would backstop a $150 million revolving credit facility.[18]

TPG's management then began to diagnose the wafer company's problems. It found three big areas for improvement.

Manufacturing costs were one area with huge potential savings. If MEMC could bring wafering productivity up to the top quartile of the industry, it could save $28 million in costs. Other improvements—yield management, aggressive attention to procurement, and changes in manufacturing processes—could add many millions more.

A second area: overhead. Detailed functional analysis of overhead expenditures—IT, finance, human resources, and so on—indicated potential savings of between $10 million and $19 million in annual costs. These changes would put MEMC in line with industry benchmarks.

Capital expenditures could also be reduced substantially. The company had already made capital expenditures of some $900 million in five years, and now believed that demand for its wafers could be serviced with only a modest level of expenditure. In this respect, management determined that it did not need to reinvest in the newest technology and could continue to drive its costs aggressively down the experience curve.

These improvements had quick and dramatic effects. With the wafer market recovering, MEMC moved from a loss of $21 million in 2001 to a profit of $117 million in 2003, and in 2004 had the highest operating margins in the industry. TPG, which had bought into MEMC for no more than a token cash investment and the assumption of risk related to the company's debt, was able to sell its shares for a very substantial gain. In late 2007, the market value of MEMC's equity stood at $19 billion.

USE THE BAND TO MANAGE A PORTFOLIO FOR HIGHER RETURNS

If you are a general manager of one business, you are most likely to encounter the issues described in the previous sections of this chapter. If you manage a portfolio of different businesses, some additional perspectives will likely apply. Like the experience curve, the band is essentially a diagnostic tool: it lets you see where companies stand vis-à-vis their competitors. It's a particularly powerful tool for analyzing and managing a diversified company's portfolio of businesses.

Suppose a company is facing a major shift in the market environment—deregulation, say, or a new treaty exposing a business to foreign competition. Band analysis can tell managers which business units are likely to survive and thrive after the change and which are unlikely to do so.

In 1989, for instance, the big Mexican conglomerate Alfa maintained twelve businesses in its portfolio—divisions as diverse as steel, carpets, and fresh meats. Its steel business, well above the band, was particularly profitable because of regulatory constraints set by the Mexican government. But then the government proposed opening up the steel industry to foreign competition. An analysis revealed that steel earnings would plummet because Alfa's units couldn't compete. But Alfa declined to sell its steel-related division, then known as Hylsamex, and so was hit hard both by new competition and by the unaccustomed market fluctuations in steel prices. It then tried to sell the division but it was too late: it couldn't find a buyer and in 2005 spun it off as a separate company. Before the North American Free Trade Agreement (NAFTA), incidentally, Alfa's other businesses were spread all over the ROA/RMS map. Since NAFTA, they have all migrated to the band.

M&A with the Band

Using the band, corporate management can also reshape a portfolio to generate substantially faster growth and higher returns over time. The underlying rationale of this approach is counterintuitive. Companies above the band are candidates for divestiture, since it's unlikely they will all be able to maintain their position without significant investment to stave off competitive attacks. Companies below the band are candidates for acquisition, since their performance can be improved. A private-equity firm we're familiar with uses this insight as the basis for its acquisition strategy, focusing on buying below-band market leaders, then improving their performance to the point where the acquirees can be merged with another underperforming follower, resold, or taken public. The firm has compiled an enviable track record with such a strategy.

As Dun & Bradstreet showed many years ago, any diversified company can put itself on a remarkable growth trajectory through this method and sustain it over time. D&B, best known for its credit reports, has in fact been a company with many different businesses—printing, broadcasting, audience research, and others. From 1968 to 1978 it enjoyed a decade of 15 percent growth in both profits and share price. At that point a man named Harrington "Duke" Drake took over as CEO. Drake knew his job was to continue D&B's growth, but he wondered how best to go about it.

The answer turned out to be a band-based portfolio-management strategy of the sort we have just described. Drake and Dick Schmidt, Drake's CFO and head of strategy, discovered that most of D&B's portfolio at the time was made up of highly independent business units spaced out along the entire ROA/RMS map. Fully one-third were overperformers with high margins and relatively low RMS, while many others either were in the band or were below-band leaders. In the following ten years, Drake and Schmidt sold fifty-two companies and purchased seventy-two others.

They did this with a carefully planned strategic goal in mind. The *divestitures* were almost all overperformers. They were not number one or number two in their markets. Their profits or market value were at historic—and probably unsustainable—highs. Because of potential cost sharing, experience sharing, or other synergies, the businesses were worth more to other companies than they were to D&B. CFO Schmidt understood that many of D&B's businesses, even if profitable or growing quickly, might be worth less to D&B's shareholders than to others—and that his job was to find the company anywhere in the world to whom a given business was worth most.

The *acquisitions* were businesses that better fit with D&B. Some were potential standalone companies, a new core for the acquirer. Others were related to an existing group of businesses or could be directly integrated with an existing business and therefore were worth more to D&B than to their current owners, even if the purchase price was high. Most were underperformers, below the band. But D&B used its expertise and disciplined management to improve these companies' performance, and they soon migrated upwards into the band.

As a result of all this acquisition and divestiture, D&B was able to continue its exceptional performance: revenue grew 12.7 percent annually while net income grew 13.1 percent a year over the next decade. The stock price grew at a compound annual rate of about 24 percent.

A general manager needs to know his or her business unit's position in the band compared with the rest of the company's portfolio. It will affect expectations and investment levels as well as strategic options.

AS WE HAVE SEEN IN THIS CHAPTER, THE LESSONS OF THE BAND are really twofold. One conclusion is the second law itself: competitive position determines your options. The other, however, is that your competitive position can't be taken for granted. Companies can move about on the ROA/RMS chart, elbowing competitors out of the way or themselves being elbowed aside.

But there is another complication as well: the markets in which companies compete don't remain stable, either. Customers' needs and wants are always evolving. Companies that understand their customer segments, identify the most attractive ones, learn how to attract and retain precisely the customers they want to attract and retain, and know how to serve those customers better than anybody else always have an advantage over competitors without those capabilities. The following chapter shows how companies can use such capabilities to keep up with a changing marketplace.

IMPLICATIONS FOR THE GENERAL MANAGER

- Use the ROA/RMS chart to assess your competitive position.

- Your competitive position (number one to number five on the chart) determines your options for realistic performance improvement. It also determines the likely resource requirements and performance expectations for your business. Your competitors' positions determine theirs. Know the opportunities and vulnerabilities you and your competitors face, and make decisions accordingly.

- Consider all the potential improvement options for advancing your position in key customer segments, including innovation actions, high-road tactics, niche strategies, and tactics to increase customer loyalty.

- If you're in corporate management, use the band to assess your portfolio and determine any changes you might consider based on a business unit's value to you as compared with its value to others.

- Don't take your competitive position for granted. Leadership is probably your most important asset, and your competitors (both traditional and nontraditional) are likely to employ some or all of the performance-improvement strategies listed in this chapter to unseat you.

FOUR

Third Law: Customers and Profit Pools Don't Stand Still

Change is the law of life. And those who look only to the past or present are certain to miss the future.

—JOHN F. KENNEDY

NOW AND THEN COMPANIES THAT SEEM TO BE WELL MANAGED— companies that obey the first two laws, that manage to the experience curve and tailor their performance-improvement plan to their competitive position—find themselves in serious trouble. They are caught flatfooted by what appears to be a sudden shift in the marketplace. That's what happened in the mid-1990s in the consumer photography business.

We described in chapter 2 how Polaroid failed to execute quickly enough on the consumer shift to digital photography. This particular shift had actually been going on for a while as consumers began experimenting with the new technology. But now the trickle was turning into a flood: more and more people were learning to appreciate the fact that they could save photos digitally, edit their own shots, print out just the ones they wanted, and even put them on mugs and T-shirts. Polaroid missed the boat, and its shareholders essentially saw their investment evaporate in the five-year period from 1996 to 2001. But Polaroid, which had been troubled for years, was hardly the only victim. Kodak, for example, had delivered a satisfying 106 percent total shareholder return (TSR) from 1990 through 1995. In the following five years, as digital took hold, Kodak's TSR was −52 percent. Kodak's Japanese competitors fared only a little better. Canon dropped from 224 percent in 1990–1995 to −13 percent in the following five years. Nikon went from −5 percent to −64 percent, Fujifilm from 49 percent to −6 percent.

And who was winning as these well-known companies were losing? One winner was a company called SanDisk, which makes memory cards for digital cameras. SanDisk delivered an impressive 92 percent total return to shareholders during the period from 1996 to 2001. Before 1995, SanDisk wasn't even in the photography business. It emerged as a major winner by combining its capabilities with insights into what digital photographers would find convenient.

Markets undergo sea changes of this sort all the time, mostly because customers don't stand still. Customers' wants and needs evolve. They decide they really like one set of products or services rather than another. They grow dissatisfied with what they're getting from one company and decide to buy from someone else. They rush to companies that offer innovative products and services, and to those whose innovative business models or processes allow them to offer greater value at lower cost. Customers are the most important source of market changes, but there are other sources as well. Power shifts occur along a value chain, as companies consolidate or enter new markets. Governments can reshape markets quickly, with the stroke of a pen, or slowly, by pursuing one set of long-term policies rather than another.

For many such reasons, companies repeatedly discover that the landscape they operate in has altered significantly, and that the plans and strategies that worked so well yesterday no longer work today. They find that the *profit pool* from which they were drawing their earnings has dried up or attracted new competitors, or that deep new pools of profit have appeared.

Companies that are closest to their customers have at least three factors going for them as they face this kind of challenge. First, they are best positioned to seize the remaining potential within their own profit pool; they better understand who their customers are, what influences the customers' behavior, and how they can attract more of the customers' business. Second, by capitalizing on these insights, they deny those same profits to their competitors and so can afford to outinvest them over time, widening the profit gap further. Third, they can often recognize changes that signal a shift in the profit pool far earlier than their competitors, giving them a head start on revising their strategy. If they act decisively, they can undermine market leaders and smash price umbrellas. They can move up the band or earn a place above the band, in the overperformer category. In effect, they can use *customer insight* to escape the gravitational pull of the price experience curve.

MAPPING THE PROFIT POOL

One of the most useful tools to help you assess shifting needs and preferences among customers is known as a "profit-pool map." Its primary value is that it can help you identify the full potential of the market you are playing in. You can also use it both to analyze your industry and to assess your own company's situation.

Drawing the Map

An industry profit-pool map shows all the profit that can be earned in an entire industry at each point along the value chain. (Our colleagues Orit Gadiesh and James L. Gilbert introduced and explained the concept in a 1998 *Harvard Business Review* article.[1]) Figure 4.1, for example, shows a map of the profit pool for the U.S. coffee industry in 2005.

The total revenue represented by the map is $31 billion. The horizontal dimension of each bar represents the portion of the $31 billion received at that stage of the value chain. The vertical dimension represents the average

FIGURE 4.1

Profit Pools
in the U.S. Coffee Industry in 2005

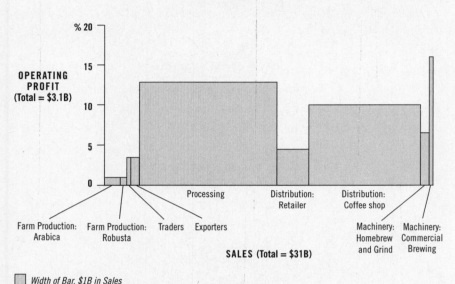

OPERATING
PROFIT
(Total = $3.1B)

% 20

Processing

Distribution:
Retailer

Distribution:
Coffee shop

Farm Production:
Arabica

Farm Production:
Robusta

Traders   Exporters

Machinery:
Homebrew
and Grind

Machinery:
Commercial
Brewing

SALES (Total = $31B)

☐ Width of Bar, $1B in Sales

Sources: Bain & Company analysis, PBS, International Coffee Organization, Company 10-Ks, and analyst reports

operating profit (as a percent of revenue) earned at that stage. The total profit in the pool is $3.1 billion.

Right away you can see who was making money in the coffee business and how they were making it. Farmers didn't get much, regardless of whether they were raising arabica or robusta varieties of beans. Exporters and traders made less of the total profit, but had a better return on sales. Distributors didn't do too badly, and machinery makers (particularly in commercial brewing) earned decent returns, though their overall share of the profit pool was small. In 2005, it was the processors and the coffee-shop operators who were making the real money in the coffee business. Their share of the profit pool dwarfed everybody else's.

Any industry lends itself to profit-pool mapping: health care, consumer electronics, telecommunications, commercial building products, athletic shoes, you name it. Creating such a map is simple in principle, though the research and calculations involved can be complex. You begin by listing all the value-chain activities in the industry, in sequential order, and you develop a baseline estimate of the total profits generated by all these activities together. You then estimate the distribution of profits at each stage of the value chain from raw materials through to the end user, and you reconcile this estimate with the total. Begin with the largest companies; that may give you much of the information that you need. Note that companies at different points of the chain may focus on different definitions of profit—accounting profit, return on invested capital, EBITDA, and so on. You may need to reconcile these different definitions so that you have apples-to-apples comparisons. (For more details, see the article by Gadiesh and Gilbert.)

What the Map Reveals

A profit-pool map is a useful tool on many fronts. Besides helping to identify strategic opportunities and threats, it can also show whatever potential may remain in the profit pool in which you participate. This is one place where many companies leave money on the table. Then, too, the map can reveal unfilled needs and weak links in serving customers. And it can show the relative economic strength of your suppliers and distributors, thus alerting you to potential encroachment from either direction.

If you mapped the automobile business, for instance, you would find deep profit pools and shallow (or dry) pools, both within auto manufacturing itself and across the entire auto value chain. To take just one example, Ford Motor Co. has earned healthy profits on its North American truck business in recent years, with a margin on large and luxury pickups an estimated seven percentage points above the company's cost of capital. According to our analysis, Ford's North American car business, by contrast, has not earned a profit above the cost of capital since before 1990, and the company's losses on cars have outweighed its earnings on trucks. So manufacturing, for Ford, has been a net destroyer of value.

Some companies do make money on manufacturing cars. But if you were to look at the entire auto value chain, you would find that manufacturing is not the most lucrative segment. On the contrary: the three points on the chain with the highest margins are financing, insurance, and wholesale parts. These three segments alone account for more than 50 percent of the industry's profit pool. Ford, for one, figured out early on that customers wanted the convenience of getting their financing at the point of sale and were willing to pay a premium to do so. That insight encouraged Ford to grow its financing division. Recently the division has accounted for *all* of Ford's profits in North America, even though it provides less than 20 percent of the company's North American revenues.

Astute general managers know their industry's profit-pool map cold, and act accordingly. For example, Kathleen Ligocki, then an up-and-coming executive at Ford, took over the company's business in Mexico in the year 2000, and found that she was facing a projected loss of $89 million in the first year alone. Running a subsidiary, she had little control over the basic quality of the product, which models she could offer, and how many cars would be made available to dealerships. But she understood where profits come from in the industry, and how much Ford was capturing from each segment. So she focused primarily on growing Ford of Mexico's financing and insurance business. She brought in experts, trained local salespeople, and made it happen. At the end of the year Ford of Mexico had made $200 million, a turnaround of nearly $300 million compared with what had been projected. And this was in a business where a more conventional manager might be tempted to throw her hands up, figuring she had few levers to pull that would make any difference.

The distribution of profits in an industry can be very different from the distribution of revenues. U-Haul has always competed fiercely in the truck-rental business, and has kept its rental prices (and margins) low in order to attract customers. Rental fees account for the vast majority of U-Haul's revenues, but little of its profits. U-Haul, however, developed a sizable complementary business in moving accessories and services—boxes and storage facilities, for example—which could be sold at its rental locations at higher margins than the equipment rental itself. The insight was that customers placed high value on convenience with regard to moving supplies. Many do-it-yourself movers either forgot to purchase supplies before renting a truck or didn't know they needed them, and so were willing to pay a premium to purchase everything they needed in one fell swoop. The company thus found a way to tap into a different segment of the profit pool, simply by turning the front of its store into a supply shop for convenience-driven customers.[2]

Mapping Your Own Company's Situation

A profit-pool map tailored to an individual company's situation can also reveal both threats and opportunities. For instance, a company we'll call FitEquipCo—a leader in the home fitness-equipment industry—wanted to figure out why its earnings were lagging despite strong sales. So managers created a profit-pool map charting units sold and profits by channel (see figure 4.2). The map made the problem clear: FitEquipCo's sales were weighted toward low-growth, lower-margin channels; in fact, 60 percent of its U.S. sales were to department stores or discount retailers. Meanwhile, a relatively small percentage of sales was through high-margin and growing channels such as specialty fitness stores and the Internet. Although FitEquipCo sold 39 percent of all units in the industry, it captured only 20 percent of industry profits. (Later in the chapter we'll examine how FitEquipCo addressed this situation.)

So the profit-pool map is a tool you can put to work right away. But the real challenge over time will be to develop your customer insight: to spot how customer preferences and behaviors, hence profit pools, are changing in your business; understand the threats and opportunities those shifts may represent; and take action accordingly.

Customers and Profit Pools Shift Over Time

The easiest way to spot historical shifts in customer preferences and behavior is simply to compare profit pools at two different points in time.

For instance, compare the 2005 profit pool in coffee with the 1995 profit pool (see figure 4.3). Processors even in 1995 were earning a large share of the pool. But the pool itself was far smaller than it would be in 2005, and the coffee-shop segment was smaller still. As the maps reveal,

FIGURE 4.2

FitEquipCo Is the Market Leader, but Is Currently Selling Through Low-Margin Channels

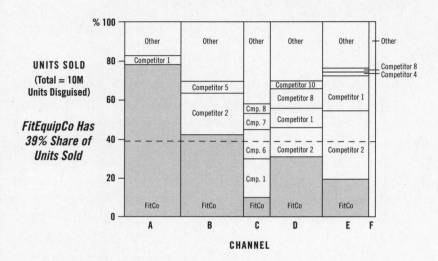

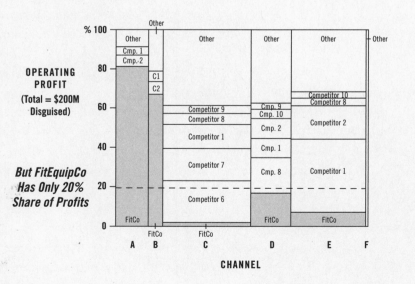

nearly all the profit growth in the industry over the period from 1995 to 2005 was propelled by the growth in just one point on the value chain: coffee shops. That shift was precipitated and led, of course, by Starbucks.

Starbucks followed a high-road strategy based on three insights. First, consumers like the experience of buying and consuming coffee drinks. Second, the coffee-shop channel was highly fragmented, and few branded players offered consistent quality. Third, convenience is everything—even for gourmet-coffee lovers. Starbucks created an innovative coffeehouse format offering a "specialty" experience, developed training and operational processes that ensured consistency at any location, and put a coffee shop within a block or so of most commuters' regular travel routes. All that enabled the company to charge premium prices for a cup of coffee. Starbucks thus created a premium segment of the coffee retailing market, growing the overall profit pool and winning a significant share for itself. In recent years the company has not only continued that strategy, it has also dipped into adjacent profit pools. It has introduced new products (flavored espresso drinks, baked goods, and sandwiches), new occasions (afternoon tea), new channels (grocery store sales of ground coffee, vending-machine sales of Frappuccino® blended drinks and other products), and new locations (adding stores in densely populated areas like downtown San Francisco every half-block or so).

Other companies have benefited from the "Starbucks effect." Many smaller competitors, including privately owned single locations and mini-chains, have prospered by meeting consumers' newfound desire for espresso and other gourmet-coffee drinks. The old supermarket coffee brands—Maxwell House and others—lost share to Starbucks initially, but they too have been able to introduce innovative products with higher margins than the old canned coffee. Even Dunkin' Donuts and McDonald's have found ways to cash in on the gourmet-coffee trend, offering upgraded flavors and even espresso drinks in many locations.

Since customers' needs and profit pools are shifting in this manner all the time, the task for general managers is to predict where the pools in their industry might be headed and act accordingly. That requires an understanding of the reasons customers and profit pools don't stand still, along with the actions appropriate to each situation.

FIGURE 4.3

U.S. Coffee Industry Profit Pool Shifted Dramatically from 1995 to 2005

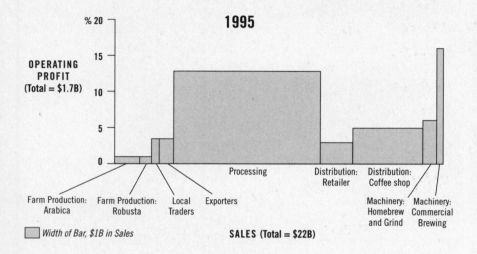

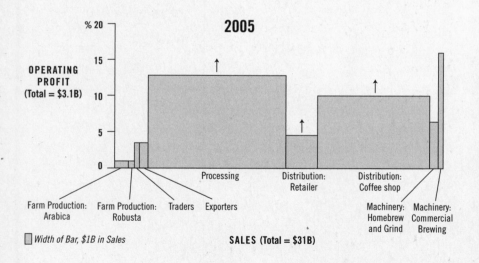

1995 profits and sales reported in 2005 dollars
↑ indicated over 50% change in profit since 1995
Sources: Bain & Company analysis, PBS, International Coffee Organization, Company 10-Ks, and analyst reports

THE FOUR DRIVERS OF CUSTOMER AND PROFIT-POOL SHIFTS

There are four broad drivers that shift customers, and that are likely to have implications for profit pools:

1. Everyday changes in customer preferences and behavior

2. Innovations, both from within your industry and outside it, that drive longer-term customer shifts

3. Changes in the bargaining power of customers and suppliers

4. Changes in the business environment

Understanding these drivers will help you spot threats to your own pool and opportunities to expand into deeper ones. You may see price umbrellas waiting to be broken. You may find demographic trends or customer segments that offer fertile ground for innovation. You may avoid being blindsided by a newly powerful set of players in the value chain or by shifts in the business environment.

As you study the four drivers and the examples of each one, you will undoubtedly notice three things.

The first is that some profit-pool shifts are big, comprehensive, and probably permanent, while others are more limited in scope, impact, or time. The big, permanent ones can affect the size and composition of the entire pool, from the customer on back. The change in photography from film to digital was this kind of shift. Smaller, less permanent profit-pool shifts may merely affect the share of the pool that goes to individual players. One player, for example, may develop the ability to capture more of a profit pool through a patent or through first-mover advantage. This kind of change may not last—it depends on how the market develops and on the actions of the different players. We will find both kinds of shifts in the examples that follow.

Second, you will note that profit-pool shifts are rarely driven by just one factor. We might list an example under one driver, but the chances are good that other factors are also helping to drain or fill up the profit pool in question. The drivers always interact with one another. So take the list of the four factors we described as what it is: an aid to analysis and under-standing. As the examples will show, few shifts can be traced to just one cause.

Third, the pace of change can be very different by industry. For exam-ple, the cycle time of biotech product development is so long that "you often have to give a CEO three or four years on the job before you know how he or she is doing," says Gabe Schmergel, former CEO of Genetics Institute. But the shifts in Internet-based industries are still taking place with astonishing rapidity. "Our business changes every three months," says Meg Whitman, president and CEO of eBay. "It's the same for Yahoo, Google, MySpace, and the others. The biggest single characteristic we look for in our managers is strategic agility. Because what was true yesterday won't be true today or tomorrow." If conventional business is like chess with a two-minute timer for each move, Internet businesses are like speed chess, with a fifteen-second timer. The opposite can be true in biotech, which is more like chess with an hour timer. (Whatever your business, of course, processes that reduce your time to market can be a significant competitive lever, as we will discuss in chapter 5.)

1. Everyday Changes in Customer Preferences and Behavior

Day in and day out, regardless of anything else that might be happening in the marketplace, people change what they want and what they decide to buy. You can see the phenomenon most clearly in fashion-dominated in-dustries such as apparel, popular music, and toys, where fads abound and styles change with every selling season. Fashion makes or breaks compa-nies in these industries. One reason for Nike's success was its shoes' popu-larity among urban teenagers, and the fact that those teenagers came to be seen as style-setters for their suburban counterparts.

Of course, preferences and behaviors shift for many reasons other than pure fashion. Consumers learned that conventional soft drinks contain a lot of sweetener and little nutrition, so many began switching to bottled water, juices, and energy drinks. Over time, the beverage profit pool shifted accordingly. Homeowners learned that "green" homebuilding techniques and products can save energy and help preserve the environment. In 2006, much of the homebuilding industry was in a slump—but the markets for green products (such as roof shingles made from recycled rubber) were booming.[3] Business customers, for their part, are always developing new products and services, opening new facilities, and making new decisions to outsource. So they, too, are always ready to do business with new suppliers.

From a company's point of view, one of the most significant factors shifting behavior is simple customer dissatisfaction. Businesses regularly change suppliers because they decide they don't like existing suppliers' prices, quality, or levels of service, and because they think they can do better elsewhere. Consumers often switch brands or service providers to get a better deal or to improve their image somehow. Customers will switch in large numbers, over time, if one company or set of companies gains a reputational advantage over another. To return for a moment to the auto industry, many U.S. drivers in the 1970s and 1980s didn't want to buy a car made by a Japanese manufacturer. Some felt that the Japanese cars were too small or otherwise unappealing. Others were loyal to Detroit's Big Three. But the Japanese companies kept improving their products, and soon gained a reputation for providing higher-quality vehicles at lower prices than Detroit's. They also introduced innovative vehicles such as Toyota's Prius hybrid. Between 1989 and 2006, General Motors's share of the U.S. market decreased from 35 percent to 24 percent and Ford's from 22 percent to 16. Meanwhile, Toyota's share increased from 7 percent to 15 and Honda's from 8 percent to 9. This kind of shift can transform a company's fortunes. In 1989, all four companies had operating margins within two percentage points of each other. Fifteen years later, Toyota's and Honda's operating margins were in the high single digits, while GM's and Ford's were zero.

Nonprofit organizations face a different kind of customer shift. These organizations typically have clients—the people they serve—and donors, the people or institutions who provide funding. In some ways, the donor population is the correct analog to a business's customers: they provide the "profit pool" that generates the funds supporting the organization. These profit pools can shift as they do in any marketplace. The priorities of foundations and agencies change over time. Individual causes go in and out of fashion. Experienced managers of nonprofits have to monitor these shifts closely so that they aren't caught unaware when one source of funds dries up. For example, Wendy Kopp, founder and CEO of the pathbreaking nonprofit Teach For America, described to us the evolution of her funding strategy over time:

> In our initial three years, we raised budgets of $2.5 million, $5 million, and $7.5 million largely from national corporations and foundations. We were aided not only by the fact that we were new, but by the fact that many corporations had just made new national commitments to education re-form and were looking for organizations to support.
>
> Our national funding sources started dropping off in subsequent years, due to three major factors: unwillingness to provide ongoing oper-ating support beyond the initial start-up, the trend among corporations to push their giving out to their local communities, and the trend among national foundations to fund "systemic" reform in lieu of other strategies.
>
> We worked to respond to this reality through building a highly diver-sified funding base. Recognizing the trends in corporate and foundation funding for education, we built very strong and diversified local funding bases in each of our local corps member placement sites, which account today for 70 percent of our budget. We also developed a federal funding stream.
>
> By our tenth year, we had built a stable organization and a stable fund-ing base. We were ready to grow organizationally, and realized that, while many of the national foundations were unwilling to provide ongoing op-erating support, they would be willing to consider one-time grants to grow our impact, if we could prove that we wouldn't need to rely on those grants for our ongoing sustainability. To respond to this opportunity, we sought "growth funding" and raised $25 million in pledges to be paid out over five years, for the purposes of making upfront investments that would enable us to grow as an organization and of building a reserve fund that would ensure our stability even as we grew. We have recently completed our second growth funding drive from national sources, this time raising $60 million over five years for the same purpose.

2. Innovations That Drive Customer Shifts

Sometimes customers change their preferences and behavior because one company, or a group of companies, offers them something distinctly different. They respond to *innovation*.

Innovation, as we saw in the previous chapter, can offer a follower a powerful vehicle by which to overtake a leader. It's often the only way a new entrant can gain a toehold. So managers naturally expect a constant stream of innovations from competitors and from start-up entrepreneurs looking to elbow their way into a market. A common mistake is to assume that these innovations will always be no more than incremental improvements—new product features, a modest increase in service, a new brand extension—that can easily be copied or fended off. Managers need to remind themselves of a fact of business: some innovations don't just put one company above another for a while; they literally change the rules of the game. They dramatically change customer preferences and behavior, and so move the profit pool in the direction of the innovator. If the innovator plays its cards right, the pool may never shift back.

Here's an example. In the late 1960s, a young Hanes executive named Paul Fulton realized that women shopping for hosiery faced a nightmare. They had to make a trip to a department store (and find the right department, not always easy) or to a specialty clothing store. They had to find the particular size and style they wanted. The hosiery was packaged in drab, flat cardboard packages, with only a little plastic window showing the color. The packages might be behind the counter, or they might be displayed on a rack—and if they were on a rack, half were likely to have already been opened by shoppers checking size and knit. Hosiery at the time frequently snagged, ran, and developed holes, which meant that quality-sensitive shoppers had to replace it often.

Armed with these insights, Fulton put together a skunkworks at Hanes charged with two objectives. One was to come up with high-quality pantyhose with greater functionality than traditional hosiery. The pantyhose had to be more durable, and it had to sell for less than women were paying at the time. The other was to solve the point-of-sale merchandising problem: to make it easy and pleasant for women to buy hosiery. If the team could do that, Hanes could sell pantyhose in fast-growing channels such as drugstores, supermarkets, and discount retailers.

So Fulton's engineers worked on reducing cost and improving quality. They planned new manufacturing processes, relying on the experience curve to drive costs down over time. His designers came up with a brilliant packaging idea: put the pantyhose in a bright plastic egg, color-coded by size and style. Hanes could build a distinctive point-of-sale display to hold the eggs, and retailers could use the display as an end-cap. It would be eye catching, easy to select from, and easy to restock. The whole idea cost about $500,000 to develop and test.

And the result? The test markets proved wildly successful, beyond even Fulton's expectations. Consumers "were totally infatuated with that egg," he remembers. They liked the price, which was lower than most conventional pantyhose. They liked the convenience and the ease of choice. They were glad to buy pantyhose in supermarkets and drugstores, as part of their regular weekly shopping. When L'eggs, as Hanes dubbed the new pantyhose, was rolled out nationwide, it quickly became the number-one brand in hosiery. Hanes's competitors were caught utterly by surprise.

So Fulton and his team shifted the profit pool in two ways. Hanes's share of the total hosiery profit pool skyrocketed, with sales of L'eggs soon reaching an estimated $500 million.[4] L'eggs also shifted the distribution profit pool away from traditional department and clothing stores and toward mass merchandisers. Of course, none of that could have happened unless women had an unmet need for convenience and price and were willing to change their preferences about where and how to buy pantyhose—an example of two forces interacting. It turned out that the determining factors were convenience of selecting and buying on the one hand and economic value (price per use) on the other.

Of course, innovation can take many forms other than the introduction of a new product. But it is often based on similar insights into customers. For instance:

New business models. Southwest Airlines founders Rollin King, Herb Kelleher, and Lamar Muse had a particular insight into customer needs: they believed that many travelers who ordinarily drove their cars or took a bus for short trips would fly instead, provided the airfare was low enough and the service was reliable and convenient. So they created an airline that was built around keeping costs at rock bottom while offering frequent service to many Texas cities.

To keep costs low, the airline offered no frills, such as movies or meals. It flew only one kind of aircraft, minimizing training and maintenance costs. As Southwest grew, it maintained this focus. It flew point-to-point and learned how to "turn" its planes in twenty minutes or less, keeping time on the ground short and increasing the utilization of its airplanes. It operated out of less-expensive secondary airports, and it kept its fare structure simple. It built a whatever-it-takes culture of cooperation among its employees, encouraging high productivity. And it always passed the savings along to customers, keeping fares as low as possible. The founders' insight into customer needs was correct: Southwest's low fares always expanded the market, a phenomenon still known in the industry as the "Southwest effect."[5]

Every low-cost carrier created since then—JetBlue and AirTran in the United States, Ryanair and easyJet in Europe, Virgin Blue and AirAsia and many others—has emulated much of this model, and most have taken the lead in finding other ways to save money (selling and distributing tickets over the Internet, for instance). The legacy carriers, by contrast, were never able to play the same game. Their attempts to emulate Southwest fell short because they were burdened with many elements of the old model, such as hub-and-spoke routes, many different types of airplanes, and adversarial labor relations. The difference in productivity between legacies and low-cost carriers can be startling. Southwest's airplanes fly an average 11.2 hours a day, compared with an industry average of 7.2. It has eighty employees per aircraft, compared with an industry average of 130. The resulting differences in cost are significant. It cost American Airlines 10.50 cents to fly one seat one mile in 2005. The same "seat mile" cost Southwest 8.05 cents—a cost advantage of 23 percent.[6]

As more passengers flew with the low-cost carriers, these carriers captured a larger share of the profit pool. In 2005, for instance, the profit pool for U.S. airlines as a group was a net loss of $2.7 billion. Delta, Northwest, and the other so-called legacy airlines accounted for $3.8 billion worth of losses. Southwest, JetBlue, and AirTran accounted for $1.1 billion in profits. Because of the shift in the profit pool, the low-cost carriers enjoyed substantially higher market capitalization per passenger than the traditional carriers. As a group they were able to invest in purchasing more planes, adding cities to their route networks, and thereby growing their share of the market still further.

Value-chain and process innovations. Women shopping for clothing often can't find fashionable items in their size because the items are sold out. But stores are usually unable to order restocks—the goods might be manufactured halfway around the world, and there isn't enough time in one selling season to replenish the shelves. Zara, the Spanish clothing retailer, found a way to restructure the value chain so that customers have a better chance of finding what they want when they want it.

Zara has two different production pipelines, one that is similar to other retailers' and one that is locally based and integrated. The company expects all of the suppliers in the integrated pipeline to be capable of rapid turnarounds; in fact, it worked with Toyota to learn how to produce small batches of clothing efficiently and quickly. As a result, Zara can move clothing from design to manufacturing to its store shelves in two weeks. Every store receives new garments and restocks twice a week. While other retailers must rely on the skill of their merchants to make big inventory bets every season, Zara's managers have created a value-chain model that offers built-in customer insight—they can see what sells well before they have to restock the stores, reducing their need to bet right on fashion trends.

The fast turnaround changes the economics of the business in other ways as well. Zara can introduce new products rapidly, and the regular introduction of new products helps draw shoppers into the stores. Because Zara is more likely than its competitors to have hot-selling items on its shelves, stores can sell more goods at full price. Because it places smaller initial bets on fashion, it has fewer markdowns—goods that don't sell can be discontinued rapidly. Because it turns its inventory faster than its traditional competitors, Zara needs far less working capital. Its ratio of working capital to sales in 2005 was 3.0 percent, as compared with 30.4 percent and 20.6 percent for two of its major competitors.

Zara grew at a compound annual rate of 17.4 percent for the years 2000 through 2006, compared with 10 percent a year for traditional apparel retailers in the United States and Europe and only 0.4 percent for U.S. department stores. But what really shifted was the profit pool. Zara's earnings before interest and taxes in those years were about 16 percent, compared with 7 percent for traditional retailers and 9 percent for department stores. Zara and other fast-fashion companies were driving the market's growth *and* appropriating a growing share of the industry's profits to themselves— all because they developed an innovative system of producing goods and bringing them to market.

Innovation from outside: companies with different skill sets. Companies from outside an industry are often faster than insiders to gain new, unexpected insights into customer behavior and to capitalize on them. For example, the economics of Amazon.com—nearly endless virtual shelf space, little physical infrastructure relative to sales volume, and so on— transformed the bookselling business and allowed the company to grow rapidly. Bricks-and-mortar chains such as Barnes & Noble and Borders were great at running bookstores, but they didn't have the same level of Internet-related skills as Amazon's Jeff Bezos and his team. When BarnesandNoble.com, a joint venture between the chain and the German company Bertelsmann, went public in 1999, it held only about 18 percent of the online book market compared with 75 percent or more for Amazon. (Barnes & Noble has since acquired Bertelsmann's share of the online venture.) For its part, Borders outsourced its Web strategy to Amazon itself. As Amazon grew, it turned profitable and appropriated a large share of the book-retailing profit pool. In 2006, Amazon's operating profits (from books and other items) were almost as large as the profits of Barnes & Noble and Borders combined.

Sometimes the companies with different skill sets arrive from adjacent markets. When Wal-Mart moved from hard-goods and apparel retailing into groceries, for instance, the giant company was able to capture a sizable fraction of the grocery profit pool simply because it was so skilled at every facet of retailing. The compound annual growth rate of Wal-Mart's grocery business between 2000 and 2004 was 18 percent; the growth rate of traditional grocery chains was zero. On average—and despite the experience of H-E-B, reported in the previous chapter—a new Wal-Mart Supercenter reduced sales at competitors' stores between 5 percent and 15 percent.

In a few cases, companies can move into adjacency after adjacency because they possess a set of distinct skills that allows them to succeed in each one. Olam International, for example, grew into a $3 billion agricultural-commodity company in less than twenty years without making a single acquisition. The secret to that phenomenal growth was a repeatable formula: Olam's ability to move into one country after another and one agricultural commodity after another. The formula, CEO Sunny Verghese told us, rested on three capabilities. One was the company's ability to set up stable, reliable sources of supply in countries that were underdeveloped and often unstable. A second was the development of world-class risk-management skills—the ability to assess and manage not just economic and financial risks but also political risks. The third was a particular kind of customer insight: learning which additional services, such as traceability of a given shipment from farm to factory gate, were valued by the customer and then learning to deliver those services. These capabilities have allowed Olam to succeed in a wide variety of markets, from cocoa and edible nuts to spices and wood products.

Outside competitors offering substitute products or services. The compact disc replaced tape cassettes as the preferred medium for music lovers during the 1990s; by 2003 the cassette had virtually vanished from the marketplace. That changeover shifted the profit pool for manufacturers of recording media. But it had little effect on music publishers or music retailers, both of which adapted quickly to the new medium. Then, in 1998, a Korean company named Saehan Information Systems introduced the first digital audio player, better known as an MP3 player. Others quickly followed. Among them were Diamond Multimedia's Rio PMP300 (also in 1998), Compaq's Personal Jukebox (1999, the first one with a hard drive instead of flash memory), and, in 2001, Apple Computer's iPod. The iPod was more attractive and easier to use than other players, and it got a lot of favorable publicity.

But even Apple's new iPod business didn't take off until the company figured out how to take advantage of an insight into changing customer behavior, namely the fact that more and more people were learning how to download songs. In 2003, Apple was able to convince four of the biggest record companies to offer their songs through its new iTunes music store, where users could download a song for 99 cents. By making legal music downloads easy and affordable, the company created a new business model: turning the old razor-and-blades model upside down, it sold the songs essentially at break-even in order to encourage sales of the high-margin iPods.[7] Overall, it created a product and distribution system that could substitute not just for CDs but for the entire industry that manufactured and distributed recorded music and for parts of the industry that manufactured and distributed portable and in-home CD players. The fallout has been significant: for example, major retailers such as Tower Records, already under assault by large retailers and illegal music downloaders, have been forced to seek bankruptcy protection. Apple hastened the process along.

Apple, in short, dramatically changed customer behavior and played a role in shifting the entire profit pool for this segment of the consumer electronics market. With about 70 percent of the global market for digital music players (in 2005), and with the iTunes store selling more than a billion songs in 2006 alone, the company appropriated much of that shift for itself. Apple, accordingly, experienced dramatic revenue and earnings growth from 2001 to 2006; its stock rose from below $10 in early 2003 to more than $87 in early 2007. The record companies did well, too. "Because most of Apple's online music revenues go back to the record companies, the iTunes store has significantly boosted overall industry profits," notes Adrian Slywotzky.[8]

3. Changes in the Bargaining Power of Customers and Suppliers

Profit pools can shift for reasons other than changes in customer preferences and behavior. For example, sellers in a value chain may increase their bargaining power to the point where customers no longer have the options that they once had.

Here's a particularly graphic example. The first movie in the famous Harry Potter series, *Harry Potter and the Sorcerer's Stone*, was released in 2001. It grossed more than $1 billion worldwide, which placed it number four on Hollywood's all-time list. When Warner Bros. cast that first movie, it chose Daniel Radcliffe, then eleven years old, to play Harry. Warner paid Daniel £150,000 (about $220,000 at the time) for his efforts. The fourth movie in the series, *Harry Potter and the Goblet of Fire*, was released in 2005 and grossed close to $900 million. By then, however, Radcliffe had a lock on the role: Warner couldn't replace him without provoking howls of protest from the fictional Harry's millions of fans. So Radcliffe's bargaining power had increased considerably. This time around, Warner paid Radcliffe about $9 million.

Warner Bros. and other studios don't release profit figures for individual movies, so we don't know the exact margins for the two films. But we know that Radcliffe and the other actors were able to garner a larger slice of the revenue pool over time—and if the costs of the two movies were more or less comparable, it is likely that Warner's margins were lower on the second movie than on the first one. The actors, led by Radcliffe, had increased their power in the marketplace from one movie to the next. Warner, the customer for their services, had to go along. (In July 2007, Radcliffe signed a $50 million deal to act in the final two movies of the series.)

So it is in more conventional businesses: the balance of power among participants in the value chain can shift, and can alter the profit pool significantly. Often the reason is consolidation of one set of players. Food-processing companies—in meatpacking, flour milling, and soybean processing, for instance—have been consolidating in recent years, to the point where the top four firms in each of these categories control half or more of the market. Consolidation increases these firms' economic power vis-à-vis farmers on the one hand and downstream producers and distributors on the other. In the same time frame, however, the top five grocery retailers in the United States have nearly doubled their share of the market, increasing their own economic power relative to suppliers. Analysts have expected these leaders to continue growing at a faster rate than their smaller competitors, thus gaining additional share.

Once in a while, an innovative product helps a company shift the balance of power in the value chain. Take the iPhone—"a revolutionary and magical product that is literally five years ahead of any other mobile phone," as Apple CEO Steven Jobs described it with his usual hyperbole. Ordinarily, cell-phone carriers "hold enormous sway over how phones are developed and marketed," said the *Wall Street Journal*, "controlling every detail from processing power to the various features that come with the phone." Not this time. Apple cut an exclusive deal with AT&T (then Cingular). The carrier agreed not to put its name on the phone, and further agreed that the phone would not carry its software for Web surfing and other services. Most surprising of all, according to the *Journal*, Apple would share in revenue from subscribers. It was an unusual deal in the industry, giving the manufacturer far more control over product development and marketing than was customary, and shifting at least part of the profit pool in the manufacturer's direction.[9] (AT&T, however, did not subsidize the development of the phone, as carriers often do, and it expected to garner more revenue per subscriber on iPhone plans than on plans involving other handsets.)

4. Changes in the Business Environment

There is one last set of forces that can shift profit pools: changes in the business environment. We are referring to events that take place outside an industry, rather than events that are due to the actions of customers or companies. Usually the driving force is a government policy. Governments can shift profit pools quickly, by changing rules or programs or tariffs. They can also shift pools slowly, by pursuing one set of long-term policies rather than another.

A change in laws or regulations may abruptly drain a profit pool, create a new one, or both. When the Australian government eliminated import quotas and dropped tariffs on vehicles from 70 percent to 15 percent, Jacques Nasser—general manager of Ford's Australian operations at the time—quickly capitalized on an existing partnership with Kia and brought in one of the Korean company's smaller models. "Overnight," he remembers, "we had a world-class small product for our customers and our dealers," not to mention a brand-new profit pool. When the U.S. government deregulated the financial-services industry in May 1975, a struggling thirty-seven-year-old brokerage-house owner named Charles Schwab saw the opportunity to create one of the first discount brokerages. In just a few years, Schwab and other discount houses were drawing large segments of the brokerage-industry profit pool away from traditional full-service competitors.

Longer-term government policies, interacting with other trends, can lead to striking shifts in the business environment. The biggest such development of our day is the (nearly) worldwide governmental commitment to participation in international trade. That has laid the foundation for a global economy. It has also enabled a host of previously underdeveloped countries to emerge as major players in this global economy because of their low costs. In 2004, for example, manufacturers in China were paying wages 97 percent lower, on average, than those in the United States. The wage gap was even larger in the Philippines, Indonesia, and elsewhere.

All told, more than half the world's population has recently entered the global marketplace. The sheer size of the population in these emerging markets suggests that there will be a large supply of low-cost labor for many years to come. As trade grows, moreover, logistics costs have steadily (and predictably) declined along the experience curve. The cost of shipping goods from Asia to North America, for instance, dropped an average of 4.5 percent a year between 1994 and 2005.

The rise of the low-cost countries (LCCs) has provoked a massive shift in the profit pools of virtually every industry where production can be moved overseas. Companies that never moved their sourcing or manufacturing to the LCCs, or were slow to do so, have gone under. Companies that were quickest or most successful in capitalizing on the LCCs' advantages have prospered. The Canadian T-shirt company Gildan, for instance, moved production to LCCs in Central America in the early 1990s. Its sales and earnings grew rapidly over the next several years, and it became the number-two player in the T-shirt business after Hanes. Gildan's stock increased by a factor of 29 during the period following its 1998 initial public offering. Meanwhile, a company that was once a market leader—Fruit of the Loom—was slow to move production overseas, and eventually did so hastily, without sufficient quality control or training. Fruit of the Loom filed for bankruptcy in 1999.

HOW GREAT MANAGERS CAPTURE PROFIT POOLS— AND ANTICIPATE OR PRECIPITATE SHIFTS

As a general manager, your job is to devise a strategy for performance improvement. Insight into your customers' preferences and behaviors, and into how those preferences and behaviors might change over time, is essential. It can help you take full advantage of your competitive position. It may even give you the ability to counteract the advantages of leaders who are farther down the experience curve and thus move up (or over) the ROA/RMS band. There are a number of valuable analytical tools that will help you turn up data and insights about all the sources of profit-pool shifts (see table 4.1).

What to Do About Changes in Customer Preferences and Behavior

An important source of shifts in profit pools, we said, is everyday changes in the preferences and behaviors of customers. Most of the tools we will discuss here are designed to help you anticipate and respond to such changes.

Customer segmentation. Customer segmentation is an indispensable tool for performance improvement, because it answers fundamental questions any company must face. Are we selling to the right customers? Which segments should be the primary target of our product-development efforts, and of our sales and marketing activities? In which regions and countries should we be competing? In which markets can we create differential value? How should we differentially allocate our sales and

TABLE 4.1

How Great Managers Exploit Profit Pool Shifts

	CHANGES IN CUSTOMER PREFERENCES AND BEHAVIOR	INNOVATIONS FROM WITHIN OR OUTSIDE YOUR INDUSTRY	CHANGES IN BARGAINING POWER OF CUSTOMERS AND SUPPLIERS	CHANGES IN BUSINESS ENVIRONMENT
Why Profits Shift	– *Customer preferences* change for many reasons (dissatisfaction, fashion, lifestyle, spending, etc.), thus creating, shifting, or draining profit pools	– *Innovations* cut costs and prices, permit new types of distribution, or create new combinations of existing offerings, and as a result, change customer preferences or behavior – *Outside competitors* offer substitute products or services – *New competitors* move into adjacent businesses	– *Power shifts* between stages of the value chain, e. g., from consolidation of customers or suppliers	– *Government or regulatory actions* change competitive environment – *Broad economic, political, and social changes* influence industry dynamics (e.g., global trade and low-cost countries)
Implications for General Managers	— Immediately *create a map of the profit pools* in your industry – Relentlessly *track changes* in your industry, company, customers, and competitors			
	– *Segment* your customers and track changing customer needs and preferences by segment (e.g., through customer ethnographic research and surveys) – Periodically perform segment needs and performance *(SNAP)* analysis – Perform *revenue sieve* analysis to identify hidden customer opportunities	– Engage in *scenario planning* – Incorporate value of *real options* in your investment decisions – Conduct *"war games"* to engage senior management team in creative thinking on potential moves by competitors, customers, and suppliers – *Map adjacent markets* to determine opportunities and threats from outside your industry – Examine your industry's profit-pool map for possible *price umbrellas*	– *Look for consolidation* of players in the profit pools up and down the value chain	– *Track economic factors* that create opportunities (e.g., factor cost changes globally) – *Monitor economic, political, and social developments* in countries where you do business and other potential markets *(chart continues)*

	CHANGES IN CUSTOMER PREFERENCES AND BEHAVIOR	INNOVATIONS FROM WITHIN OR OUTSIDE YOUR INDUSTRY	CHANGES IN BARGAINING POWER OF CUSTOMERS AND SUPPLIERS	CHANGES IN BUSINESS ENVIRONMENT
Implications for General Managers *(Cont.)*		*– Seek dissatisfied customers* and understand why *– Analyze your entire supply chain* for inefficiencies – Determine appropriate *investment in innovation* *– Track competitor developments* inside and outside your industry	*– Talk regularly* with your distributors, customers, lenders, investors, and industry experts to determine likely shifts in profit pools	*– Monitor regulatory issues* and changes in your industry; appropriately lobby or work to influence the direction and details
	– Measure customer retention, share of wallet, and Net Promoter Score (NPS) as early warning signals of changes in customer loyalty and spending			
	– Unite your team behind the short list of top priority actions + Develop cost and price leadership in your industry + Focus on specific potential competitors that threaten your position + Invest to build the capabilities you require + Lobby to influence regulations and translate trade agreements into specific tactics			

marketing resources to various segments? To answer such questions, a management team must understand which customer segments are most attractive in terms of size, profitability, and growth. They must also make an honest assessment of their company's capabilities to meet each segment's needs relative to the competition. Some segments "fit" a company better than others—that is, the company has greater ability to serve these segments in a way that is differentiated from competitors. Some segments are more profitable, either because they generate higher revenues, because they can be served at lower cost, or both. And some segments are growing faster. Segments with high growth, high profitability, and sufficiently large revenue potential are a company's natural focus (see figure 4.4, upper right quadrant; the size of the circle indicates the size of the segment). But the company may also be able to adjust its value proposition to serve high-growth customers that are not currently very profitable (see figure 4.4, lower right).

Remember FitEquipCo's profit-pool map, mentioned earlier in the chapter? The analysis revealed that the company's share of revenue was less than its share of units sold, and its share of profits was less than its share of revenue. So FitEquipCo's management team concluded they needed to refocus the company on winning more customers in higher-spending segments. To do this, they worked to gain a deeper understanding of those customers' needs and how they differed from the needs of other segments. They then invested in product development, sales resources, and service approaches designed to meet those needs better than the competition. In our experience, companies frequently misallocate their sales and marketing resources relative to the priorities suggested by analyses like those reflected in figure 4.4.

Effective segmentation can also reveal underexploited opportunities

FIGURE 4.4

Which Are the Biggest, Fastest-Growing, and Most Profitable Customer Segments?

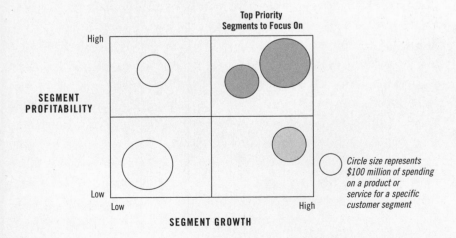

within your customer base. By "de-averaging" your customers and prospects, you can often find hidden pools of profit that could be more fully exploited. A great starting point for this sort of analysis is to identify segments that are willing to choose your product over others, or that are willing to pay more for the bundle of needs and wants that your product represents. Have you fully penetrated all the customers in the market who have similar characteristics? Among those you have penetrated, have you earned and captured 100 percent of their purchases?

In chapter 3 we discussed a simple scheme that divided customers into three camps: those who buy primarily on price, those who are looking for some combination of quality and service, and those who are looking for some form of prestige through buying a particular brand. Of course, much more complicated segmentation schemes can be developed, but this simple one can be powerful.

Dow Corning is a good example. Dow Corning makes silicone-based products that are used as a raw material in many different industries, from cosmetics to electronics to food and beverages. In 2001, the company was facing a series of challenges. Its revenue growth had been flat for several years, and its profits were below expectations.

As it turned out, Dow Corning had attempted to differentiate its products over time by adding more and more value-added services, pushing up costs and prices. But in talking to customers, Dow Corning managers discovered that some large customers didn't need those services; they understood the product, used it effectively themselves, and really just wanted the best possible price. In response, Dow Corning developed a line known

ndard silicone products that could be ordered over the traditional customer service, marketing and sales support and engineering support. This move allowed the company to take significant amount of cost out and reduce lead times. In fact, could offer these plain-vanilla products at a lower price than market, and gained share as a result.

Many of the company's customers wanted and needed technical and other services. So Dow Corning began offering these services at prices that would cover its costs. This two-brand strategy enabled the company to be clearer internally about the needs of its customers, both the "price-seekers" group and the "custom-solution" group. Both groups turned out to be more satisfied with what they received from the company. The results were remarkable. By 2006, Dow Corning had grown by more than 60 percent and multiplied its profits. In 2005 the research firm Frost & Sullivan named Dow Corning the specialty chemicals company of the year.

Segment Needs and Performance (SNAP) charts. Different customer segments will have different wants and needs. If you compare your offerings for particular segments with those of your competitors and substitute products as they are viewed by these customers, you are likely to glimpse what will happen to your profit pools and relative market shares down the road.

How to assess the needs of different segments over time? One simple tool—we call it a "SNAP chart"—can often get you 80 percent of the answer. First, you define the specific attributes of the products or services you offer that might be important to the customer segments you want to target. Second, you conduct research aimed at determining how important each of these actually is to these customers. A bank, for instance, might study everything from its hours of business or its loan rates to the quality of the advice it offers and the ease of access to its ATMs. Third, you assess your performance on each attribute as viewed by the customers and where each of your competitors performs on these dimensions as well (see figure 4.5).

The resulting chart shows how you measure up to the competition *in the eyes of your key customer segments.* You can use it to identify which gaps are most important to close (if you're behind) or widen (if you're ahead). You can also see where you might be overshooting the mark. Figure 4.5 shows sample data for FitEquipCo. The company exceeds customers' requirements on innovation and assortment, two attributes that rank number four and number six in importance to the customer. It is thus incurring costs that may not earn a return in the marketplace. Meanwhile, it is slightly underperforming competitors on quality, which is number one in importance, and significantly underperforming on customer service, which is number three. It probably needs to take action to close those gaps.

FIGURE 4.5

How Are Customer Needs Changing?
How Well Do You Meet Those Needs?

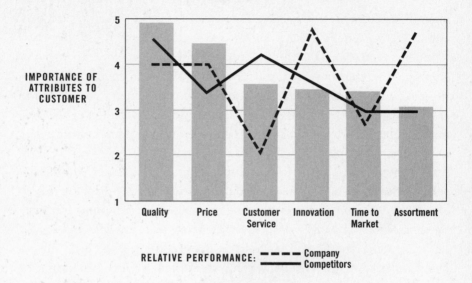

RELATIVE PERFORMANCE: ---- Company
——— Competitors

SNAP charts, incidentally, underscore the importance of an effective segmentation strategy. To oversimplify only a little: if you have only one undifferentiated offering, you are unlikely to meet the needs of your customers as well as competitors that have offerings tailored to each significant segment. You will also probably incur unnecessary costs in overserving needs that are not highly valued by some customers.

Customer ethnographic research. Traditional quantitative and qualitative research techniques can help identify and size customer segments and characterize their needs. But in fast-changing markets, or in situations where innovation is required, customers often have trouble articulating or even recognizing their own needs. Consumer-products and technology companies have pioneered the use of a tool known as *customer ethnographic research* to address this kind of situation. It's a way of identifying unmet needs that customers might not be wholly aware of. Researchers spend time with customers in their homes, backyards, or cars. They watch what customers do—the frustrations they encounter, the jury-rigged devices they come up with to solve their problems. That helps the companies develop products that customers wouldn't necessarily have been able to describe.

Executives at Procter & Gamble, for example, knew they wanted a product that could clean carpets the way the company's Swiffer cleaned floors. In 2003, chemist Bob Godfroid led a team into homes, where they took pictures and talked to people about how they cleaned their carpets. A young mother said the vacuum cleaner's noise scared her child. An older woman had to have two vacuums, a heavy one for regular cleaning (once a week, when she could take painkillers for a sore knee) and a lighter one for spot cleaning. Nobody liked carpet sweepers—too cumbersome, too ineffective. Focusing on the needs they had uncovered, Godfroid and his team experimented with dozens of possibilities, eventually coming up with a lightweight device that caused dirt particles to spring off the carpet like Tiddlywinks and then trapped the dirt behind a removable element. Further laboratory and consumer testing led the team to add a sticky layer to the element, to catch hair or lint that didn't flick up. The P&G Carpet-Flick was an immediate hit, generating an estimated $750 million in revenues by 2005.[10]

The revenue sieve. Once you know more about your customers, you need to figure out the appropriate actions. One tool that can help you capture more value from your segmentation is known as the "revenue sieve."

The revenue sieve starts by asking the question: what customers represent 100 percent of the market we could serve, and why do we not have all of it? This technique breaks down the difference between the full addressable market and a company's current sales. The concept can best be illustrated through the story of Grainger, the industrial-goods distributor.

Distributors of industrial goods were mostly mom-and-pop operations for much of the twentieth century. By the 1980s, however, Grainger had emerged as a strong national leader in maintenance, repair, and operating (MRO) supplies. The company had 200 branches selling 30,000 products, many of them aimed at the contractor market. But in the mid-1980s, it seemed to be hitting a plateau. Sales growth in the 1970s had averaged 12 percent a year. From 1979 to 1986, as the economy turned down, growth averaged less than 1 percent a year. Grainger at the time had a sizable share of what seemed to be a $3 billion market, and some managers weren't sure they could increase that share.

At this point, the company took a fresh and detailed look at the addressable market and applied the revenue sieve. It first noticed that MRO products were being purchased by a far broader range of customers than just contractors. Manufacturers, wholesalers, and institutional and commercial organizations all bought MRO supplies, though Grainger had not been targeting these customers. In fact, the total market for the products Grainger distributed was $40 billion, eight times the size of the market that the company had traditionally addressed. Starting with that $40 billion total market, Grainger could identify the points of leakage between that and its current sales (see figure 4.6).

As Grainger managers analyzed the full-potential set of customers and their buying patterns, they discovered that the various customer segments had different needs. But all had one thing in common: a lot of unplanned

FIGURE 4.6

The Revenue Sieve Helps Companies See Where Market Share Leaks Away

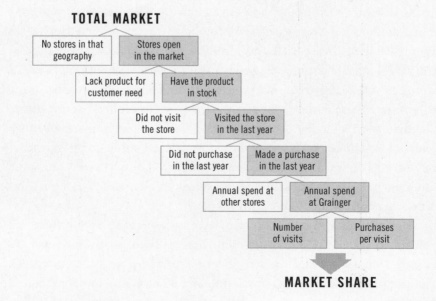

purchases. They would suddenly discover they needed something, and would then look for the most convenient location to buy the products. The distances customers were willing to drive, however, was generally limited.

So Grainger took a number of actions to address the full-potential market. It dramatically increased the number of branches, so that more were within a thirty-minute drive from concentrations of customers. It refocused its product lines onto the convenience items that were most often the object of unplanned purchases. It restructured the salesforce and applied best practices for each type of customer. It improved customer service and streamlined its ordering procedures.

The result was a rekindling of growth: through the 1990s, Grainger was able to grow at an average annual rate of more than 7 percent a year, or about twice the underlying industry growth rate for Grainger's basic products. By understanding the leakage between full potential and current sales, the company could take concrete actions to grow when the conventional wisdom suggested it was doing as well as it could.

Loyalty and retention. Our colleague Fred Reichheld is well known for showing that customer retention and loyalty can be enormous boons to growth and profitability.[11] Think about how rapidly your company grew last year. How much of the growth came from new customers, and how much did you lose from customers who left you for a competitor? Most companies' revenues are like a leaky bucket. As you add revenue in the top, you lose it out the bottom. This happens for a variety of reasons. Some of your customers have bad experiences and move to someone else. Some enter a new phase in their life cycle and now find your offerings less attractive than those of a competitor. Others experiment with the innovations offered by competitors. In many industries, increasing customer retention can be the biggest single driver of profitability. In credit cards and some other financial-services businesses, for example, increasing retention by as little as 5 percent can double profits.

An obvious starting point, of course, is to measure accurately how well you retain your customers and what share of their purchases you have earned. Understanding customer retention in each segment of customers, and mapping the differences in retention rates among customers acquired through different channels, on different products, pricing or service plans, and with different customer experiences can help locate "hot spots" for focus. But while this is an important technique for figuring out what has happened in the past, managers have long struggled to find a way to anticipate future issues. Traditional measures of customer satisfaction have failed to gain the trust of management teams for a variety of reasons. The measures often rely on complicated, hard-to-understand indices. They are often based on small samples of customers, and they may become available only after a long lag time because they require months of data collection and analysis. The measures may also fail to explain and predict variations in customer behavior and profitability.

In recent years Reichheld and others developed a metric and approach known as Net Promoter® Score (NPS), which measures loyalty and can help predict customer retention and share of wallet.[12] One of the simplest, most practical, and most powerful approaches to customer metrics, NPS is derived from asking your customers just one question: how likely they would be (on a zero-to-ten scale) to recommend your company, product, or service to a friend or colleague. Typically, companies using the NPS approach follow up with only one to five additional questions. That keeps the survey short and respectful of a customer's time. Speeding up the feedback enables the metric to become an embedded operational process rather than remaining an isolated piece of research. Used wisely and in the right circumstances, NPS can supplement or even replace some of the more complicated customer-feedback approaches companies have traditionally used.

Looking at your Net Promoter Score over time is the best way we have found to assess and predict customer loyalty, and greater loyalty is the best way of plugging the leaky bucket. You can calculate your NPS by customer segment, and you can compare your scores with those of your competitors simply by surveying customers of all the relevant companies. Average scores naturally vary by industry, but the leading companies in many industries are likely to have an NPS greater than 50 to 60 percent. If you are ten percentage points below the best competitor in your industry, you may have an opportunity to improve performance through a strategy designed to increase customer loyalty.

If you find that your NPS is declining over time, additional research into your customers' experience may reveal the reasons and may help show how to improve things. In businesses with many customer touch points this can be challenging, but the reward is worth it. St.George Bank in Australia, for instance, discovered that its promoters—those who said they would definitely recommend it to a friend or colleague—were twice as profitable as an average customer: they used more of the bank's products, on average, and gave it a greater share of wallet. But the bank's retention rates for promoters were not as high as they should have been. Root-cause analysis showed that poor service was the major cause of defection. So managers attacked service issues aggressively, focusing on touch points likely to have the greatest effect. They used best-practice examples to set goals and develop initiatives. They developed detailed implementation plans, including training and recognition-and-rewards programs. They created a dashboard of measures so that they could monitor their progress. Three years later the bank's NPS had risen, and its stock price had outperformed a peer index by a factor of 1.4.

In all such cases, the key to success is identifying the factors that are most important to the customer. Analyzing why customers defect can be an effective way to learn exactly what is most important. Customer satisfaction is usually a combination of many complex factors that are difficult for a customer to articulate and prioritize—but when customers decide to leave you, they can usually tell you exactly why. So focusing on identifying and eliminating the root causes of defection is a powerful tool.

You can supplement your NPS analysis with a host of diagnostic tools related to loyalty: share-of-wallet analysis, analysis of the lifetime value of a customer, customer migration analysis, and so on. There are also many other sophisticated tools for learning about your customers these days—tools such as the S curve (discussed in chapter 6), cluster analysis, perceptual mapping, CHAID (chi-squared automatic interaction detection, a method of answering questions such as which factors best explain the behavior of a given variable), and discrete choice.[13] Depending on your situation, you will want to use a variety of tools to understand your customers in depth. It's a key to both diagnosing your current performance and evaluating opportunities for the future. We will have more to say on the process of diagnosis in chapter 6.

Segmentation and retention efforts are at the ends of a six-link chain of activity that enables a company to earn more profits per customer than its competitors, and then to outinvest the competitors to generate greater growth. The first links are 1. to identify the most attractive target segments and 2. to design the best value propositions to meet their needs. The next steps are 3. to acquire more of the target segment and 4. to deliver a superior customer experience. That enables the company 5. to grow its share of wallet, and finally 6. to drive loyalty and retention, with more promoters and fewer detractors (figure 4.7).

FIGURE 4.7

Profitable High-Growth Companies
Do Six Things Especially Well

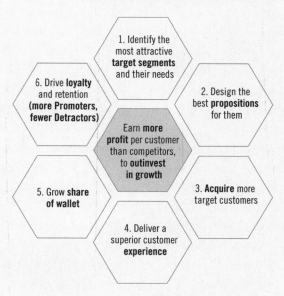

What to Do About Innovations That Drive Customer Shifts

Game-changing innovations don't appear—and certainly don't succeed—randomly. They succeed when the old game isn't working as well as it could. Customers may be "satisfied," but they still have unmet needs. Existing competitors have created a price umbrella and have grown complacent. The supply chain is inefficient. A new technology has developed that might provide similar products or services at lower cost. New competitors see these vulnerabilities and challenge the incumbents. If you're an incumbent, it isn't enough to respond once the innovation appears. By then it may be too late. Rather, you need to take three proactive steps.

First, examine your industry's profit-pool map and experience curve for possible price umbrellas. For example, if you are playing in a segment that accounts for a disproportionate share of the profit pool at rates of return far in excess of the cost of capital, a price umbrella may exist that could attract the attention of competitors or potential innovators. If you find one, you may be able to exploit it for a while, or you may be able to undermine it. Stay on top of all developments that could affect costs or prices. If there is a price umbrella, you can be confident that someone, at some point, will force it to collapse. In the United States, the low-cost airlines have been undermining the legacy carriers' price umbrellas for years now, and have helped to drive most of them into at least one bout with bankruptcy protection.

Second, seek out customers who are dissatisfied, or even satisfied but not enthusiastic advocates. A decrease in NPS over time is a sure sign of increasing customer dissatisfaction, and is usually corroborated by increases in customer defection. In fact, a low overall Net Promoter Score relative to your competitors or to substitute products or services is usually a good sign of vulnerability, signaling few enthusiastic promoters of your products or services. Of course, there are other methods you can use to identify vulnerability to innovation and stay ahead of it as well. Paul Fulton spent time in stores watching how women bought hosiery. Procter & Gamble's Bob Godfroid went into people's homes. Hal Sperlich watched drivers parking and loading their vehicles in shopping mall lots. EBay hears from customers through its message boards and e-mails; it also brings groups of twelve to eighteen customers to its San Jose, California, headquarters for daylong discussions and brainstorming. These customers "talk to managers from virtually every department, including customer support, product development, marketing, technology, and community outreach. They spend an hour or two with the executive staff; later, a group of executives joins them for dinner. After the trip, the group reconvenes by conference call every month for the next six months."[14] Intuit, like eBay, sponsors online discussions of its products; it also uses what's known as a "Follow Me Home" methodology, in which managers ask new customers if they can watch them as the customers open, install, and begin to use Intuit's software.

Third, analyze your entire supply chain for inefficiencies. If you don't have the capabilities you need to eliminate those inefficiencies, build or acquire them as quickly as you can. Half-measures are usually insufficient. As Zara was rising to prominence, the apparel industry as a whole was taking some measures of its own to speed up time to market, including a collection of initiatives known as "Quick Response." Quick Response made for a faster game but not a different game. Retailers practicing Quick Response techniques were able to register incremental improvements, but not the kind of dramatic gains registered by Zara.

In addition, you should closely monitor what is happening in the global marketplace. You should consider every step in the value chain to determine whether your activity there is truly superior to the competition. If there are other companies that can do something better or more cheaply than you, you might consider having them do it for you.

Research of this sort may identify threats or opportunities from shifting profit pools. But you need not only the relevant information; you need to be prepared to act effectively to ward off the threat or capitalize on the opportunity. General Electric under CEO Jeffrey Immelt has a program it calls "Imagination Breakthroughs"—essentially, ideas for new products or services that would take GE into a new business, customer segment, or geographic area and that would provide incremental revenue of at least $100 million. GE's business leaders must submit at least three such ideas per year, and the company promises to test the best among them. The process thus gives GE a stock of well-thought-out proposals for innovation, and the ability to respond relatively quickly when profit pools begin to shift. It was the Imagination Breakthrough process, for instance, that led to GE's partnership with Bechtel to develop a cleaner-burning coal-fired generating plant.[15]

The viability of a new idea often depends on how the competition responds to it—yet another source of uncertainty. You can plan for competitors' responses, but if the responses are different from what you anticipated you may lose the initiative. To get around this problem, some companies have borrowed a process practiced by the U.S. Department of Defense (DoD): they engage in "war games." The games attempt to simulate how competitors will respond to performance-improvement moves; they then give company executives a chance to map out their own responses. One team of managers launches the new product or service. Another team maps a counteroffensive. The first team responds, and so on. "Many teams have a strategy crisis after being shocked by a clever competitor's response to their first moves," write Jeff Cares and Jim Miskel, who have worked with DoD. "Such crises compel the teams to think more deeply about the dynamics of the competition so they can make more robust moves in the future." Cares and Miskel add that teams often find strategies that will work, but not until the third or fourth set of moves. Then, in the real world, they can "take their third move first."[16]

Threats from outside your industry. Shifts in the profit pool due to innovation or new competition from outside your industry can be the hardest to anticipate. As we suggested earlier in the chapter, attacks can come from innovators with different skill sets or technologies, or from new competitors offering products or services that can substitute for your own. Both factors were at work in reshaping the music business. In a few short years it went from a business based largely on CDs sold in stores to a business based mostly on downloading songs to portable music players.

Though such shifts may be hard to anticipate, they are not impossible. Typically, a new technology or a new set of consumer preferences takes years to evolve. Often the forces that reshape one industry reshape others. The record-store chains, for example, had already watched bricks-and-mortar bookstores lose significant market share to online retailers such as Amazon. Then along came Napster, which enabled music fans to swap songs (albeit illegally) and revealed a huge potential market for downloaded music. At that point the potential threat from Internet-based distribution should have been apparent. That the industry profit pool would shift dramatically should not have been in question. What hadn't yet been answered, however, were questions such as how quickly the illegal approach would cannibalize traditional sales, whether a legal substitute could be developed, and how traditional music industry companies could capture a significant part of the shifting profit pool. Is there anything comparable on the horizon that could have a similar effect on your company? It is always worth asking, "What is happening right now that, if brought to our industry, would devastate our business?"

Usually, of course, threats from outside your industry come from closer to home—from companies moving into what for them are adjacent markets. *Adjacency planning*—mapping and evaluating adjacent markets—can reveal both threats and opportunities.

There are six broad categories of adjacencies, as Chris Zook suggests in *Beyond the Core*: product adjacencies, geographic adjacencies, value-chain adjacencies, channel adjacencies, customer adjacencies, and new-business adjacencies. (The latter is rare; the classic example, Zook notes, is the creation of the Sabre reservation system by American Airlines.) Each one can be mapped and subdivided. Product adjacencies, for instance, might include next-generation technologies, complements to existing products, support services for existing products, or "new to the world" products. Customer adjacencies could include wholly new segments, segments the company serves but has not yet penetrated, and microsegmentation of current segments.

Adjacency moves always involve some risk. The most successful ones build on already strong cores and don't move too far away from the core. They capitalize on more-robust profit pools, and they take advantage of opportunities to establish leadership economics. Some companies, such as Olam and Nike, develop that ability to make repeatable adjacency moves. If you are in an industry close to an Olam or a Nike, watch out: these are the types of competitors most likely to threaten you. By the same token, you may be able to use adjacency mapping to find promising new opportunities for growth in any of the six categories, provided that the analysis reveals favorable economics. Successful adjacency moves always shift the profit pool.

What to Do About Changes in the Bargaining Power of Customers and Suppliers

As you study your profit-pool maps, look for consolidation of players in the profit pools up and down the value chain. How attractive is your pool? Does it represent a tantalizing opportunity for your suppliers or customers? And from your own point of view, are there equally tantalizing pools up and down the value chain that you could and should share in?

You should be able to detect the trends early on. This is your industry, after all. You are watching competitors closely in hopes of anticipating their next move. You are in constant contact with suppliers and customers. Salespeople may talk about what is happening in their companies. Distributors and customers will let you know if they are starting to see better products or better prices elsewhere. You also may talk regularly with lenders and investors, with consultants and other industry experts, and so on. Regular informal information gathering and assessment is the best tool you have for anticipating this kind of shift in the profit pool. Jerry Kahn, former CEO of Holmes Products, could see that the big-box retailers his company sold to were coming to exercise more and more power in the marketplace. Holmes—a maker of air purifiers, fans, and other products for the home—quickly moved its production to China (well ahead of its competitors) and stepped up the pace of innovation. Without a well-known brand, Kahn knew, frequent product innovation and the world's lowest cost position were the only ways to maintain a large share of the profit pool.

That said, competitive battles involving suppliers and customers can be like a high-stakes game of chess between two masters: fiercely intense, and with an uncertain outcome. Consider the ongoing struggle between auto manufacturers and the companies that supply them with parts and sub-assemblies. The auto companies regularly demand steep price cuts from their suppliers. In response, most of the suppliers have moved aggressively to reduce their own costs (often by moving production to lower-cost countries) and to manage costs and prices with their own suppliers. They have also moved to protect their share of the profit pool against incursions from their customers. Some might agree to a lower price per part, for instance, but then impose steep charges on their customers when the customers issue change orders, as they almost always do. Some have begun to develop proprietary—and in some cases patented—products, and have attempted to develop brand awareness around these products with the consumer. (An example is Harman International's brands of car-audio systems, such as Becker. To the extent they are successful, they can earn a higher margin because auto buyers look for the brand.) Still other suppliers have migrated toward producing larger subsystems of the vehicle. Johnson Controls, for instance, moved from manufacturing seats to making interiors to providing its customers with full cockpit systems, thereby helping to achieve lower system costs for customers.

Moves and countermoves such as these will continue, and will help determine the share of the total profit pool that various companies enjoy in any given year. And unlike chess, of course, the game of business never ends. So when one battle between participants in a value chain quiets down, another is likely to heat up.

What to Do About Changes in the Business Environment

General managers have to monitor the possibility of quick shifts brought about by government actions, and influence those actions when possible. What are your company's or your industry's lobbyists working on right now? What is the likelihood that something will change in the next six or twelve months? A seemingly tiny regulatory reform—a modest shift in quotas or tariffs, for instance—can reshape sourcing decisions overnight. A change in safety rules or consumer-protection laws can catch companies unprepared. All such changes can have substantial effects on profit pools.

Managers also need to keep a close eye on longer-term trends in the business environment. By now, for example, the trend toward sourcing and manufacturing (as well as selling) in China and other LCCs is well developed. But what's next? Already countries such as India have created burgeoning software, engineering, and service industries, suggesting that overseas sourcing will extend to more and more business segments. More LCCs are beginning to participate in the global economy—Bangladesh and Vietnam, for instance, and even a few nations in sub-Saharan Africa. Managers have always had to watch what is happening in countries where they already do business. They now have to pay close attention to exactly how changes in the rest of the world economy are likely to affect their industry. Many profit pools that seem safe today are likely to come under attack by lower-cost foreign sources, so it is essential for you to understand and monitor these changes and develop appropriate action plans. These plans necessarily involve two kinds of decisions. One is the traditional make-or-buy decision: do we do something ourselves or do we find a lower-cost or higher-quality supplier? The other is *where* to locate production or service functions. As we have argued elsewhere, "outsourcing" is not necessarily the same as "offshoring"—and both need to be considered.[17]

Trend analysis and sourcing decisions of this sort are necessary. But they aren't sufficient, if only because wholly unforeseen events and developments can throw the global economy into turmoil. This category includes sudden shocks, like the 1973 oil embargo or the September 11, 2001, attacks. It also includes trends with no clear direction. (Will the furor in Europe over genetically modified foods die down, or will it intensify?) To cope with such uncertainty, companies have found it helpful to use sophisticated tools such as "scenario planning" and "real options analysis."

Scenario planning is quite different from forecasting. Instead of trying to determine what is most likely to happen, scenario planners offer a range of alternatives as to what *might* happen. They tell different stories of the future, using narratives as well as data. Company executives then brainstorm how their strategies might need to shift if various scenarios actually play out. Royal Dutch Shell has been a leader in the field, and in recent years began exploring alternative scenarios for the global economy. "Open Doors," as one Shell scenario was called, represented "a world in which a transnational society develops around market incentives." "Flags," by contrast, was a "world of nations and causes," with widespread backlash against globalization.[18] The profit pools available to a company such as Shell could be quite different in the two scenarios. Managers who have given some thought to these and other possibilities are less likely to be blindsided by large-scale profit-pool shifts due to unexpected changes in the business environment.

But how can these managers keep their options open? After all, when a company makes a big investment decision, it has essentially decided to gamble on a particular view of the future. Other views of the future, apparently less likely, don't figure into such decisions. If you think Country X is likely to be mired in civil war for the foreseeable future, any proposed project for Country X will carry a prohibitively high discount rate and won't pass the net-present-value hurdle. But you might want to have the right—not the obligation—to make such investments in the future if things turn out different from what you expected. That's analogous to buying an option on a stock, and financial analysts in recent years have figured out ways to assign a price to such an option. "Real-options analysis," as the method is known, allows you to quantify the cost of steps you might take to protect the possibility of making investments in a highly uncertain environment.[19]

FACE REALITY—AND MOVE TO A NEW POOL WHEN NECESSARY

Good general managers watch for potential shifts in profit pools and try to anticipate them. But sometimes a company gets stuck in a pool that is drying up, and the manager then has no choice but to bite the bullet and move, even in the face of intense internal resistance. This can be an immense challenge. Still, a determined leader can move even the largest of companies into a more productive pool, as the story of IBM shows.

IBM Creates a New Profit Pool

IBM was once the leading computer company on the planet, so dominant in its markets that both the U.S. Department of Justice and IBM's competitors mounted antitrust actions against it. Between 1980 and 1989 it made more after-tax profit than any company in the world. In 1984 it captured 70 percent of global computer-industry profits. Its big mainframe computers, based on proprietary technologies, generated gross margins of more than 50 percent.

But IBM was taking those rich profit pools for granted, and other players took advantage of its lack of vigilance. Digital Equipment Corp., Data General, and others introduced smaller minicomputers in the 1960s. Apple brought out the first popular microcomputer in 1977. New mainframe competitors such as Amdahl, Fujitsu, and Hitachi were bringing their products to market faster than IBM and pricing them lower, thereby shifting the profit pool and eroding IBM's margins. IBM, with twenty separate business units selling 5,000 hardware items and 20,000 software products, was slow to respond to these threats. Its midrange products flopped, partly because managers and sales reps were reluctant to cannibalize mainframe sales by pushing smaller computers.

And then there were PCs. IBM was the first major company into the market after Apple, bringing out its IBM Personal Computer in 1981. But the business didn't work out quite as the company expected. To be sure, the profit pool in computers shifted away from mainframes and minis and toward PCs: the PC industry grew at a 74 percent compound annual rate during the 1980s. But IBM licensed its PC technology to other manufacturers, and before long some 200 companies were turning out low-cost IBM clones. Big Blue's share of the IBM-compatible PC market fell from 100 percent in the early 1980s to 11 percent in 1993. Meanwhile, IBM had itself licensed the PC's operating system from a little company called Microsoft, and IBM's managers soon realized that the fees they and their competitors were paying Microsoft had created a huge new profit pool that Microsoft owned. IBM put 1,700 programmers to work on building a proprietary operating system, OS/2. But Microsoft beat IBM to market with its own innovation, Windows, and OS/2 died on the vine.

In the early 1990s, IBM's growth was stalling, and its margins had turned negative. In 1993 the board fired the CEO, John Akers, and hired Louis V. Gerstner, former head of RJR Nabisco. Gerstner, with no emotional attachment to the hardware company that IBM had been in the past, cast a fresh eye on the profit pool in computers and spotted a trend: more and more companies needed not just hardware but complex, large-scale IT services. He decided he would move IBM aggressively into that market—and a growing profit pool—as a provider of software, services, and end-to-end solutions.

It was a bold move. Services in 1992 accounted for a relatively small share of IBM's revenue and an even smaller share of its gross profit. But Gerstner and his team began building up IBM's capabilities. They hired thousands of new people and signed billions of dollars' worth of service contracts and strategic outsourcing agreements with companies such as Prudential Insurance and AT&T. Eventually they acquired the global consulting and technology-services unit of PricewaterhouseCoopers, the accounting firm. Soon IBM Global Services had become the largest IT-services business in the world, with 150,000 employees and $35 billion in revenue.

Sam Palmisano, who succeeded Gerstner as CEO, continued in this direction. In 2005, IBM sold its PC business to the Chinese company Lenovo. The PC business wasn't growing as fast as the IT-services business, and the profit pool in the latter was far deeper. IBM, said CFO Mark Loughridge, "is getting out of the PC manufacturing business because it sees greater profits in the services market." Today IBM Global Services accounts for more than half of the company's revenue. In 2006, the division enjoyed a gross margin of 27.5 percent, and its relative market share was 2.3.

It is rare for a company as large as IBM to switch direction so dramatically and so successfully. What made it possible was Gerstner's ability to see that IBM's existing profit pool had dried up, and that there was a deeper pool awaiting at a different point in the value chain.

THERE ARE PROFIT-POOL SHIFTS TAKING PLACE AS WE WRITE, AND time will tell if the managers in the affected companies succeed in altering their strategies and execution appropriately. For example, Kodak is entering the market for consumer inkjet printers, believing that it sees an opportunity both to break a price umbrella in ink and to take advantage of a significant profit pool. Meanwhile, the PC market is shifting to consumers who want to "kick the tires" and see a computer in a store before buying.

It will be interesting to see if this trend continues, and how Dell responds to the threat it poses. There are countless other examples we could cite, no doubt including some in your industry.

Successful pursuit of growing profit pools almost always requires an aggressive and focused effort to succeed against the competition in carefully selected battlegrounds. Because profit pools are not trivial to map and project, and because of the inherent complexity of how they shift, most organizations discover they need a way to bring the threats and opportunities into focus. How can you drive down the experience curve, manage your strategy, and constantly monitor profit pools without overwhelming your organization? The next chapter discusses the necessity of a simple approach. Finding the answers may take plenty of time and analysis, but it must ultimately lead to a simple path forward.

IMPLICATIONS FOR THE GENERAL MANAGER

- Develop a fact-driven map of the profit pools, current and time-phased, within your industry and throughout your value chain. The map will show you who's making money in your industry, how they're making it, and how the pools are shifting.

- Analyze your industry for threats and opportunities along the four dimensions outlined in this chapter, and assume your competitors are doing the same. The dimensions are 1. everyday changes in customer preferences and behavior; 2. innovations from inside and/or outside your industry that drive customer shifts; 3. changes in the bargaining power of customers and suppliers; and 4. changes in the business environment.

- Utilize the tools mentioned in this book to segment your customer base effectively, understand their specific needs, and assess both your own and your competitors' performance against those needs. Assess future growth rates of those segments and their impact on the profit pools most relevant for your business. Then develop clear actions to shore up your weaknesses and capitalize on competitor weaknesses.

- Develop a robust strategy to optimize your share of the future profit pool, and look for other high-growth pools where you may have the capabilities you need to be successful. Assume that your competitors are doing the same.

- Be purposeful and relentless in assessing and tracking both evolving customer needs and threats from competitors and changes in the environment.

FIVE

Fourth Law: Simplicity Gets Results

Simplicity is an exact medium between too little and too much.

—SIR JOSHUA REYNOLDS

ONE DAY, SO WE ARE TOLD, KING ARTHUR ADDRESSED THE KNIGHTS of the Round Table. He charged them to be "ever true and noble knights":

> to do neither outrage nor murder, nor any unjust violence, and always to flee treason; also by no means ever to be cruel, but give mercy unto him that asked for mercy, upon pain of forfeiting the liberty of his court for evermore. Moreover, at all times, on pain of death, to give all succour unto ladies and young damsels; and lastly, never to take part in any wrongful quarrel, for reward or payment. And to all this he swore them knight by knight.[1]

Whew. Sir Lancelot and his colleagues might be forgiven if they came out of that meeting a little daunted. We can imagine the poor knights trying valiantly to remember every principle that their king wanted them to live by, and usually coming up short. If only King Arthur had been able to capture the key words and structure all the admonitions in an easy-to-remember graphic (see figure 5.1). Then the knights could have committed the graphic to memory before setting out, confident that they wouldn't forget the king's precepts.

The fact is, we human beings aren't very good at carrying long lists of things around in our heads. We aren't very good at following complex interactions or making decisions based on a large number of criteria. We need simple organizing principles and other ways of structuring information and action. Imagine trying to follow a soccer game if the two teams weren't wearing uniforms to tell us at a glance who was who. "The span of absolute judgment and the span of immediate memory impose severe limitations on the amount of information that we are able to receive, process, and remember," wrote George Miller, a Princeton University professor who was a founder of the field of cognitive psychology. "By organizing the stimulus input simultaneously into several dimensions and successively into a sequence or chunks, we manage to break (or at least stretch) this information bottleneck."[2]

How many "chunks" can we take in at once? The familiar "Rule of Three"—well known to teachers, speakers, and everyone else who tries to

FIGURE 5.1

King Arthur Charged His Knights to Be:

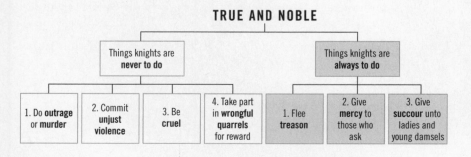

Source: James Knowles, *The Legends of King Arthur and His Knights*, Chapter 6, accessed 6/28/04, Project Gutenberg eBook, www.gutenberg.net

impart information—holds that audiences won't remember more than three points in a presentation. Recent scientific research takes this principle one (but only one) step farther: the rough consensus among many psychologists is that people can hold about four chunks of input—visual objects, items in a list, or other pieces of information—in their short-term memory.[3] King Arthur's imaginary graphic relies on this principle: it simplifies the king's list by creating two categories, each with no more than four chunks.

Remember this little lesson in the human need for simplicity as we return to the business world. The fourth law says that simplicity gets results. As the famous dictum usually ascribed to Albert Einstein puts it, "Any intelligent fool can make things bigger, more complex, and more violent. It takes a touch of genius—and a lot of courage—to move in the opposite direction."

THE PRICE OF COMPLEXITY

In recent years, people's need for simple structures and principles—for limits on the number of things we have to deal with and the number of choices we have to make—has run smack up against the astonishing growth of complexity in the business world.

The Trend Toward Complexity

To get a sense of this trend, travel back in time three decades.

Thirty years ago, people chose from just a few brands of toothpaste, each with a few different flavors. Today people choose among the same few brands—but each one is likely to come in dozens of different variations and flavors. We counted forty-three separate varieties of Crest on the product's Web site, ranging from Kids' Spider-Man Super Action Liquid Gel to Baking Soda Peroxide Whitening with Tartar Protection, and fifteen different sizes.[4] What's true of toothpaste is true of other products as well. In consumer goods alone, the number of new products put on the shelf was 51 percent greater in 2004 than in 1994.

Thirty years ago, people ordered a telephone from a national phone company, and could choose among a relative handful of models and colors. Today people must not only select home phones and cell phones, they must also choose a carrier and a plan for each. In late 2006, the four major U.S. wireless carriers were offering between thirty-five and fifty-five choices in handsets and forty to eighty-six different plans, with new options appearing seemingly every week. A large wireline carrier we worked with, more or less typical for the industry, offered a wide variety of business plans, consumer plans, long-distance packages, local packages, high-speed Internet plans, international calling plans, and optional individual features such as call-waiting and voice mail. All told, the number of theoretically possible product combinations came to 377 million. Not surprisingly, many of these combinations were never ordered by a customer.

Thirty years ago, most people kept their savings in a bank account. The account might have been in the same local bank that held their twenty-year, fixed-rate mortgage, typically the only kind available. Relatively few people held credit cards. For the most part, only wealthy individuals and institutions bought stocks or other financial investments. Today, even the middle class can (and must) choose among a mind-boggling array of credit cards, mortgages, and investment alternatives. MBNA (now part of Bank of America) offers 155 different credit cards. Wells Fargo offers close to 200 varieties of mortgage. Fidelity Investments offers 168 different mutual funds. And each of these companies is only one provider in a large, diverse industry.

This list of comparisons could go on almost indefinitely. People once had access to just a few channels on their television sets. Today we have access to hundreds. People once shopped at book and record stores, some with as little as a few thousand titles. Today many of us buy books from Amazon.com, which probably has close to three million unique titles, and music from iTunes, which at this writing sells more than four million different songs (not to mention feature films, television shows, and podcasts). Once the biggest shopping channels of any sort were probably the Sears, Roebuck & Co. catalog for consumers and the multivolume *Thomas Register of American Manufacturers* for businesses. Today we can buy just about everything in the world from one Web site or another—provided that we have time to do all the comparison shopping that being a good consumer seems to entail.[5]

Is complexity good? The "long tail" theory. The proliferation of products and the growth of product complexity have a natural source. Companies always have an incentive to innovate—to come out with a product or service that competitors don't yet offer, or that somehow outperforms the competition. Introducing distinctive offerings is often the easiest way to compete for shelf space, protect market share, or repel a rival's attack. Companies also like the idea of offering customers exactly what they want, and so are constantly creating or re-creating variations on their basic products or services in hopes of finding a segment of customers that wants just that variation. Meanwhile, technology has made it possible for businesses to increase the number of different goods or services they offer, and to keep track of much larger inventories and information databases than in the past.

All of this has led some management commentators to conclude that smaller and smaller market segments are the wave of the future. They write of "segments of one," of "mass customization," and of the "long tail." (The last phrase refers to all the products a company might carry that are not top sellers.) Thanks to technology, their argument runs, the days of mass production and marketing of relatively few items are over. Individuals and business customers today want products and services tailored precisely to their needs, and companies can now provide exactly that. The best business strategy, therefore, is to focus on selling large numbers of different products and services, even if each one has a low sales volume. "All those [market] niches add up," writes Chris Anderson in *The Long Tail: Why the Future of Business Is Selling Less of More*. "Although none sell in huge numbers, there are so many niche products and collectively they can comprise a market rivaling the hits."[6]

Rising Costs, Dissatisfied Customers, Slower Growth

But this argument applies at best to a small number of situations—businesses such as iTunes, where the product is itself digital (and where the marginal cost of production and storage is therefore close to zero), or businesses such as eBay and Amazon, where inventory costs can be pushed backward to suppliers. Consumers' desire for variety has no doubt encouraged the adoption of the new technologies that make these businesses possible. Still, even in those cases, a company's prime job is to make it easy for customers to find exactly what they are looking for, which is often a hit tune or popular item. That's why successful Web-based vendors offer so many recommendations and top-ten lists—it helps customers cut through the complexity.

For most businesses, though, the idea of a segment of one or a long tail is fraught with peril. Companies that try to offer something for everybody wind up with big, unwieldy catalogs and lists of options. Salespeople have difficulty keeping track of them; distributors have difficulty stocking them. Customers get confused and angry. Shoppers might decide that they like a new toothpaste—maybe Crest's Whitening Plus Scope Extreme Mint Explosion—but then can never find it again. (In an admittedly unscientific experiment, we recently shopped at six grocery and drug stores and found that the average store in our sample carried only about half the varieties, half the flavors, and a quarter of total Crest stock-keeping units [SKUs].) Cell-phone buyers might turn to a sales rep for help comparing their old plan to the company's new offerings, only to learn that the rep can't possibly explain or even understand the differences among the thousand or so plans and promotions that her company has offered during the past couple of years. As dissatisfaction rises, some customers seek simpler alternatives. Sometimes, the companies that offer the most new products and services can actually lose market share, exactly the opposite of what their managers intended.

Within a company, meanwhile, the proliferation of products or service offerings often wreaks havoc. It increases lead times and causes late or incomplete deliveries. It undermines scale and experience economies and operational efficiencies. It complicates forecasting and production decisions, leading to stockouts and unsold items. At the extreme, the experience curve no longer applies: if everything is unique, experience never doubles and costs never decrease. Anyway, conventional accounting doesn't capture the full costs associated with this kind of complexity. A new offering might seem lucrative when considered by itself. But the more products or services a company offers, the more complex its purchasing, its inventory management, its production management and scheduling, and its sales process. These costs are rarely figured into the business planning, but they nearly always rise significantly.[7]

The Spanish clothing company Zara, discussed in the previous chapter, reduces the problem of complexity: even though its stores may carry as many SKUs as other specialty-apparel stores, they have relatively few products on the shelves at any one time. Zara can respond quickly to consumers' changing tastes, so it doesn't try to offer everything to everyone all at once. But many other companies have found themselves bogged down by the complexity of products, features, and options.

The case of the tinted windshield. Look, for example, at what happened when one automaker started offering tinted windshields as an individual stand-alone option.

On the surface, the move looked like a clear winner. The company's marketers calculated that nearly 40 percent of customers would buy the option for $120, while the supplier would charge just $8 per unit. Moreover, installing tinted glass rather than clear glass seemed to add no labor costs on the assembly line. With new revenue far outstripping direct costs, adding the new option seemed to guarantee a quick profit boost. On the basis of these economics, any manager would decide to add the option.

But adding the new option as a unique and separate choice was likely a mistake because it was built on a false premise. For illustration: if the automaker was already offering 100 packages of options, the new one added 100 more possibilities, because each of the original packages could now come with a tinted windshield. So the new option led to a geometric increase in the number of possible combinations a customer could buy, and thus contributed to a whole range of higher costs. If it were the only option on the car, it might make sense. But tinted windows was only one of a lengthy list of options.

As the number of options grew, the company had to adjust its work flows, add new quality-control tests, and even change the routes of its forklifts, all of which added to production costs. Purchasing and materials-handling costs increased to accommodate added parts. Assembly-line errors crept upward as proliferating options made workers' jobs less predictable. Every new option also added complexity to the company's operating and accounting software, which already produced millions of option codes to account for often-minor variations in assembly. The increased customization led to unexpected peaks in demand for certain options and combinations, which in turn produced more errors as workers rushed to finish tasks. Forecasting, too, became more complex and prone to error, so the company produced cars with options packages no one wanted, which then sat unsold on dealers' lots.

The result? The "clear winner" contributed to the company's operating complexity and probably ended up costing it money. In this case, we calculated the costs of all the complexity for all options in the plant to be 25 percent of the total costs. The unnecessary complexity probably reduced sales by as much as 20 percent. The company would have done far better to understand its customers well enough so that it could offer relatively few options packages, each one including individual options that particular customer segments most wanted. The tinted windshield, for instance, might have been part of a climate-control package or a sporty-design package.

The problem in this kind of situation is that the decision to add product complexity is almost always based on *incremental* economics. But as a company adds more and more options, its *systemic* costs rise. Suddenly it must add significantly more capability (perhaps a $50 million scheduling module from SAP) to try to handle the unpredictability of orders. Or maybe machine utilization drops significantly, or the company can't balance its lines. These additional costs are viewed by management as part of the cost of doing business; they aren't (and cannot be) tied directly to the addition of any one option. But they are nonetheless real.

Ironically, perhaps, consumers often feel they have more choice when fewer options are available. The supermarket chain H-E-B, mentioned in chapter 3, reduced the number of SKUs significantly in some departments of a select number of pilot stores. Asked for their response, most customers didn't notice—but more felt there were more choices in the store than felt there were fewer. Comparable sales increased significantly.

The statistics on complexity. The effects of complexity are not lost on managers. A couple of years ago, Bain researchers surveyed executives in 960 companies around the world, asking them about complexity in their organizations. Nearly 70 percent of the survey's respondents told us that complexity was raising their companies' costs and hindering growth (see appendix 1).

The managers' belief, moreover, seems to be justified. Another team of researchers studied the impact of complexity on the growth rates of 110 companies in seventeen different industries. The industries included business-to-business categories, such as aerospace and chemicals, and consumer industries, such as fast-food restaurants and pharmaceuticals. The team devised a complexity metric that was relevant to each industry. For fast-food restaurants, for instance, the metric was the number of entrees on each restaurant's menu. The researchers found that the least-complex companies grew between 30 and 50 percent faster than companies with average levels of complexity, and between 80 and 100 percent faster than the most complex companies. In one particularly dramatic example, a telecommunications company that offered consumers only about one-fifth the number of options offered by a competitor was growing almost ten times as fast as the other company (see appendix 1). This quantitative analysis flies directly in the face of popular enthusiasm for a "segment of one."

Diagnosing a Complexity Problem

In the second part of this chapter we will show you some tools to use to reduce complexity. But first, the general manager must assess whether the organization has a complexity challenge.

Complexity doesn't show up on a balance sheet or an income statement. It isn't likely to come up spontaneously in management meetings. It is stealthy: it can sneak up on an organization without being noticed. That means you have to search it out wherever it may arise. To determine the complexity of your business, begin by looking at your number of offerings (including all options) and the sales volume for each. If 20 percent of your products or services account for more than 80 percent of your revenue, it's likely your business could be less complex. Look, too, at your sales reps' performance and your pricing. If salespeople struggle to communicate your most profitable offerings to customers, or if you must often discount to sell slow-moving products, you may have a chance to reduce complexity.

In figure 5.2, we offer a simple set of diagnostic questions for manufacturers, retailers, and service businesses. If you answer "yes" to any of these questions, your business is likely to be overly complex.

FIGURE 5.2

How Do You Know You've Got a Complexity Opportunity?

CONSIDERATIONS	MANUFACTURING	RETAIL	SERVICES
Number of offerings	Is your total number of SKUs or possible product configurations greater than 1,000 or over 50% more than that of your lowest-complexity competitor?	Do your fastest-turning SKUs sell more than twice as often as your slowest? Are your inventory turns more than 10% slower than your lowest-complexity competitor?	Does your sales force struggle to understand and communicate your most profitable offerings to core customers because of the complexity of these product offerings?
Sales volume	Do less than 20% of SKUs, build combinations, or product configurations make up more than 80% of your sales volume?	Do less than 20% of SKUs make up more than 80% of your sales volume?	Do less than 20% of service configurations make up more than 80% of your sales volume?
Modularity	Have any of your competitors created modular or bundled products?	Is your approach to customer segmentation aimed at "offerings for many to attract the many" rather than "delighting the few to attract the many"?	Can you bundle offerings to meet specific segment needs?
Where complexity shows up	Does complexity show up early in the process, such as in engineering (creating change orders) or in assembly (creating unpredictability in the operation)? Do you have low or erratic effective capacity utilization?	Do you find that you frequently have to discount to sell slow-moving inventory?	Do you have excessive error rates, low close rates, or frequent customer abandonment due to customer confusion?

Source: Gottfredson and Aspinall, "Innovation vs. Complexity," *Harvard Business Review*, November 2005.

To diagnose and address complexity, it helps to divide the issue up into four categories: 1. strategic or business complexity; 2. product complexity; 3. organizational and decision-making complexity; and 4. process complexity. We have discovered in our work that addressing them roughly in this sequence is critically important. Just about every company we know, for example, is working on process complexity, and many aren't seeing much in the way of results. The reason? The underlying systemic issues that created the process complexity have not been dealt with, so the effort is like pushing on a balloon: if you push in one area, another gets bigger. The complex processes in insurance companies, for instance, are usually linked to a variety of different products, to the exceptions associated with them, and to regulations. An insurance company can't simplify its processes much without changing the product line that drives the process complexity.

In other cases, a poorly designed organization or unclear decision-making structures and procedures may be leading to process complexity. A good example of this was a major oil company we are familiar with. The company had invested in literally hundreds of process-reengineering initiatives throughout its vast network of operations. It could and did point to examples of great success all over the place. But somehow they didn't add up to much. As one manager in the company told us, "If we had actually achieved all the benefits reported by the process-reengineering initiatives, we would have negative costs today." In fact, the company's SG&A (selling, general, and administrative) costs were rising at 15 percent a year, and overall output was flat.

As we analyzed what was going on, we discovered that there were big gaps in the company's performance-management system, in its decision-making processes, and in its organizational structure. For example, the company had decided to centralize information-technology systems, along with decision making and budgeting relating to IT. Business-unit heads, no longer accountable for IT expenditures, began using more and more IT, driving up costs. Many such anomalies conspired to frustrate the individual reengineering initiatives.

So the company's first task was to simplify and reengineer the organization, including clarifying decision rights and accountability. It had to find simple metrics (such as benchmarks against key competitors) that aligned the organization so that everyone could work effectively toward improving processes. If you have found yourself constantly reengineering without noticeable effect on your organization's complex processes, you may want to look at product and organizational complexity as possible systemic root causes.

FINDING THE RIGHT BALANCE

While we could write a whole book on complexity, we will provide only a brief overview of each category. As you will see, the task in each case isn't just to simplify. Rather, it is to establish the right balance between innovation and simplicity, between delivering what customers want and keeping complexity under control.

1. Strategic Simplicity

"When business becomes complicated," wrote management professors Kathleen M. Eisenhardt and Donald Sull, "strategy should be simple."[8] We couldn't agree more. Product simplicity, organizational simplicity, and process simplicity all depend on a simple overall strategy for performance improvement, one that everyone in the organization can easily grasp and support. Great managers understand this intuitively and focus their organization on just a few key objectives. "The first thing I did was to make sure the team that works with me understood the three to five items to focus on," said David Noko, not long after he became managing director of De Beers Consolidated Mines. Jürgen von Kuczkowski, former CEO of Vodafone Germany, echoed Noko's view. "It makes no sense to give the organization more than three really important actions and follow up. You have to have success with, let's say, three actions—and then you can start another one. Don't do too much at the same time!" Others repeated the same point. As we'll see in a moment, Gordon Bethune and Greg Brenneman developed a turnaround plan for Continental Airlines with just four critical action imperatives.

Complexity can creep into strategy for the same reasons it creeps in everywhere else. Companies respond on an ad hoc basis to competitors' moves. They take advantage of opportunities that suddenly appear on the horizon. They lose their focus on their most loyal and most profitable customers. They fail to match their strategy with their capabilities.

When a company sticks to it, however, strategic simplicity is one of the most powerful forces in driving business performance, mainly because everybody in the organization can see where they're headed and how they can get there, and so can buy into the journey. We'll give a couple of examples that we think illustrate the point very well.

Gordon Bethune and Greg Brenneman revamp Continental Airlines. Greg Brenneman joined Continental in 1994, becoming chief operating officer in 1995 and president in 1996. He and then-CEO Gordon Bethune devised a simple new strategy, dubbed the "Go Forward Plan," for the troubled company. It had just four parts, but every decision the senior leaders made and every policy they implemented was designed to further the plan.[9]

Part one of the plan—the market plan—was called "Fly to Win." Bethune and Brenneman focused their marketing efforts on business travelers. They eliminated money-losing flights and added flights on profitable routes. "We needed to stop flying 120-seat planes with only thirty passengers on them," Brenneman later wrote.

Part two, the financial plan, was "Fund the Future." The company had serious liquidity problems, far worse than Brenneman imagined when he took the job. Bethune and Brenneman restructured its debt and sold unneeded assets. They began tracking cash assiduously.

The product plan—part three—was "Make Reliability a Reality." Bethune and Brenneman wanted to change the perception (and the reality) that Continental delivered poor service in unpleasant airplanes. They got the planes repainted and the interiors refurbished. They increased scheduled cleanings and improved the meal service. They began tracking metrics such as late arrivals and lost bags. They handed out bonuses to every employee each month the airline finished in the top five of the Department of Transportation rankings of on-time performance.

Part four, finally, was the people plan, dubbed "Working Together." Bethune and Brenneman wanted to make Continental a great place to work. They publicly burned a particularly obnoxious rulebook. They created a profit-sharing plan, thereby aligning employee incentives with performance. They began listening to employees' ideas, and they communicated relentlessly—weekly voice mails, monthly open houses, and 650 bulletin boards throughout the system. The bulletin boards carried "everything an employee needs to know about the company, from a daily news update to Continental's operating results over the last twenty-four hours."

Soon Continental's operating income had turned positive. Over the next five years, the company's stock outperformed the S&P 500 by a factor of four.

Turning around Continental was obviously a complex process. Other good managers had tried and failed. What made it possible for this team was that Bethune and Brenneman organized the complexity into simple, memorable strategic categories. The power of simplicity lay in the fact that they, their managers, and the employees could then focus on those tasks and no others. "In any company I've been in," Brenneman said, "there haven't been very many people who are capable of standing back and making the complicated things very simple. Yet that's where the real value is."

Paul Farmer and Jim Kim attack drug-resistant TB. Great managers of nonprofits also understand the importance of simple strategies. Partners In Health, led by Paul Farmer and Jim Yong Kim, mounted a project in Peru to treat patients with multi-drug-resistant tuberculosis (MDR-TB). The project presented challenges of all sorts. The medicines for treatment at first cost $25,000 per patient. Peruvian government officials believed they already had an effective TB-control program and didn't welcome the outsiders. (Kim acknowledges that Peru's program even then was one of the best in the developing world at treating drug-sensitive TB that could be cured using the standard first-line drugs. But the program provided no treatment for the growing epidemic of MDR-TB that had taken root in the shanty towns outside Lima.) MDR-TB was and remains a difficult disease to treat. At the time, the World Health Organization (WHO) frowned on aggressive treatment programs in developing countries for fear that the programs would distract attention from its efforts to treat drug-sensitive TB and could also generate strains of TB that were more and more resistant to drugs.

"What we realized we had to do," Kim explains, "was three things. First, we needed to show that treatment was actually possible, that we could treat patients and get good clinical outcomes. Second, we had to lower the price of the drugs. Third, we had to change WHO policy." The strategy, he adds, "seemed very straightforward." Partners In Health began treating people at clinics and institutionalized an effective protocol. It worked with the World Health Organization and other NGOs to negotiate lower prices with the relevant pharmaceutical companies, eventually lowering the cost per patient to as little as $1,500. Another Partners In Health team member took a job with WHO and served as the point person for work aimed at changing WHO policy. "Now," says Kim, "the Peruvian government itself is treating MDR-TB everywhere."

2. Product Simplicity: The Model T Approach

A company that made only one product with no options wouldn't have any product complexity. Nor would it have much in the way of strategic, organizational, or process complexity. The classic example in most people's minds is Ford Motor Co., back in the days when the only car it produced was the Model T. In fact Model T vehicles came in several different body styles and with several possible options; at some points in time Ford even produced them in different colors, despite Henry Ford's famous declaration that customers could have any color automobile they liked, so long as it was black. Still, the Model T has long been a symbol of product simplicity, and we will use it as such here. Certainly, the company's production process was simple, one assembly line per plant. Its decision making was equally simple: Henry made the decisions. The company's strategy was to make as many Model Ts as it could, and to drive down the price so that more customers could afford them. Henry Ford intuitively understood both the experience curve and the negative impact that complexity might have. Between 1908 and 1927, Ford relentlessly drove down the experience curve: the retail price of a typical Model I touring car dropped from $850 to $380. Allowing for inflation, it's a reasonable estimate that Ford took out about 80 percent of the cost of manufacturing an automobile.

Ford, of course, was immensely successful—until General Motors came along and began offering customers a wide variety of brands and models with many different options and colors. GM soon commanded close to three-quarters of the U.S. market, and Ford was never able to catch up.

So it isn't enough to simplify your product offerings blindly. Customers want choices, and companies must offer variety. The challenge for every company is to find its *innovation fulcrum*, the point where products or services meet customer needs with the lowest possible level of complexity. The tool we present here shows you how to find your innovation fulcrum. We call it the "Model T approach" because it evolved from our work with the auto industry in the 1980s. But companies in nearly every industry have used it since then to cut costs and boost sales by reducing complexity (see figure 5.3).

The first step in this approach is to ask yourself and your management team: "What would our company look like if it offered only one product or service, like Ford in the days of the Model T?"

The reason we recommend asking this question isn't that we expect you to go back to those days. Rather, imagining just one product or service allows you to zero-base your costs, to cut through all of your company's existing complexity and see exactly what would remain. This is the only way we have found for management teams to get at the systemic costs that

FIGURE 5.3

Model T Approach to Finding Your Innovation Fulcrum

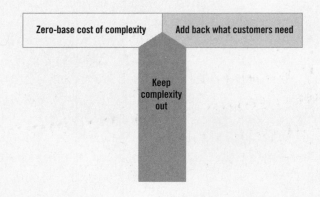

Zero-base cost of complexity   Add back what customers need

Keep complexity out

have grown up in the business. By asking the question of how your costs and processes would change if you had only one product, you and your team can reimagine what the business could look like.

Cost out your "Model T." So begin by determining what your one product or service would be. For Hewlett-Packard it might be a midrange printer. For a bank it might be the most popular kind of checking account. For a neighborhood health clinic it might be a simple walk-in pediatric visit. A good way to determine your Model T–equivalent is to consider your highest-volume products or SKUs and pick an item that is roughly average in terms of content, cost, and cycle time. Big companies that operate in many markets may find it difficult to isolate a single item and so may have more than one Model T, perhaps one for each set of products that are aimed at different customer segments and that don't share manufacturing processes or supply chains.

Now ask yourself: "What would our costs be if we made only this one product or delivered this one service?"

A manufacturer would still need a supply chain, a factory, a distribution network, and a sales-and-marketing function. But managers of a one-product company could streamline processes. They could greatly simplify entire IT systems. They could simplify distribution and sales (no more worrying about getting enough shelf space for all the different models). One manager we spoke with noted that making only one product would utterly transform his forecasting process. Each night this manager took an inventory of all 46,000 parts in his plant to ensure he had what he needed to manufacture any of the 10 billion permutations that customers could theoretically request. "If we don't have enough in stock or arriving by truck in time to meet the next day's schedule, then we have parts flown in," he said. "On average, fifteen planes a day fly in to the plant from our suppliers around the country. All those costs would disappear instantaneously."

Once you have determined your Model T costs, you can assess the costs of adding variety back in. But that requires a different kind of thought experiment: figuring out what your customers really want.

Determine customers' true preferences: the "Killer ABCs." The automotive legend Hal Sperlich, who helped create the original Mustang at Ford and then the first minivan at Chrysler, had a gut-level appreciation of simplicity. As we noted in chapter 1, he liked to point out that car buyers, immediately after making a purchasing decision, could remember no more than three criteria that were critical in making the decision. So if you want to sell a lot of cars, he added, you'd better make cars that stand out distinctly on the three things the target customer segment really cares about. If you do that, you need only match the competition on other attributes.

Sperlich called those three dimensions the "Killer ABCs" and applied them to everything he developed. The minivan's Killer ABCs were its carrying capacity, convenience (especially for parents), and value. The Mustang's Killer ABCs were performance (symbolized by its name), design, and price. The iconic ad for the original Mustang—aimed at male drivers—featured just a few items on an otherwise white page: the company's name with a picture of a shiny Mustang convertible looking like it was moving while standing still; an attractive young woman in an evening gown, suggesting luxury and style; and the figure $2,368, which even at the time was a widely affordable price. Killer ABCs, Sperlich said, meant standing out starkly from the competition on the attributes the customer segment really valued. The attributes had to be obvious to the customer, almost to the point of caricature.

Of course, not every segment of customers cares about the same three dimensions. That's why companies such as Honda offer stripped-down, midline, and higher-end models. But they do not go after "segments of one." In fact, the Honda Accord today comes in only three styles (sedan, coupe, and hybrid) with a total of just sixty-four option configurations, excluding body color. If you include color, the number of possible configurations rises to 484. A Bain & Company analysis in a recent year concluded that the Ford Fusion was theoretically available in 35,908 possible configurations, including color. While Honda would require half a day to build all possible Accords, Ford would take ninety-two days to build all possible Fusions. Honda's sales have been growing 6 percent a year while Ford's have been shrinking 1 percent a year.

As we have worked with companies over the years, we have come to believe that high complexity is a priori evidence of a lack of customer understanding. Organizations too often add options and products in hopes of finding one more customer who will buy the product, or increasing the company's share of wallet by a marginal amount. Huge catalogs of SKUs or configurations are really a way of saying, "I don't know what you want, but I have a whole range of options for you to choose from. I hope you can find something you like."

So adding in that tinted windshield and each of fifty or sixty other options really may not be necessary to meet customers' needs. In fact, companies that have cut back on product variety have found that their performance improved significantly. One of the major computer-printer manufacturers helped its retail-channel partners pick the company's top-selling printers, then supplied them with fewer models. That reduced stockouts, kept customers from switching to competitors' products, and cut back on the need to discount slow movers. Navistar's Diamond SPEC™ program, introduced in the mid-1990s, allowed buyers of a certain class of truck to choose from just sixteen preengineered modules rather than from thousands of individual components. The shorter ordering process (hours rather than days), together with improvements in quality and performance, led customers in the pilot program to place more than twice as many orders as forecast. Not long after its launch, Diamond SPEC accounted for 80 percent of dealer orders for that class of truck.

Again, we are not suggesting that you blindly reduce the number of options or SKUs. Doing this right requires that you know your customer well. Your sales and marketing organizations will let you know very quickly that if you don't understand your customer segments and what the Killer ABCs are for them, you actually do increase your risk. Going through a product-complexity-reduction exercise always requires detailed customer research.

But when it is done right, the payoff can be substantial. We have studied more than 500 situations where companies have gone through some version of this product-simplification process. The savings have ranged between 10 and 35 percent of total costs. We have found that most sales and marketing departments are initially skeptical of the approach. But they shouldn't be: we also found that, when done properly, revenue actually rises when customer needs are met with a set of Killer ABCs. In these 500 cases, the range of revenue increase was anywhere from 5 to 40 percent.

Customers, for their part, value simplicity. Google, for instance, has kept its powerful search engine so simple that a child can use it. "Google understands that simplicity is both sacred and central to its competitive advantage," wrote a reporter. Its spare home page, said a company official, "gives you what you want, when you want it, rather than everything you could ever want, even when you don't."[10] One of the most memorable and successful ad campaigns in recent years is auto insurer GEICO's "caveman" campaign, with its slogan "So easy a caveman can do it." The campaign helped GEICO increase its national market share from 4.6 percent in 2001 to 6.3 percent in 2005.

So remember Hal Sperlich, who knew that customers do not really want to design their own car, and don't take it for granted that your customers really want everything your company has been offering them. They may be fully satisfied with a more modest array of choices—so long as the choices you do offer have those Killer ABCs and deliver superior price/value propositions for the customer segments you are targeting.

Calculate the costs of adding some variety back in. The key to this step is to take a methodical approach, adding only a single element of complexity at a time and then tracing the effect through the value chain. That should allow you to identify exactly where the costs of complexity begin to outweigh the benefits. In a tractor plant, for example, you wouldn't need a scheduling system with just one model. You might not need much more for two models, but you probably would for four. Often the cost curve has a "knee"—a step change triggered by adding another particular model (see figure 5.4 [left-hand side]). An industrial supplier, for example, found that adding seven options for a particular part to its product effectively doubled the cost of that part for the Model T unit. That was acceptable, given the company's pricing possibilities. The eighth option, however, triggered another doubling, making the part cost now four times that of the Model T, and higher than the company could recover through pricing. Seven options was that company's innovation fulcrum, the right number of choices to offer its customers. It also turned out that customers could be completely satisfied with seven or fewer options. Once more, the key to finding the fulcrum is truly understanding your customer. By definition you are making trade-offs. You must ensure that the trade-offs you choose are precisely those that your target customer would make.

One cost of complexity that general managers frequently miss is exactly what we noticed in the tinted-windshield case: revenue may ultimately decline as the number of options increases. We have already listed the reasons: sales reps get confused, distributors can't stock all the varieties, customers can't find what they are looking for and won't buy what they don't want. To be sure, technology has made it easier in many businesses to keep track of variety, and so may affect the shape and position of the curve shown in figure 5.4 (right-hand side). But wherever the point of decreasing revenue may be, you can be sure that it exists—and that you'd better take it into account in your planning.

The judgment about which offerings to keep and which to jettison is rarely as simple as just "cutting off the tail." Many companies, for instance, chart the profitability of their products or customers and find that the results are highly skewed. A retailer might discover that the top 5 percent of SKUs account for nearly 100 percent of operating income. An insurance

FIGURE 5.4

Complexity Impacts Both Costs and Revenues

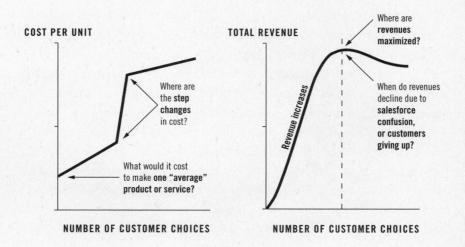

company might find that 60 percent of its clients are unprofitable, and that the top 5 percent account for the lion's share of profits. It might also discover that the accounts in the top 5 percent are the most loyal. One response to this situation is to propose cutting off the tail—to say, "Let's get rid of all the products or customers on the unprofitable side of the graph." That is seldom the right answer. Many products or clients look unprofitable because they are carrying some allocation of fixed costs. Those fixed costs don't suddenly disappear if you eliminate the unprofitable tail of the curve. Also, some products might help bring customers in the door, even if they themselves don't make money. The British supermarket chain Tesco, for example, keeps slow-moving products on the shelves if (and only if) they are important to the store's most loyal customers. The chain's Clubcard system, a frequent-shopper program, identifies and categorizes shoppers and purchases, including a group known to the company as "Premium Loyals." If Premium Loyals like an item, it will stay on the shelf even if other demand for it is slow. There's no substitute, unfortunately, for doing a careful product-by-product analysis.

Manage the balance point. Complexity tends to creep back in to product lines, for the reasons we mentioned earlier. You can help prevent that by simplifying your decision making and your processes, topics that we will take up in a moment. But there are measures to take on the product front as well. We have seen four models work:

1. Set absolute targets. In Europe this is known as the Aldi principle, after the German retailer that removes one SKU every time it adds one. Hisense, an electronics manufacturer, sets a maximum number of SKUs for each model of television it produces. If there are more, managers have noticed that R&D spending creeps upward and it is hard for consumers to choose among the competing variations on the basic model.

2. Raise the hurdle rate for new products. Requiring a higher rate of return on new products makes it more difficult for marketers to add SKUs. One clothing company dropped thousands of SKUs and millions of dollars in unprofitable sales, thereby increasing its gross margins. To keep a lid on complexity, it increased the required return for a new SKU from 15 to 25 percent.

3. Use pricing and ordering rules to guide customer behavior. A major producer of telecommunications components, finding that many of its sales were unprofitable, raised its minimum order quantity. That by itself led to a 27 percent reduction in transaction costs. The company also upgraded its cost-accounting system, recalculated its standard margin, and renegotiated prices with priority customers. These moves contributed to an annual profit improvement of 15 percent. At Navistar, a 5 percent discount guided customers to low-complexity options, and most customers availed themselves of the discount. That was a sign, as one manager wryly put it, that "customers definitely care about having all the choices in the world unless it's a nickel cheaper not to have them."

Astute use of technology can also help guide customer behavior. Say you are looking for a computer, and you log on to Dell's Web site. You won't have to scroll through thousands of options. The first screen simply asks what kind of customer you are: large enterprise, small enterprise, government, education, or home user. From there you are directed automatically to the options and configurations bought most frequently by customers in your segment. You can always customize the standard configurations that Dell offers—but Dell understands the costs of complexity and prices those options to cover the costs. Many customers revert back to the standard package when they see the price rapidly rising.

Another opportunity arises if a company understands the costs of complexity better than its competitors. That can enable it to price lower and attract the segments that are most suited to its products. It can decide not to offer products that are costly just to serve customer demand; instead it can shift those customers to competitors who do not really understand the full cost of serving the customers' specific needs. Navistar, again, wasn't interested in serving customers who wanted a very wide range of choice. The company understood that those customers might want a lot of choices but were unwilling to pay the full cost of the resulting complexity.

4. Weed the garden. The innovation fulcrum can easily get out of balance. Technologies change. Customer needs evolve. A company may have gone past the optimal point of complexity. Crest, for all its many varieties,

seems not to have passed that point. Its introduction of new products has been done carefully, and has helped the brand take over leadership in the U.S. toothpaste market from Colgate. By contrast, Nestlé in 2006 introduced a "dizzying array" of variations on its basic KitKat candy bar in the United Kingdom, according to the *Wall Street Journal*. The varieties included "strawberries and cream, passion fruit and mango and even red berry versions," plus "Christmas pudding" and tiramisu flavors in the winter. But the introduction of so many varieties had exactly the opposite effect from what the company hoped: sales dropped 18 percent in the course of the year.[11] KitKat was way past its innovation fulcrum, and the company soon abandoned nearly all of the exotic flavors.

Reduce the underlying complexity. Not all product complexity is the same. A company can offer customers a wide variety of products while minimizing the level of complexity in the production process. Here are two tools smart general managers have employed effectively:

1. Postpone customization until later in the value chain. Necessary variation in a company's product line can often be put off until later in the production or service-delivery process, where it may cost less. A simple example comes from Master Lock, the padlock manufacturer. In the past, Master Lock had customized its locks from the very first step in the manufacturing process, and by the second step already had 256 separate SKUs. Conversion to a modular product allowed Master Lock to build only a few standard models in the first steps, to postpone customization until step four, and to move packaging from the factory to its distribution centers, where labor costs were lower. The postponement lowered both inventories and labor costs, thereby doubling profitability.

Operating in global markets always introduces complexity, but postponement can often reduce it in this context as well. Take the situation of an electrical-appliance manufacturer we'll call ApplianceCo. ApplianceCo sold its wares all over the world, and needed region-specific SKUs because of variation in electrical outlets, packaging, regional color preferences, and so forth. The complexity—built into the products from the beginning—had led to high inventory levels and obsolescence rates, and had generated unnecessary costs. Much of the solution to ApplianceCo's difficulties lay in postponement. The company moved market-specific printing and coding of products to later in the production process. It created a universal electrical base with "smart plug" technology, allowing the appropriate plug to be put on at a late stage. It bulk-shipped unfinished products to local and regional hubs, where they were finished, sealed, and packaged to the specifications of the local market. The number of SKUs in manufacturing declined, as did inventory days. Yet the company was still able to meet its customers' needs.

2. Rely on common platforms, modules, and parts. Many companies simplify production by introducing—and enforcing—the use of common platforms and parts. Toyota, for instance, has a "parts store" for designers to draw from when they design a new model. Absent a very good reason to the contrary, a designer is expected to use standard parts. Thus Toyota has only two door hinges, one for its cars and one for its trucks. Its experience in making these hinges has allowed it to lower costs and improve quality, making for a quieter ride, fewer leaks, and faster design. You want to customize something only when it is a key attribute for the customer, one of the Killer ABCs. Door hinges aren't on anybody's list of Killer ABCs.

Modularity—designing and building individual modules that can be assembled or configured into different products—is another way to simplify processes. The U.S. Navy, which is required to buy from American shipbuilders and must deal with a variety of political considerations in its procurement decisions, has been plagued by high levels of complexity and high costs, and the secretary of the navy has proposed a new system for designing and building its ships. Under the new system, the navy would reduce the number of different ships it requires, change the design of these ships so that they can be built partly from preassembled modules, and invest in technologies (such as extensive use of composites) to simplify construction and reduce life-cycle cost. "Construction modularity," says one report, "affords a navy two key advantages. It helps to reduce class construction costs, and it allows different yards to simultaneously perform work on the hull and different modules for the same ship." [12]

3. Organizational and Decision-Making Simplicity

The more complex your strategy and your products, the more likely your organizational structures will be infected as well. We have to tell one last anecdote from the auto industry, because it speaks so clearly to this issue.

Chrysler Corp. undertook a major product-complexity optimization effort in the 1980s and eventually began to examine its organizational procedures for similar simplification opportunities. A bellwether example was found in the organizational processes surrounding the wiring harnesses of the vehicles.

A wiring harness is the electrical distribution system of a car—a bundle of wires, usually inserted early in the assembly process, that connects all the parts requiring electricity to the power source. It has a big trunk cable with a major branch to the engine and subbundles containing individual wires leading to the dashboard, the lights, and other parts of the car. Chrysler had thousands of different wiring harnesses at the time. Individual engineers designed a basic harness for each car model. But the exact harness installed in a car would depend on the configuration of options in that car. A car with a rear-window defogger, for instance, would get a different harness from one with no rear-window defogger. Assemblers had not only to get the right harness for each car on the line, they had to pull the harnesses all the way through the frame and firewall of the car. That sometimes broke wires or stripped off insulation. In fact, electrical problems relating to wiring harnesses were one of the most common kinds of quality defect, occasioning expensive rework costs after the car had been assembled, and sometimes leading to electrical problems for the consumer that were difficult to diagnose and expensive to correct.

It obviously made sense to standardize the wiring harnesses, and suppliers had been suggesting that. But this is where they ran into the real source of complexity: Chrysler's decision making. Some 240 different people had to approve a wiring harness.

When Chrysler tried to diagram all the touch points necessary for approval of the designs, it wound up with a picture that looked like a mass of spaghetti connecting boxes marked "body," "supplier 1," "engineering," and so on. No supplier had been able to walk through that decision-making process to get things simplified.

So Chrysler's problem wasn't just the option complexity and the impact on the number of wiring harnesses, it was the dysfunctional decision-making system that made it nearly impossible to fix the harness situation. We'll come back to Chrysler in a moment—but in the meantime, we want to introduce two tools that can help you fix such a situation.

Clarify and simplify decision making. The key step in untangling too-complex decision-making processes is to assign clear roles and responsibilities. Few decisions in a large organization can be made by one person. Nearly all must involve a variety of people in different positions. But not everyone who takes part in a decision plays the same role. Some are responsible for *recommending* a particular course of action—for making a proposal or offering alternatives. Others have responsibility for *input*; they are consulted about the proposed alternatives, and they provide relevant facts and judgments from their vantage points. Still others must *agree* to the recommendation. They must sign off on it before it can move forward.

Eventually one person will *decide* and others will assume responsibility for *performing*—for carrying out the decision.

We and our colleagues at Bain have developed an analytical process that incorporates all five roles. For the sake of a memorable acronym—particularly important since it's five steps rather than four—we have taken liberty with the order in which the steps are performed: we call it "RAPID," for Recommend, Agree, Perform, Input, and Decide. RAPID and similar procedures, as our colleagues Paul Rogers and Marcia Blenko wrote in *Harvard Business Review*, "give senior management teams a method for assigning roles and involving the relevant people." The key, they add, "is to be clear who has input, who gets to decide, and who gets it done."[13]

Charles Schwab is one company that revamped its decision-making process by assessing roles in this way. Schwab had come to see that its marketing organization was slow and ineffective in launching new products. There were too many internal handoffs and no clear decision makers. So a project team interviewed directors, vice presidents, and senior vice presidents, asking them which decisions they were involved in, where the major pain points were, and which decisions they felt they ought to be involved in. The team then mapped organizational roles to each of the top decisions, using the principle that each decision should have an accountable owner and that other people's roles in the decision needed to be specified. It then developed a high-level decision calendar, including clearly defined activities and processes for each role in the decision.

Chrysler did something similar with its wiring harness. Hal Sperlich established a wiring-harness steering committee, with members representing all the functional organizations. The committee ranked and selected the vendors with the best combination of technical talent and costs. It then selected vehicle models for a test, and it evaluated two or three suppliers to see who did the best job of simplifying the harnesses, reducing costs (including assembly line costs), and improving quality. The committee also tested a new decision process for how those suppliers interacted with Chrysler. By clarifying decision rights and involving the "input givers" and the "recommenders" earlier, it was able to reduce the touch points for a decision by almost a factor of ten, and to locate responsibility with just one decision maker. Based on these tests, Chrysler eventually rolled out the new vendor base and new decision process across the company. Wiring harness costs (including assembly) and electrical quality problems dropped dramatically.

"The courage to decide is a virtue not many people have," says Pier Francesco Guarguaglini, CEO of the Italian aerospace company Finmeccanica. Once decision roles are clear, you can see whether your people have that courage or not.

Optimize spans and layers. One way to assess organizational and decision-making efficiency is to analyze management *spans*—the number of people each manager is responsible for—and management *layers*, the number of levels between the bottom rung of workers and the CEO. It will help you determine where you may have too many people and too much organizational complexity.

There is no fixed guideline for management spans; it depends on the company and the industry. General Electric's guideline, for example, is that no manager should have more than ten to fifteen direct reports. The company keeps the number of management layers under control as well, reducing layers in some parts of the company from ten to four.

In analyzing spans and layers, you need to pay attention both to your industry benchmarks and to the types of managers you are assessing. Line supervisors, for instance, are likely to be responsible for more people than staff managers. An individual manager's span may vary depending on the extent to which he or she is involved in tasks such as planning, coaching and training, and monitoring and control. The approach we recommend includes several steps. In the diagnostic phase, team members analyze the company's organization charts to determine the reporting structure. They conduct internal interviews to verify the charts and to identify informal reporting links, then they create a map of spans and layers. In the analysis phase, members identify appropriate benchmarks and compare the company's spans and layers with the benchmarks for both management and nonmanagement personnel. That process allows the team to map out potential changes and add up the savings they will bring. In the implementation phase, the team and company management redesign the organizational map, set a timeline for implementation, communicate the plan to everybody affected, and train workers in their new job descriptions when necessary.

Like so much complexity reduction, these steps can lead to enormous savings. But it isn't just costs that are affected. A more efficient arrangement of spans and layers leads to quicker, better decisions; fewer unnecessary meetings; and more-empowered, more-motivated people. "When there are a lot of layers, it usually means managers have too few people reporting to them," write Jack and Suzy Welch in *BusinessWeek.* "They end up babysitting their direct reports, or worse, doing their jobs for them. Talk about killing morale and initiative!" [14]

At a privately held airline we'll call AirCo, revenue per employee was 20 percent less than at its peers. A survey of employees turned up a variety of complaints, ranging from "We are getting data and creating reports that no one reads" to "Overall we are overstaffed . . . we just don't know where." A detailed analysis of management spans revealed that senior managers' spans typically averaged five or fewer direct reports, while the average for the entire company was eight direct reports per manager. That compared with ten to twelve direct reports at AirCo's competitors. The company also had nine layers of management—the same number as a competitor with more than ten times AirCo's revenues. Its smaller competitors, meanwhile, had between four and six layers.

Quantitative analysis of AirCo's spans and layers, comparing the actual with a target level, revealed a potential headcount reduction of some 500 people. Qualitative analysis turned up significant overlap of activities across departments. The level of redundancy led to unnecessary meetings, processes, and reports, and to poor decision making. Analysts also assessed people's activities on the extent to which they actually delivered value to the customer. Put together, these analyses suggested that AirCo could cut its workforce by about 1,400, or about 13 percent of the total, for a potential savings of $150 million. When AirCo implemented these and other changes, its estimated market value appreciated by 80 percent. Its main competitors' stock prices, meanwhile, grew in single digits or declined.

4. Process Simplicity

As with products, complexity creeps into a company's operational processes for understandable reasons. Processes, after all, evolve over time. Managers and engineers regularly add steps to a process in hopes of saving money, avoiding errors, solving a current problem, or ensuring that customers get exactly what they want. Manufacturing processes are notorious for their complexity—remember the manager who had to keep track of 46,000 parts and fly them in from around the country if he ran short. But process complexity turns up in many other industries as well. A brokerage company, for example, allowed prospective customers to fill out an application on the Web. The application required prospects to plow through some sixty screens, however, and about 70 percent of prospects gave up before finishing the application. No doubt the screens were complex for good reasons—to understand customer profiles, meet regulatory demands, and so on. But the whole process became too complicated for the customer. Before Hal Sperlich reduced complexity at Chrysler, consumers were so baffled by the choices the company offered that they ordered cars directly from the factory only 7 percent of the time. The rest of the time they chose from whatever the dealer had in stock. The presumed value of choice ("any car you want") was being rejected by most of the intended beneficiaries, who ended up choosing from among four to eight cars on a given dealer's lot.

You can take a variety of measures to simplify your processes and keep complexity from reappearing. For example:

Use technology. The great advantage of modern information technology isn't that it allows products and services to proliferate. The real advantage is that IT can help simplify processes.

Some service industries have been remarkably slow to simplify processes through technology. An example is the claims function in auto insurance. Claims "is the single largest and most onerous overhead in an insurance company, accounting for between 75 percent and 90 percent of total administrative costs," write the researchers Ricardo Arruda and Benjamin Ensor. "Wasted resources . . . drive these costs: many processes are still based on old legacy or manual systems, and insurance workers spend a large amount of time on associated routine interactions that have little or no impact on the outcome of a claim."[15]

The Progressive Group of Insurance Companies, based in Ohio, has been a leader in changing this state of affairs. In 1990, Progressive was the first car insurer to introduce 24/7 claims. It put claims representatives in mobile offices, called Immediate Response® Vehicles. It equipped the vehicles with wireless laptops, printers, and cell phones. The laptops have software that claims representatives use to write an estimate and settle the claim on the spot at the customer's work, home, the accident scene, or the body shop, drastically reducing the amount of time necessary to settle a claim. As a result, Progressive has lowered its cost of doing business and is able to pass those savings on to customers in the form of lower premiums. Progressive has consistently been more profitable than the industry average because of lower costs and superior customer service.

Redesign your processes. In recent years, financial services companies such as Progressive have been among the leaders in reconfiguring processes to remove complexity. That brokerage company with the sixty screens for an applicant, for instance, redesigned the process so that it required only thirty screens—25 percent fewer than its closest competitor. The firm's Web revenues rose 120 percent, and the cost of allowing customers to open accounts on the Web declined 20 percent. Another insurance company found that its handling of applications and other input from sales agents was slower and less efficient than that of its key competitors. Analyzing the situation, it found that its "one-on-one" model—a case coordinator for each agent—delivered great service but was costly in terms of time and money. The company then redesigned processes so that small teams of case coordinators and administrators worked together to serve a group of agents; it also added Internet functionality so that routine inquiries could be diverted to a Web site. The redesign cut staff costs for bringing in new business by 50 percent. Yet service levels didn't suffer; on the contrary, revenue actually increased.

Companies in other industries have also learned the payoffs from redesigning processes. Here's one dramatic example concerning one of those U.S. companies that builds ships for the navy. This company had found that its average total cost was double that of commercial competitors. One critical problem lay in its planning and scheduling processes. The "bills," as work orders in the industry are known, were not always sequenced correctly. Employees often found that the materials they needed weren't available. A lot of the company's paid labor time was simply unproductive—workers were waiting around to get started on what they were supposed to do next.

So the company launched projects to revamp the planning and scheduling process. Project teams scoped the bills to individual work units and compartments rather than to the entire ship. They scheduled tasks based on capacity constraints, and released them to craft workers only when material, labor, and equipment were available. Maybe most important, they sequenced the bills correctly—the planning group itself took responsibility for sequencing, rather than leaving the sequencing to field-operations personnel. The results of several pilot projects have been truly startling: nearly a 50 percent reduction in open (uncompleted) bills, a reduction of time necessary to complete the bills of up to 30 percent, and an 11 percent increase in capacity utilization. Ultimately, the process reengineering is expected to cut unproductive labor by 40 percent, leading to savings of hundreds of millions of dollars.

Another advantage of achieving process simplicity is that it increases a company's nimbleness, and so can significantly improve the time to market. As we noted earlier, shorter time to market helps you reduce costs such as inventory and rework, and it lets you learn more quickly what your customers prefer.

Many companies are aware of unnecessary complexities in their processes, and so attack them through the kind of reengineering initiatives we mentioned earlier. But the right time to do this is after you have learned to simplify your strategy, your product offerings, and your organizational structures. Otherwise, process complexity will creep back in as fast as you can eliminate it. Like managers at the energy company, you may find that you simplify process after process and still can't see the results.

KING ARTHUR MIGHT HAVE KNOWN THE TRUTH: HIS LIST OF IN-structions as to what knights should and should not do was too long. It needed to be simplified. Human beings can't remember long lists, and so they focus on a few things anyway.

For business, the meaning is clear: excess complexity is the enemy of results. Complexity comes from a lack of clarity about strategy and/or what customers really value. It comes from ignoring the innovation fulcrum and creating too many products and services. It comes from inefficient organizational structure, and from poorly designed processes. An overly complex organization is an organization that can't move forward, and that can't satisfy its customers. A general manager's job is to simplify, simplify, simplify—to obey the fourth law—and to create an organization that continues to operate in as simple a fashion as possible. This is the key to minimizing costs, maximizing revenue, and energizing a company's people.

So there are the four laws. In the next part of this book we will turn to the question of how you can apply their lessons to your organization.

IMPLICATIONS FOR THE GENERAL MANAGER

- Use the Model T approach to calculate the systemic costs of strategic, product, organizational, and process complexity that have crept into your business. Determine lost opportunities for revenue and price optimization.

- Study your customers' needs in detail, and find the Killer ABCs for each segment that you are serving. Focus your resources intensely on outperforming your competitors in these segments.

- Based on the above, simplify, redesign, and restructure to meet your company's innovation fulcrum. You can expect significant reductions in costs and significant increases in revenue and growth.

- Set no more than three to five critical imperatives for your organization, and communicate them so that every employee can remember, recite, and buy into what the company is trying to accomplish.

- Streamline your organizational structure, decision-making responsibilities, and critical business processes to ensure clarity, speed, and efficiency in meeting customer needs better than your competitors.

SIX

Where You're Starting From: Diagnosing Your Point of Departure

We can have facts without thinking, but we cannot have thinking without facts.

—JOHN DEWEY

IT'S MONDAY MORNING AT EIGHT O'CLOCK, YOUR FIRST DAY ON the job as the new CEO or general manager. You are responsible for running the business. You understand the four laws we have described. What do you do first?

You may find this question answered for you, almost before you have time to think. As we noted at the beginning of the book, people will want to see you—urgently. There are decisions to be made, appointments to be kept, fires to be put out. The cacophony of voices calling for your immediate attention can be overwhelming. Many items are actually marked "urgent," and their priority is often determined by the order in which they land on your desk.

But we urge you to sort through all the agenda items carefully and to put off anything that can be put off. Because you have two other critical tasks to perform during your first few months on the job. In all likelihood, nobody will put these tasks on your calendar. You have to put them there yourself, and you have to reorder your priorities so that they get top billing. They can help make the difference between success and failure.

The first step is to assess the business's condition accurately—to conduct a diagnosis of your *point of departure.*

You need to know exactly what has been going on, where your organization stands in the marketplace, what its internal capabilities are, what threats and opportunities it faces. That's your starting point. Someone once said that if you don't know where you're starting from, you'll never get where you're going. The maxim applies doubly to running a business or indeed any sort of team. In this chapter we will walk you through the process of making a thorough, detailed, analytical, fact-based assessment of your point of departure, using the lens of the four laws. This is what we are calling the full-potential performance-improvement diagnostic process, or just the performance-improvement diagnostic. The role of the diagnostic is to help you understand what the full-potential performance of your business can be. It will help you see exactly where you *can* improve and where you should set your priorities.

Your second task is to craft a destination, a *point of arrival*, and a plan for getting there.

After all, you want to improve the business, and you are expected to do just that. You want to boost performance, build on past successes, set out in a new direction, turn things around, beat the competition, achieve the vision agreed on with your boss or the board. As we noted earlier in the book, you don't have much time to make your mark. Your goal has to fit your time frame, probably no more than two or three years. We will show you how to develop a point of arrival that does fit it, and that is based on the four laws.

After you develop your point of departure and point of arrival, you will be mapping out and leading certain actions and initiatives—just a few at

FIGURE 6.1

The Point of Departure, Point of Arrival, and Road to Results Are Your Blueprint for Success

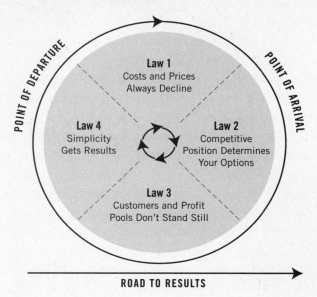

any given time—to move the business from one point to the other. That's your *road to results*, and it too will affect whether you succeed or fail (see figure 6.1). In chapter 7 we'll show you how to develop your point of arrival and make a plan for getting there. In chapter 8 we'll show you how to implement the plan.

THE SIMPLE PATH TO *DRAMATIC* SUCCESS

Point of departure, point of arrival, road to results: this is the simple path to success we mentioned in the beginning of the book. Again, in calling it simple we don't mean to imply that achieving great results is easy. If it were easy, everybody would be doing it all the time. But great managers can make it *look* easy. They can make it look easy because they know what they are doing—and at times, what they accomplish is astonishing. Let's remind ourselves of what a few of them have achieved, then map out the template of analysis and actions that shows how they went about it.

Warren Knowlton, for instance, spent just over three and a half years at Morgan Crucible. As we noted earlier in the book, he was the architect of a dramatic improvement in the company's performance. Morgan Crucible is "now a focused, world-leading business with a clear strategy in place to deliver top-line growth . . . [and] operating margins of 15 percent," wrote one admiring analyst in February 2006. "Add in the net cash in the balance sheet and it represents one of the biggest turnarounds in recent capital goods history." [1]

Or take Ken Chenault, who thoroughly revamped American Express's core card business by offering customers options and services its competitors were unable to match. In the five years after Chenault took over as CEO, he also generated $1 billion in benefits from reengineering each year. During that time, American Express's revenue grew an average of 10.6 percent a year, while earnings per share rose 16.9 percent annually. An investment of $100 in Chenault's American Express in 2001 would have been worth $202 in 2006, compared with $135 for the S&P 500.

Or consider Mitt Romney's accomplishments as CEO of the Salt Lake Organizing Committee (SLOC), the nonprofit organization that put on the 2002 Winter Olympics. (Romney is a former colleague of ours: a onetime partner at Bain & Company, he left to found Bain Capital, which he led until taking on the Olympics and then beginning his political career.) SLOC's previous leaders had been indicted for allegedly fixing bids. Board members had been forced out, and insiders feared that the Department of Justice might indict the entire organization. SLOC was also in the hole to the tune of hundreds of millions of dollars. Costs were skyrocketing, and the organization's bankers were nervous. [2]

But when the games ended in February 2002—again, just a little more than three years after Romney took the job—everyone declared them a resounding success. NBC Olympic Sports chief Dick Ebersol said the Olympics were "far and away the best Games I have ever been involved in." SLOC got its costs under control, then beat its goals for ticket sales, revenue from sponsors, and even sales of Olympic merchandise. The games ended with a *surplus* of $56 million—and SLOC returned $10.5 million to a surprised federal government.[3]

The fact is, such stories aren't as unusual as you might think. Look at the business history of the past few decades. Lee Iacocca, Hal Sperlich, Gerald Greenwald, and their teams completely turned around Chrysler in the 1980s, a fact that has been overshadowed by the company's later troubles. More recently, the Burger King team took a struggling brand and made it once again into a profitable, solid number two among hamburger chains. Gail Kelly led a notable improvement in performance at St.George Bank in Australia, delivering double-digit earnings gains for five straight years before her departure in 2007. Fred Rowan led a team that took Carter's, the children's clothing company, from a position as a sleepy, old-line manufacturer to the top of its industry. (We will revisit Carter's in chapter 8, because Rowan is responsible for not just one but a series of performance-improvement cycles.)

Or simply look around you. As we wrote this in mid-2007, we could see CEOs and general managers in any number of industries who were in the process of making their businesses into performance leaders. Philip Teel not only brought Northrop Grumman Ship Systems back from the devastation wrought by Hurricane Katrina, he improved on its prehurricane performance as well. Sol Trujillo, after stints as CEO at US West and the European telecommunications company Orange, had initiated in 2005 a five-year change program at Telstra, the largest telecom in Australia. Even in the face of political and regulatory opposition, Trujillo seemed likely to remake Telstra from an underperforming government-owned business into a technology and performance leader. In chemicals, David Weidman and his team took Celanese from a point where it was earning less than its peers in the early 2000s to performance in line with peers by 2006. In plastics, John Taylor brought Vienna-based Borealis from a loss position in 2001 to robust profitability by 2004, with continued strong profit growth through to 2007.

Good things were happening even in one of the most troubled industries, airlines, both in the United States and overseas. Gerard Arpey became chief executive of AMR Corp., parent of American Airlines, in April 2003, a job that was almost unimaginably challenging because of the carrier's high cost position and huge losses. But Arpey engineered the beginnings of a serious turnaround: in 2006, AMR recorded EBITDA (earnings before interest, taxes, depreciation, and amortization) of $2.1 billion and net income of $231 million. Meanwhile, a former Royal Dutch Shell executive named Idris Jala became chief executive of Malaysia Airlines in December 2005, when the troubled carrier was nearly insolvent. In just twelve months he resolved the airline's cash crisis and put it on track for sustained profitability. In the last two quarters of 2006, Malaysia Airlines earned total net profit of 362 million ringgit (about $99 million).

Many different people, many different industries, many different specifics. But they are all great managers, and they all followed—or were following—some variant of the simple path to success. The path always begins with a fact-based performance-improvement diagnosis of the point of departure. Knowlton had a list of diagnostic questions, which we'll come back to later in this chapter. Romney's first step was a "strategic audit," his term for a performance-improvement diagnosis. Other CEOs underscore the point. Trujillo says, "My first action at Telstra was to bring together the real facts and data about the business—to strip away what we might want to believe about the business to get to what was real. In sixty days we understood where the company stood strategically, what the cost take-out opportunity was, what the organization and cultural roadblocks were. I had to understand what the real starting point was so that I could make the hard choices early and help our leadership team, the board, and ultimately the market reset their expectations." Arpey says, "If you don't figure out honestly and ruthlessly what you are up against and what needs to be done, then you will not be able to execute on what needs to be accomplished." Weidman puts it only a little differently: "First, we needed to articulate the areas where we were falling behind. So we went to external benchmarks to determine in key areas exactly where we stood."

The examples show that significant performance improvement is possible. So, of course, is failure, where by failure we mean not just catastrophe but simply not improving the business toward its full potential. When we have seen failure, we have nearly always been able to trace it to the lack of a simple, compelling framework informed by the four laws. A leader who fails may have ignored the experience curve or a shifting profit pool.

He may have been overwhelmed by the complexity of his organization, and have failed to take the steps needed to simplify it. Even if he was aware of the laws, he may have failed to map out where he was starting from, where he wanted to go, and how he proposed to get there.

So it's important to get the path right. The path begins with a diagnosis of the point of departure, and the diagnosis must begin with the four laws.

POINT-OF-DEPARTURE PERFORMANCE-IMPROVEMENT DIAGNOSTIC: THE TWELVE MUST-HAVE FACTS

The humorist James Thurber once said, "It is better to know some of the questions than all of the answers." A performance-improvement diagnosis is all about asking the *right* questions, then finding out the answers. It has to be based on an "honest and ruthless" assessment of facts. You study the situation as it is, not as you had hoped or wished it might be, and not as some people might like you to believe it is. Those facts, moreover, must come from the outside as well as the inside. You must know what is happening in the marketplace—with your competitors, your suppliers, your customers, and your other stakeholders. Your teams will gather data. You yourself will have conversation after conversation. "You need to listen to people in your industry, people in related industries, even people in unrelated industries," says Richard Crawford, who built Cambridge Industries into a leading manufacturer of plastic-composite components. "It helps in determining where things are going and where your business is going to fit."

But which data should your teams gather, and exactly which conversations should you have? Effective fact gathering always depends on a hypothesis that helps you understand what is important and what isn't. Doctors diagnosing patients don't gather facts randomly. They perform a basic assessment, then they drill down into what the data and their experience suggest is likely to be the problem area. That's where the four laws come in: they show you what is important to your business. Remember how Lou Gerstner turned around IBM. He didn't begin his tenure by identifying and fixing the many problems in the company's hardware divisions that presumably needed fixing. Rather, he identified the shifting profit pool in the industry and began putting his investment dollars into building up IBM's capabilities in software, services, and systems integration. Seeing the big picture through the four laws helps a manager set effective priorities.

As we have observed high-performing managers, we have developed a list of the most important questions raised by the laws. We call the answers to these questions the "twelve must-have facts" (see figure 6.2). These are the minimum that you will need to create an effective diagnosis of the business. Appendix 3 shows the basic charts that incorporate these facts. These charts are a presentation template that one company customized

FIGURE 6.2

Defining Your Points of Departure and Arrival Requires Twelve Must-Have Facts

LAW 1 Costs and Prices Always Decline	LAW 2 Competitive Position Determines Your Options	LAW 3 Customers and Profit Pools Don't Stand Still	LAW 4 Simplicity Gets Results
1. How does your cost slope compare to those of competitors? What is the slope of price changes in your industry right now and how does your cost curve compare?	**4.** Where do you and your competitors fall on the ROA/RMS chart? How are the leaders making money, and what is their approach? What is the full potential of your business position?	**7.** Which are the biggest, fastest-growing, and most profitable customer segments? How well do you meet customer needs relative to competitors and substitutes?	**10.** How complex are your products or service offerings, and what is that degree of complexity costing you? Where is your innovation fulcrum? What are the Killer ABCs in your business?
2. What are your costs compared with competitors'? Who is most efficient and effective in priority areas? Where can you improve most relative to others?	**5.** How big is your market? Which parts are growing fastest? Where are you gaining or losing share?	**8.** What proportion of customers are you retaining? How do your NPS ratings track against competitors'?	**11.** How complex is your decision making and organization relative to competitors'? What is the impact of this complexity?
3. Which of your products or services are making money (or not), and why?	**6.** What are the few capabilities that are creating a competitive advantage for you? Which are missing and are therefore holding you back, and which ones need to be strengthened or acquired?	**9.** How much of the profit pool do you have today? How is the profit pool likely to change in the future? What are the opportunities and threats?	**12.** Where does complexity reside in your processes? What is that costing you?

appropriately for each of its fifty business units and then used successfully as a diagnostic tool.

You may want to create your own template or adapt this one to the specifics of your business—and of course you will undoubtedly go after many additional facts as a result of what surfaces from the analyses. In large, complex organizations there are always plenty of areas for investigation. When we work with a company, we often use the twelve must-have facts to drill down into various functional areas to create the full-potential performance-improvement diagnostic. (We will give some examples in this chapter; the complete set of tools is outlined in appendix 3.) But the important point is that you can boil all the detail into a relatively simple set of charts that will give you an X-ray of your organization's point of departure and raise the right issues. The charts are the Killer ABCs of what you need to know. If you don't have the answers to the questions they raise, you run the risk of flying blind.

FIRST LAW: COSTS AND PRICES ALWAYS DECLINE

The first law tells us that costs and prices always decline in the long term, according to the experience curve. So you naturally need answers to some key questions relating to both.

1. Cost and Price Experience Curves

How does your cost slope compare with those of competitors? What is the slope of price changes in your industry right now—and how does your cost curve compare?

You know that prices will very likely decline in the long run. If they have been declining right along and are continuing to do so, you need only know how fast. Calculating the slope of the experience curve will allow you to predict what prices will be as cumulative experience in the industry continues to double.

In the short run, however, prices may be stable, or they may even be rising. Some companies, possibly including your own, may be maintaining a price umbrella. A temporary imbalance of supply and demand may have pushed prices up. Regulations, tariffs, and other government actions may be interfering with the normal workings of the marketplace. When you calculate the price curves, estimate what the effects will be if the environment changes.

Then compare the industry's price curves with your own cost curves (see figure 6.3). The relationship between prices and costs in any given business area will determine some of your top priorities. If prices are going down while your costs are going up or holding steady, for instance, cost improvement will likely be your single most urgent challenge. Your own costs need to be decreasing over the long term regardless of what prices are doing. An upward movement in prices will likely be only temporary.

Understanding your overall cost trends, of course, is just the first step. You must drill down into every segment of costs to determine where the

FIGURE 6.3

What Is Your Cost Slope Versus Competitors'?
What Is Your Industry Price Slope?

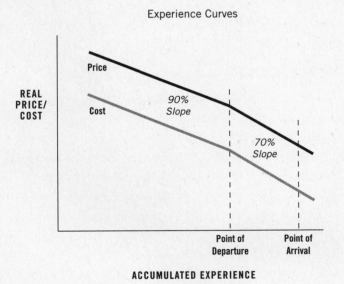

Experience Curves

REAL PRICE/COST

Price

Cost

90% Slope

70% Slope

Point of Departure

Point of Arrival

ACCUMULATED EXPERIENCE

central challenges and opportunities lie. Dig into the cost areas that are most important for your organization: manufacturing, supply chain, service operations, overhead, whatever they may be. Identify the key cost components and the trends in each one. Look for instances of failure to manage to the experience curve, such as rising unit costs for labor or rising procurement costs. This kind of detailed diagnosis will identify opportunities for improvement at the most granular level, and will provide the basis for a plan of action.

One CEO we spoke with reflected on what he called his biggest mistake in his first few months on the job. One of his company's business units was the leader in an industrial market. It had been raising prices, so it was quite profitable, and the new CEO decided to leave it alone for the time being. But new low-cost competitors from Asia were beginning to enter the market, and soon were able to collapse this business's price umbrella. The situation required urgent and dramatic action to reduce costs by at least 15 percent, an initiative that is well under way and on track as we write. The lesson he drew from the experience was stark: be sure you diagnose *every* business position carefully, particularly in units that seem to be doing well. Another CEO, Pier Francesco Guarguaglini of Finmeccanica, would agree. "Often," he says, "it's precisely where one thinks one knows everything that the biggest shortcomings are hidden."

2. Relative Cost Position—and Key Levers to Change It

What are your costs compared with competitors'? Who is most efficient and effective in priority areas? Where can you improve most relative to others?

The previous question dealt with cost trends as compared with prices. This question deals with your relative cost position—how you stack up against others in your industry—right now. An analysis of relative cost position quantifies cost differences between your business and that of your competitors; it shows which cost elements and specific practices are different. You should drill down to the point where you understand where and how you differ, and why. That, in turn, will help you understand exactly where you can close cost gaps and gain or regain competitive advantage. It will also help you formulate detailed plans to do so.

Listen, for example, to David Weidman discussing what he wanted to know when he came on board at Celanese:

> You want the facts relative to your variable margin versus your competitors. Are your conversion costs on a par with the competition's? You want to know your income statement and you want to see your best competitor's income statement—you want to know why there are differences. Is it because he has a technology advantage that you're never going to have? Is it because he's got a labor pool that is 10 percent of your hourly cost and you're never going to bridge that? Is it because you've got five times more people than he has? If he doesn't have a technology advantage and you've got more people, you ought to be able to match his headcount. And if you have something that he doesn't, then you have a winning business. Maybe you have a global market position, proprietary technology, a raw-materials contract that runs for twenty years and no one else is going to get another one. These are the types of facts that you look at.

Weidman had to make sure his people were comparing themselves to the right competitors in determining their relative cost position—not just other companies with low performance (as some were inclined to do) but leading companies with similar products, similar markets, and similar scale. "Once you got through the denial, they came back and said, 'Holy cow, our average EBITDA to sales is seven or eight percentage points lower than the competition. The competition is running around 15 percent and we're running in high single digits!' And this was not in one business, this was across every organization."

Weidman also wanted his team to identify specific areas where they could improve relative to the competition. He asked them to find out, for instance, what a key competitor was doing in maintenance, because that company's maintenance spending was far better than Celanese's. He asked them to learn how European companies managed energy utilization, because they were some of the best in the industry. "So we launched a series of initiatives that basically said, 'We are going to take it one by one, and we are going to go after areas where we can become top quartile in our performance.' "

Best demonstrated practices. As Weidman understood, this kind of analysis presents a unique opportunity. Rather than simply comparing yourself to your one best competitor, figure out which one (including you) is best in each individual area. Maybe one is world class in supply-chain logistics practices, another in a particular step in manufacturing, and so on. You can then build up a hypothetical competitor representing the best of the best, or what we call "best demonstrated practices." That hypothetical company will have lower costs and better performance than any real-world company—and you can use it as a benchmark for improvement once you know the best practices and how much they might be worth for you to adopt.

Many practitioners have used just this technique to leapfrog their competitors rather than simply trying to catch up. One example is a Houston heart surgeon. We conducted a best-demonstrated-practices analysis on open-heart surgery, looking at the highest-quality and lowest-cost practices wherever we found them. The Houston surgeon used our analysis, adopted the practices, and soon was able to perform open-heart surgery with lower mortality rates and significantly lower costs than any doctor we had seen. He put in a bid to be the primary heart surgeon for the largest insurer in Puerto Rico and ultimately won 100 percent of heart surgeries for patients in that plan.

Also, don't rely exclusively on what you have learned in the past. One thing we have noticed about new general managers—it's probably a natural human tendency—is that they often focus on what they know best. We worked with a senior executive at a well-known private-equity fund, for instance, who was responsible for performance improvement in the fund's portfolio companies. He had achieved great success in the past by fixing supply-chain management issues. So he tended to see possibilities for improving the supply chain in all the portfolio companies, to the point where every issue somehow morphed into a supply-chain problem. The trouble with this approach, of course, is that you may miss opportunities outside your power alley of expertise. That's why we suggest looking broadly at all areas of activity to understand your gap relative to best-in-class performance. It isn't that every area is equally important, it's just that you are likely to be surprised by the magnitude of opportunity in areas you might have otherwise overlooked.

In appendix 3 you will see a comprehensive list of topics to be covered on the cost front. At one level of aggregation higher, you will want to ask the questions below:

- *Selling, general, and administrative expenses*: Is each function efficient and effective relative to competitors, including IT, product development, human resources, and finance? High costs in these areas can also contribute to slow, bureaucratic decision making, hence an inability to respond to competitors' moves.

- *Manufacturing or service operations*: Are you the low-cost provider? Are you in the right locations, and do you have processes that create competitive advantage?

- *Procurement and sourcing*: Do you have a world-class team and a total-cost perspective? Are you able to help your suppliers drive down their own experience curves? Are you buying from the lowest-cost suppliers and locations anywhere in the world? For many companies, sourced materials and services can account for 40 to 80 percent of total costs.

- *Supply-chain management*: Do you have optimal distribution and transportation? Do you and your suppliers and distributors have efficient operations that help you provide better service and delivery than the competition? Do you have a high-velocity demand-pull supply-chain system operating, and how can you improve it?

American Airlines attacks its costs. Gerard Arpey did a full-blown diagnosis of both costs and revenue performance relative to competitors shortly after he took over at American Airlines. The company had just averted bankruptcy, so Arpey knew that lowering costs had to be one of his top priorities. He called the initiative "Lower Costs to Compete," and it became one of the four critical imperatives of his turnaround plan. Under Arpey's direction, employee-led teams reviewed every aspect of the company's operations. They examined costs in every nook and cranny. They compared American's performance with best-in-class competitors. The result was a comprehensive fact base vetted by both labor and management that identified gaps versus best-in-class in every area of the company.

The teams then identified the right metrics for comparison with the competition. Each metric had to include the key drivers of the costs. For example, the agreed-upon metric for pilot costs was cost per block hour. ("Block hour" means time that the plane is actually flying.) Cost per block hour could then be broken out into both direct costs, such as wages and benefits, and utilization rates, which reflected factors such as operational delays and sick time. One surprising discovery was that more than half the gap with the best-in-class low-cost carrier was due to differences in utilization rather than differences in direct costs.

American's teams completed this kind of analysis for every single cost category. They then categorized the gaps two ways: first, by difficulty and risk to change; and second, by whether the gaps could be closed soon or would take more time and investment. Figure 6.4 shows this categorization graphically, with the size of the bubbles indicating the size of the gap.

Because Arpey and his team looked at best demonstrated practices across all the players in the industry (even looking at other industries for some functions not specific to airlines), the sum of the gaps was greater than the difference between American and the industry's most profitable carrier. Thus American had the opportunity to overtake that carrier if it could adopt all of the best demonstrated practices.

This kind of comprehensive cost diagnostic process can be powerful in mobilizing an organization to action. Most people have a natural desire to be the best.

3. Product-Line Profitability

Which of your products or services are making money (or not), and why?

This is known as a "product-line profitability analysis"; its goal is to calculate the true margin of your products and services. It is a challenging but essential exercise. You need to calculate true direct costs for each

FIGURE 6.4

Detailed Diagnostic Across All Categories of Cost Identified and Ranked Gaps

Difference Compared with Best-in-Class

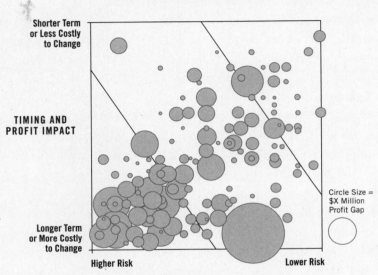

Shorter Term
or Less Costly
to Change

TIMING AND
PROFIT IMPACT

Longer Term
or More Costly
to Change

Higher Risk   Lower Risk

STRATEGIC OR OPERATIONAL RISK

Circle Size =
$X Million
Profit Gap

product based on actual activities performed, rather than using standard costing. Activity-based costing will give you a more accurate picture than you or your predecessor may have had in the past. Then you must accurately allocate indirect costs—logistics, selling expenses, general and administrative expenses—to each product line and customer segment. The analysis should reveal key cost and revenue drivers: areas where COGS (cost of goods sold), for instance, is out of line, or where revenue is below benchmark levels. The analysis should thus identify the *primary drivers of underperformance* in each product area and customer segment.

When Warren Knowlton decided to accept the job at Morgan Crucible, he knew he had a huge challenge in just this arena. The company had hundreds of SKUs ranging from crucibles and advanced piezo ceramics to body armor and state-of-the-art superconductor magnetic systems. It sold them to thousands of different customers. Which of these products were making money and which were dragging the company down?

Knowlton's approach to determining his point of departure had much in common with the one described in this chapter. He began by drawing up a long list of questions for the heads of his business units, including most of those in figure 6.2. His questions would help him get a read on the capabilities of the management team. They would also help him figure out the pressure points where he could take quick, effective action. But most of the questions were expressly designed to gather information relevant to the four laws. On costs and prices, for instance, he asked the unit heads to delineate their expectations for operating profit during the coming year, and to explain expected changes from the preceding year. Then he drilled down to learn about the factors affecting prices and costs. One question asked, "What percent of your revenues are sold to customers you would consider to have significant leverage over you?" Another was, "How much of your revenue do you believe is sold as a price-sensitive commodity-type product?" Still others focused on the cost side, asking about matters such as purchasing procedures, the ratio between fixed and variable costs, and the trendline in working capital. The answers gave him a jump start on his analysis of product-line profitability, and he subsequently made major shifts in product lines to deemphasize commodity products and unprofitable customers.

SECOND LAW: COMPETITIVE POSITION DETERMINES OPTIONS

The second law says that your competitive position determines your options for performance improvement. But what is happening in your market, and what is your real position in it? These questions will help you assess it.

4. Competitive Position Determines Options

Where do you and your competitors fall on the ROA/RMS chart? How are the leaders making money, and what is their approach? What is the full potential of your business position?

These are the questions, of course, that underlie and reflect the band that we introduced in chapter 3, showing the relationship between return on assets (ROA) and relative market share (RMS). You'll remember that companies can occupy five generic positions on the chart: in-band leaders, in-band followers, distant or below-band followers, below-band leaders, and overperformers (see figure 6.5). To create this chart, you'll need your company's revenues and operating profit for the past five years, along with the same numbers for your principal competitors. You'll also need the market leader's sales for this year so that you can calculate relative market share. The slope of the band is driven by the kind of empirical evidence we mentioned in chapter 3—for instance, the evidence found in the PIMS database—and is directly related to the slope of the experience curve in your industry.

This "band analysis" can be used as a diagnostic tool in two different contexts: assessing competitors' improvement strategies, and assessing businesses in a multiunit organization.

FIGURE 6.5

Where Do You and Your Competitors Fall on the ROA/RMS Chart?

ROA/RMS Normative Band

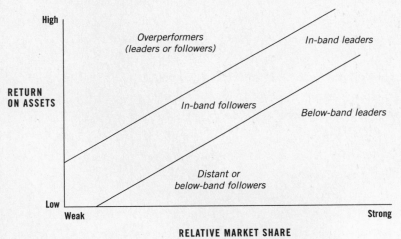

Assessing competitors' improvement strategies. Mapping your own company against its competitors on the band helps you see how each one is making money or where it is failing to do so. It helps you spot potential threats and opportunities for your own business, and it helps you assess the strategic options available to others. Changes in position over time will help you detect and assess the effects of various approaches pursued both by your own company and by its competitors.

In chapter 3, we discussed three broad strategies for performance improvement that can allow companies to outstrip competitors. Companies can seek market leadership, with all its attendant advantages. They can invest heavily in innovation and product differentiation through brand building (the "high road"). They can learn to cultivate customer loyalty, and thus enhance customer retention.

Band analysis will help you understand which of these strategies companies in your industry are pursuing. For example, when we and our colleagues first compiled this chart for credit-card companies, we could find no relationship between market share and returns. So we asked what was driving the returns of the most successful players. The analysis led us to the insight that, in this business, customer loyalty was the single most important factor in determining profitability. If every company were equally skilled at retaining customers, then market share *would* be the principal driver—but every company was not equally skilled. Because of the high cost of customer acquisition and the tendency for customers to increase their credit-card use over time, sophisticated techniques for retaining customers could overcome the advantages of scale. Still, managing costs down the experience curve remains an important variable even in this business, as competition for the most loyal and profitable customers intensifies. The competitors that are most experienced and capable in cost-effective loyalty management typically have an advantage that is hard to attack.

The high-road approach—brand building—is most common in consumer-products industries, including the everyday items you might buy in a supermarket.

The idea is to find a source of value that customers appreciate and that is not driven by the lowest cost. Products such as Gucci bags, Calvin Klein perfumes, and many other fashion-driven items fall into this category. In these instances, the companies are courting the segment of the market that is motivated by prestige or status—important values for up to one-third of customers. Products like chocolate syrup, by contrast, are driven by occasion of use. Chocolate syrup used in baking is a commodity, and can easily be replaced with substitutes like cocoa powder. On ice cream, however, it becomes a low-cost addition even when sold at a premium. Small innovations can make the product seem different, and appropriate for a particular occasion of use.

Effective branding is essential to a high-road approach. If you do not already have a well-known brand, building one can be expensive. For obvious reasons a leader is often in the best position to create a brand: it has both the resources and the breadth of distribution to take action. PepsiCo's Aquafina, for instance, is the top bottled-water brand in U.S. supermarkets. Launched in the mid-1990s, the brand was aimed at the mid-priced market, where annual volume was growing up to 20 percent a year. PepsiCo relied on its core strengths and competitive advantages; the strength of its national distribution network helped it propel Aquafina past competitors. Developing a high-road strategy typically requires an innovation of some kind. For PepsiCo it was the price point coupled with an image campaign stressing the "hipness" and accessibility of its product.

There are many categories that have been dominated by high-road strategies for long periods of time—disposable diapers (Pampers and Huggies), cola drinks (Coke and Pepsi), analgesics (Tylenol and others), and so on. Name brands have maintained large premiums in these categories despite challenges from lower-priced and virtually identical store brands. There are two explanations for this situation. Either a single brand has created enough trust in the product (based on quality or prestige) to sway all but the most price-sensitive customers, or else two leading players have accomplished the same goal. In the latter case, typically, neither of the leading players has an incentive to compete on price because doing so would actually reduce the overall profit pool for both companies. Meanwhile, commodity brands do not have either the scale or the cost position to effectively challenge consumers' trust in the product.

Assessing businesses in a multiunit organization. Band analysis can also help the leader of a multiunit organization assess his or her business units to determine whether each business is achieving close to its full-potential performance. This was the basis for the divestiture-and-acquisition strategy followed by Dun & Bradstreet some years ago (see chapter 3). It was also the heart of Knowlton's decision-making process regarding Morgan Crucible's many businesses. Placing Morgan's business units on a band chart comparing their EBITDA with their region-weighted relative market share, Knowlton could see at a glance that some units, such as the company's Industrial Rail and Traction division, were in the band—performing as expected. Others, such as Thermal Ceramics, were below the band and needed to be moved upward, typically through aggressive cost control and measures designed to grow revenue. Still others were obvious laggards in the lower left of the band and were candidates for divestiture.

5. Market Landscape and Critical Trends

How big is your market? Which parts are growing fastest? Where are you gaining or losing share?

A simple way to map your company's market size and dynamics is to draw a rectangle, then divide it into vertical segments representing your most important markets or products. The segments should be sized in proportion to revenues. Next, divide each of these vertical segments into boxes representing the share held by each principal competitor. Do this for two dates: one for three to five years ago, and one for the present (see figure 6.6).

Now you'll be able to see at a glance the market growth trends for key sectors and competitors. Depending on your situation, of course, you may need variations on the basic chart. A company selling telecommunications equipment into Asia might first map the Asian telecom market by country and by sector (wireline, wireless, and so on), only then breaking it down into competitors' market shares. Again, comparing two or more points in time will show you not only how big the market is, but where, and how fast, it is growing. Faster-growing markets attract more competitive interest, so you want to make sure that you have an aggressive plan to win your

FIGURE 6.6

How Big Is Your Market? Which Parts Are Growing Fastest? Where Are You Gaining/Losing Share?

Market Size, Growth, Share

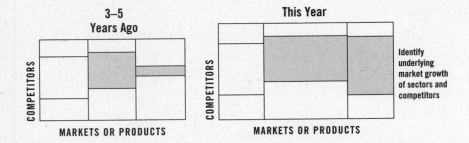

share. The revenue sieve, described in chapter 4, is a good way to compare the full-potential size of your market with its actual size. It helps you spot where you are losing customers from the segments you are addressing.

The S curve. As you uncover customer needs and watch them shift, you might be tempted to project them into the future along a straight line. This would usually be a mistake. In fact, the growth pattern of a new product or service tends to be shaped like the letter S. First come sales to early adopters. These customers purchase the product, use it, and determine whether they like it. The early adopters are often opinion leaders, and they spread word of mouth about the product. Pretty soon more and more people are buying it, and sales rise steeply. Later, as market penetration rises to high levels, the growth slows, revealing a flattened-out S pattern.

The trick, of course, is figuring out how quickly an innovation will penetrate its market. Just knowing that the shape of the curve looks like an S isn't quite enough. Managers need to be able to plan production, staffing, and distribution capacity. Moreover, they need to be able to predict how quickly experience will be accumulated, how quickly a product or service should come down the experience curve, and therefore how to price. Of course, prices that decline with experience make an innovation more affordable, which is one reason the S curve is shaped as it is.

Managers can use several techniques to determine the likely rate of adoption. First, they can plot S curves for prior innovations with similar characteristics. When music-industry executives were trying to figure out how to price DVDs, they could anticipate the adoption of the technology better by plotting the penetration curves of earlier home-entertainment technologies, such as VHS videotapes and compact discs. In 2003, for example, the data showing cumulative units sold suggested that DVD sales were roughly where VHS and CD sales had been in the early 1990s, and were likely to follow a similar trajectory upwards. Managers could also look for related adoption triggers. Sales of VHS tapes and CDs peaked between four and six years after VHS and CD players achieved 75 percent market penetration. Using this data, media-industry executives should have been able to anticipate first the explosion of DVD sales and then an eventual tail-off in DVD growth rates (and pressure on DVD pricing). Finally, managers can use customer research to gather information about the likely shape of the S curve. For example, if the Net Promoter Scores for a new product are very high, it is more likely that early adopters will influence other buyers in the market. If many consumers express interest in a new product early in its life cycle, consideration and purchase rates may be higher as well.

Take the example of electronically delivered professional health-care education, which includes online training and educational resources for hospital staff. S-curve analysis can help determine the speed of further adoption and how much investment in the industry would be appropriate. In this case, interviews and secondary analysis showed that the current adoption level was at about 35 percent, and that the market would not be saturated until adoption reached about 70 percent. The analysis also showed that adoption varied by hospital size—the smaller the hospitals, the lower the adoption rate.[4] But small hospitals were planning to catch up and large hospitals were planning to purchase more. Factors affecting adoption included a focus on reducing errors and improving patient care and safety, a constantly changing regulatory environment, resource and staff constraints, a drive for standardization, and increased acceptance of the online format. An S-curve model based on historical adoption and the saturation point showed that the industry was at an inflection point in

2006: close to 90 percent of the industry's future revenue growth would be realized over the following five years, representing a jump from 35 percent to 65 percent adoption (see figure 6.7). Think of the enormous advantage of knowing this in 2006 rather than learning it too late, in 2011.

But companies sometimes do just that: they buy a business based on its growth when it is in the middle or near the top of the S curve. The acquirer expects the acquiree to show the same growth for long periods of time, when in fact its growth is about to taper off. Smarter companies will acquire a business when data shows that the S curve is forming but hasn't hit its high-growth phase yet. Because the S curve and the math that underlies it make growth somewhat predictable, companies can use it to develop a smart acquisition strategy.

6. Key Capability Gaps

Which are the few capabilities that are creating a competitive advantage for you? Which are missing and are therefore holding you back, and which ones need to be strengthened or acquired?

FIGURE 6.7

S-Curve Analysis Used to Forecast Penetration Rates in Future

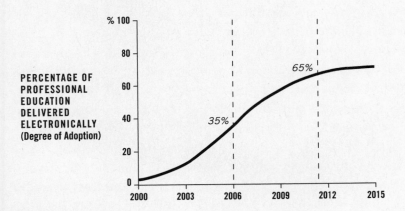

Source: Expert Interviews, S-Curve Regression Analysis

Companies frequently succeed or fail at their performance-improvement strategies on the basis of their capabilities. Emerson, for example, knows how to manage its costs so aggressively that it can acquire other businesses and then add substantial amounts of value. By contrast, Polaroid did not have the capabilities necessary to pursue the strategy it had set for itself. Companies also can succeed or fail based on their ability to develop capabilities they don't have. The iPod, for example, didn't really take off until Apple developed the capabilities to manage and sell digitized music through its iTunes store. Carter's worked on developing top-level skills in supply-chain management and global sourcing in order to prepare itself for its entry into the discount-retail channel. In his book *Unstoppable*, Chris Zook points to underutilized capabilities as a hidden asset that can renew a company's core if wisely developed and deployed. A case in point is Li & Fung, the Hong Kong–based company that evolved from a trading firm into a sourcing-and-distribution company known for its supply-chain expertise. Great managers identify the institutional capabilities that are critical to success, and they focus the organization's attention on building or maintaining these skills.

Genzyme is a company that set itself apart from competitors through capability development from the very beginning. Headquartered in Cambridge, Massachusetts, Genzyme is one of the most successful and well-respected companies in the biotechnology industry. In fiscal 2006, its revenue was $3.2 billion and its operating income more than $1 billion.[5] Its compound annual growth rate for revenues during the period 2003 to 2006 was 26 percent; for operating income it was 34 percent.

CEO Henri Termeer, who has led the company since 1983, first assembled the scientific talent and the management team he would need to lead a world-class biotech company. Those were table stakes, so to speak: nobody competes successfully in this industry without a high level of specialized talent. But Termeer then developed several other critical capabilities. He launched a decade-long campaign to raise the capital the company would need to remain independent and finance its own product development. The campaign included an initial public offering, creation of research-and-development partnerships, and many other specialized financing vehicles. He made early investments in Genzyme facilities and operations in Japan, Europe, and elsewhere, hiring local people and creating thriving local businesses. He began developing the skills the company would need to do its own large-scale manufacturing, culminating in a state-of-the-art facility in Boston. All these capabilities—financial, global operations, manufacturing—set the company apart from its competitors.

Genzyme's culture is built around values of generosity, fairness, respect, and sustainability—Termeer summarizes it as "doing things right." The culture includes providing free products to patients who can't afford them, giving stock options to every one of its 9,000-plus employees, maintaining a commitment to environmentally sound buildings and operations, and creating a world-class workplace environment. (Genzyme was named to *Fortune*'s list of the 100 best companies to work for in 2006 and 2007.) The culture helps the company attract, retain, and motivate highly talented people. It thus reinforces the capability building, and vice versa. "The economic power of doing things right is quite amazing," says Termeer. "People want to do business with you."

Capability sourcing. Genzyme made a series of decisions about which capabilities it wanted to maintain in house. Every company does this, of course, but the environment in which companies must make the decisions has changed dramatically in recent years. In many industries the primary basis of competition has shifted from ownership of assets (stores, factories, etc.) to ownership of intangibles (expertise in supply-chain or brand management, for example). At the same time, a number of vanguard companies have transformed what used to be purely internal corporate functions into entirely new industries. Thus FedEx and UPS can offer world-class logistics-management services; Flextronics and others can offer contract-manufacturing capabilities that are often superior to their customers' in-house capabilities; and Wipro and IBM can offer a variety of business and IT services that nearly every company used to consider necessary internal overhead costs.

The result of all this is that companies can no longer afford to make sourcing decisions on a piecemeal basis, nor can they be satisfied with a "good enough" approach to selecting and working with suppliers. Today, managers should assess every capability they need to produce a product or service. You should analyze every step of your value chain, from design and engineering to product or service delivery. You should compare yourself not only with competitors at every step of the chain, but with whatever company is best in the world at performing that particular step. Are you the best? Do you have some particular capability that creates a sustainable competitive advantage in a given step? If the answer to both questions is no, you need then to ask whether you can improve or acquire the relevant capability, or whether you might be better off sourcing that part of your value chain to whoever is best. It is just this kind of process that has allowed companies such as UPS to succeed as functional specialists: they have created capabilities that are among the best in the world, and so can offer their customers skills that it would be too difficult, costly, or time-consuming for most of them to develop on their own.

The 7-Eleven chain offers an example of this process. 7-Eleven analyzed its value-chain processes in the early 1990s and found that it was doing virtually everything itself. It operated its own distribution network, delivered its own gasoline, and made its own ice. It even owned the cows that produced the milk it sold. Former CEO Jim Keyes, as we noted in a *Harvard Business Review* article, found it hard to believe that the company could be best-in-class in every one of those functions.[6] So Keyes partnered with companies that could provide the best-in-class capabilities he needed. Citgo was the company's primary gasoline supplier. IRI maintained and formatted detailed data on customer purchasing behavior. Other suppliers provided and managed specialty food products, fresh produce, ATM functions, and other goods and services. 7-Eleven maintained control over the capabilities it saw as critical to its competitive differentiation, such as merchandising, pricing, and analysis of customer data. But its sourcing decisions allowed it to reduce headcount, flatten its organizational structure, and reduce its capital assets. Same-store merchandise sales grew at roughly twice the industry average, while inventory turns rose to 72 percent above the industry average. All this contributed to 7-Eleven's remarkable economic performance: its stock appreciation from 2000 to 2005 outpaced all of its major competitors.

Look once more at your company's skills in every area: are they below average, above average, world class? Customer and supplier interviews can help you answer these questions. So can analyst reports and industry surveys, along with interviews with ex-employees and other knowledgeable people. Employees themselves can provide feedback on best practices within your organization across businesses and geographies—even over time. If you don't have capabilities that you need, you may decide you want to build them through acquisition or outsource the relevant functions to companies that do have them.

Assessing your people. A company's capabilities, of course, often depend on the caliber of its people. So no matter what your critical few institutional capabilities may be, assessing the strengths and weaknesses of your team is always an essential part of the diagnostic process. Listen to what some of our interviewees told us about the importance of this process:

> "I believe that business all boils down to people. I've seen in doing turnarounds that you can take good people and put them in a horrible situation, and good managers will find a way to fix it or change it in some way and make it successful. On the other hand, you can take a great company or situation, put lousy managers in, and they will find a way to screw it up."
>
> —RICHARD CRAWFORD

> "You have to hire people who are smarter than you are, and you have to encourage people to hire people who are smarter than you are, not just people who are going to say yes to you. And if the organization does that, it can do very well."
>
> —WARREN KNOWLTON

> "You need to do a quick assessment of the people on your team, and you need to be fairly ruthless about who is going to cut it and who is not. That doesn't mean you shouldn't give people a chance. [But] you either need wholesale changes in people or wholesale changes in the attitude of the same people, one or the other, and that is why it has to start with really courageous leadership."
>
> —KATHLEEN LIGOCKI

At the Salt Lake Organizing Committee, Mitt Romney assessed his team as part of the strategic audit and found that he had to acquire many capabilities and find ways of retaining others:

> Sorting through the team that was there and assessing what I absolutely had to have, I concluded that some of the people I had were not right for the job, and they left. I hired new people; I brought in new folks to be part of the team, including the chief operating officer, the head of marketing, a chief financial officer, and several others. I would also note that some of the team members were about to go out the door—they were dispirited and were looking for other jobs. I locked them in, made sure they had every incentive to stay with us.

We'll have more to say on building your team in chapter 8. For the moment, remember that assessment of people and other capabilities is a critical part of the point-of-departure performance-improvement diagnostic.

THIRD LAW: CUSTOMERS AND PROFIT POOLS DON'T STAND STILL

Customers and profit pools don't stand still. So you'll need to assess what's happening to your customers, both existing and prospective. You'll need to examine the profit pools you currently draw on and those that might hold potential for the future.

7. The Right Customer Segments

Which are the biggest, fastest-growing, and most profitable customer segments? How well do you meet customer needs relative to competitors and substitutes?

In chapter 4 we discussed methods of analyzing customer segments and assessing the likely fit between particular segments and what your company can offer. You will need to review existing customer research, and you may need to conduct new research to analyze your segments and their differing needs. The goal, as we said in chapter 4, is to identify the most profitable segments to serve, and the areas where you can win relative to the competition.

Once you have the data in hand, a simple chart showing the profitability and growth of each segment is a good starting point for analysis. It will help you understand where you are already winning against your competitors—which customers are naturally inclined to buy from you—and how those customers stack up against other segments of the market. But of course you need to know more. What are each segment's characteristics and spending habits? What share of wallet are they currently giving you, and is there reason to think that you can increase that share? Companies typically rely on a combination of in-house and third-party research to answer such questions.

The SNAP charts we described—where SNAP stands for "segment needs and performance"—are a good way of assessing how well you are meeting the needs of the segments you are targeting. And the revenue sieve can help you determine where you might be losing, or failing to satisfy, the critical segments. All this data gathering, of course, must focus not just on how your company performs in absolute terms but also on how it performs relative to competitors. In particular, you need to know which competitors are targeting the customers you are targeting, and what advantages they may bring to the table. You have to understand why customers might choose you over the competition—or why they might choose the competition over you.

Data about customer segments can be combined with data about loyalty to create a detailed picture of your customer base—and that picture, in turn, will help you learn to serve your customers better. We'll see in a moment how American Express did just that.

8. Customer Retention and Loyalty Versus Peers

What proportion of customers are you retaining? How do your NPS ratings track against competitors'?

Customer loyalty can be a critically important factor in the economics of a business, particularly when the cost of acquiring a customer is high.

So you need to know your retention rates for each segment. Not only will it help you determine the profitability of the segment, it will help you make plans to boost retention rates where necessary.

American Express learned how to combine segmentation tools and loyalty-management tools to boost the performance of its card division. The company had launched a variety of new charge and credit cards beginning in the early 1990s, under the leadership of card-division president Ken Chenault. The cards sold well and drove top-line growth, but they didn't meet management's expectations in terms of profitability. Starting around 1997, American Express's managers launched a program to figure out why. They drilled into data about their customers. They identified segments by variables such as their overall spending behavior, their demographic characteristics, and how they used the cards. They assessed how long the customers were staying with American Express, and how their loyalty correlated with other variables.

All this data allowed American Express to take carefully targeted actions designed to stimulate card usage and loyalty. The company designed Membership Rewards enrollment campaigns—signing up new customers on the phone when they activated their cards, for instance. It learned how to stimulate early usage. One initiative, for example, gave double rewards points for purchases in outlets such as gas stations and convenience stores. It developed special products, such as Delta Sky Miles® cards, and marketed them primarily to targeted segments. These and other moves helped American Express turn around a decline in its share of the market. Between 2002 and 2005 the company added more than $100 billion in charge volume, and today earns a return on capital of 40 percent in its U.S. consumer and small-business card businesses.[7]

American Express also employs NPS to assess customers' loyalty. NPS, you will recall, measures customers' responses to the question, "How likely is it that you would recommend this company (or this product or service) to a friend or colleague?" Respondents' answers are scored on a zero-to-ten scale, where a ten means "Definitely" and a zero means "Definitely not." Those who give you a nine or a ten are your *promoters*. Research shows they spend more with you, are likely to increase their spending in the future, and sing your praises to their friends and colleagues. Those who give you a seven or eight are *passives*, while anyone ranking you zero to six is a *detractor*. Promoters are an engine of growth, but detractors are a dragline: they often cost your company more than they are worth, and they bad-mouth you to anybody who will listen.

Your Net Promoter Score is simply the proportion of promoters minus the proportion of detractors. Measured against competitors, it has been shown to correlate directly with growth rates and with other measures of customer satisfaction. It can regularly be compiled, distributed, and used as a basis for managerial decisions, just like financial reports. American Express and many other companies use NPS-like metrics throughout their organizations so that they can get a quick, regular read on customer attitudes and their likely behaviors. NPS gives you a good diagnosis of whether you are likely to be retaining your customers and whether you have momentum in the marketplace. But smart companies also chart customer flows and analyze the lifetime value of a customer so that they know how much to invest in keeping various segments. They then do the appropriate root-cause analysis of the reasons that lead people to defect from their product, and they eliminate those problems.

9. Profit-Pool Share and Trends

How much of the profit pool do you have today? How is the profit pool likely to change in the future? What are the opportunities and threats?

Creating a profit-pool map of the kind described in chapter 4 requires listing channels, products, and sequential value-chain activities in the profit pool and estimating the total profit from each of these (see figure 6.8). You can then locate your business and its competitors on the map, showing how much each company takes from each part of the profit pool. It's wise to do this for each customer segment and for each set of products.

For a conventional business, drawing up this kind of map is simple in principle, though gathering the data can be complex. The company we're calling FitEquipCo, for example, mapped the growth (historical and projected) of its industry. Then it gathered extensive data about customers' intent to purchase or repurchase, developed projected profit-pool maps by product (treadmills, ellipticals, and so on), by sales channel (mass merchants, specialty stores, and so on), and by price point (entry-level, value, and premium). The analysis revealed some telling developments. Traditional riders and treadmills were rapidly tapering off in popularity, replaced by increasingly popular machines such as ellipticals. The home market was relatively mature, but the commercial market continued to grow. FitEquipCo needed to invest in new-product development. As we noted earlier, it also needed to build up its distribution through sports specialty stores, which delivered higher margins. These and other moves, the company projected, would enable it to increase earnings by $86 million over a three-year period, more than doubling the operating profits.

For a nonprofit such as the Salt Lake Organizing Committee, the task is different: the "profit pool" comprises the various sources of funds from which the organization can raise money. For the Olympics, new CEO Mitt Romney had several potential pools to draw on, including federal support, corporate sponsorship, television revenue, and ticket sales. None of these except the committee's share of television revenue was locked in when

FIGURE 6.8

How Much of the Profit Pool Do You Have?
What Are the Opportunities and Threats?

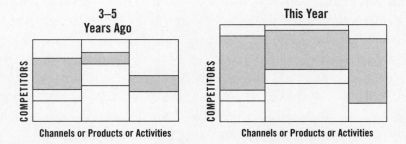

Data Needed
— List of channels, products, and sequential value-chain activities in profit pool
— Estimated total profit from all channels, all products, and all value-chain activities
— Point estimates of profit for your business and for your competitors by channel, product, and value-chain activity

Romney arrived; indeed, all were subject to potential shifts. The budget he inherited depended on massive federal support, but the scandal-tainted organization was getting a lukewarm reception in Washington. The budget also called for $859 million in sponsorship revenue, yet the committee was far short of that figure and hadn't sold a single sponsorship in several months. Finally, the budget relied on a "miraculous" level of ticket sales— a level that would depend on extraordinarily aggressive marketing and good luck. Mapping these pools showed Romney exactly where he would have to place his efforts when it came to raising money.[8] He attacked all three sources and beat his goals on each one, establishing records both for ticket sales and for sponsor revenue. That's what enabled him to record the surplus of $56 million.

As with the market map, it's also wise to compare at least two points in time so that you can see how the pools are evolving. If there is significant change, remember the possible reasons listed in the fourth chapter: 1. everyday changes in the preferences and behaviors of customers; 2. innovations that drive customer shifts; 3. changes in the bargaining power of customers and suppliers; and 4. changes in the business environment, often driven by government policies. Your segmentation and loyalty data should help you assess the first of these, but you need to be alert to the others as well. Often, for instance, a significant threat to the profit pool comes from companies that don't yet compete in your industry, or that are still too small to be noticed. Yet it is sometimes these competitors that can turn an industry upside down. Think of the effects minimill companies such as Nucor had on the American steel industry, or the effects Wal-Mart has had on the U.S. grocery business. Competitors of Firestone's EPDM roofing and competitors of L'eggs could have been more alert to the emerging threats these products represented.

Figuring out what's behind a shift in profit pools may help you assess whether the shift is likely to continue and how your company might be able to garner a larger share of the pool. In some cases, a fine-grained market analysis that compares competitors' shares a few years ago with competitors' shares today will reveal an aggressive start-up or nontraditional competitor that is shifting customer behavior in some way. You may also need to rely on qualitative assessments and judgments from industry experts. One useful way of evaluating the potential for start-ups and nontra-ditional competitors is to look at the four primary strategic levers that they may be able to pull. They may be able to create *new or distinctive products*, such as Apple's iPod and iTunes music store or a genetically engineered pharmaceutical. They may have lower-cost or more effective *distribution channels*, such as Internet-based sales. They may be able to target a *segment of customers* more effectively—for example, young people looking for a new fashion. Or they may have a strategy to shift the profit pool, such as by creating a *supply chain* with lower-cost or higher-quality sourcing, perhaps taking geographic advantage of low-cost producing countries. As a rough guide, the more of these levers a start-up or nontraditional competitor is able to pull, the stronger its potential.

You can also apply the diagnostic tools shown in appendix 3 to reveal threats and opportunities at a granular level. Analyze your customer management to see if you are utilizing appropriate segmentation strategies and cultivating loyalty among your most profitable customers. Look at your product-development and marketing processes, and at your pricing. Examine your sales channels to see if you are optimizing your channel management and getting the most from your salesforce. Companies frequently misjudge the size and growth rates of various segments of their market, and the diagnosis may reveal such a misjudgment. If you are underperforming on several of these dimensions, your full-potential market is likely to be far larger than you have imagined.

FOURTH LAW: SIMPLICITY GETS RESULTS

Simplicity gets results, so you will need to eliminate unnecessary complexity in your strategy, product line, organization, and processes. Your first job in this arena is to diagnose the degree of complexity and its impact on your company.

10. Product and Service Complexity

How complex are your products or service offerings, and what is that degree of complexity costing you? What are the Killer ABCs in your business?

Look first at your line of products and services, as we described in chapter 5, and compare what you find with the competition, just as we compared Honda and Ford. You should try to construct a "Model T" chart showing the cost of an average, basic product or service not only for your own company but for your competitors (see figure 6.9). Who has the advantage at that level? Who has the advantage as variety and complexity increase—and why? You can apply the learning from question 7 to this assessment. If you know what customers want, and what they are likely to want in the future, you can better judge what level of variety is appropriate to your marketplace.

The complexity test is a necessary counterbalance to tools such as customer segmentation. The temptation, after all, is to divide your customer base into finer and finer subcategories and tailor your offerings to each segment, all in the name of giving customers exactly what they want. That was one way Charles Schwab, the financial-services firm, got itself into a difficult situation in the early 2000s. Schwab added new divisions, including a firm specializing in institutional investments and an East Coast wealth-management company. The CEO at the time, according to *Fortune*, "deployed his marketing team to design a mind-blowing array of new offerings, targeted to so many groups that they hardly seemed targeted at all." Later, founder Charles Schwab returned to his troubled firm as CEO, and promptly took steps to reduce the complexity. He sold off most of the recent acquisitions. He reduced the number of service offerings, and streamlined internal roles and processes. "We'd intended to create an interrelated business with premium returns due to synergy," he told *Fortune*'s Betsy Morris. "What we ended up with was an interrelated business with discounted returns due to complexity."[9]

The process of asking yourself the questions highlighted in chapter 5, and then developing a set of Killer ABCs based on the customer analyses that you do, can liberate huge amounts of energy in your company. Your

FIGURE 6.9

Finding Your Innovation Fulcrum

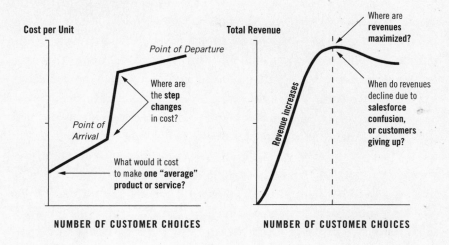

people should have "Aha!" moments as they better understand key customer needs and mobilize around meeting those needs while simultaneously simplifying operations. A good diagnosis of complexity should start you down a path that will lead to revenue increases and cost reduction as you manage your innovation fulcrum.

11. Organizational and Decision-Making Complexity

How complex is your decision making and organization relative to competitors'? What is the impact of this complexity?

Not long ago, a Bain research team surveyed more than 400 companies in seven countries. The focus of the research was the companies' organizational structure and decision making. One question was particularly significant. Did the respondents feel that their organization held them back from high performance, was sufficient for achieving reasonable success, or actually helped the business outperform its competitors? Nearly one-quarter of the respondents—23 percent—felt that their organization was holding them back. Only 15 percent answered that it helped them outperform. An examination of the outperformers' results bore out the assessment: a far higher fraction of those companies had achieved outstanding financial success.

We described some of the tools of organizational simplification in chapter 5. What we call a "RAPID analysis" allows you to assess decision-making bottlenecks, assign clear decision roles to individuals in your organization, and hold them accountable. (RAPID is a loose acronym for the different roles people can take on: Recommend, Agree, give Input, Decide, and Perform, or implement the decision.) A spans-and-layers analysis shows where your people may be deployed ineffectively or at too high a cost, and it helps you understand how to remedy the situation. You can evaluate your company on both of these dimensions, and you can often compare it with competitors. Suppliers, distributors, and customers, for example, are often good judges of how quickly and effectively you can make a decision compared with others in the industry. Employees will often be quick to tell you whether they feel supported and empowered by the organization's management structure, or whether it just gets in their way.

Ultimately, of course, organizational simplicity and effectiveness isn't just a matter of applying one or another tool; it requires a holistic approach. Our colleagues Paul Rogers and Marcia Blenko have developed such an approach, which they call the "decision-driven organization." Decision-driven organizations, Rogers and Blenko argue, do five things well (see figure 6.10).[10] They provide compelling direction and leadership, just as we have advocated in this book. They define clear decision accountabilities through tools such as RAPID. They develop and deploy talented people, they excel at front-line execution, and they have a culture that supports and reinforces organizational effectiveness. All of that allows them to make and execute good decisions quickly. If you have an organizational complexity challenge—if decision making is a perennial bottleneck, or if your organization is unable to respond nimbly and effectively to new challenges—you may need to dig deeper into these areas to find out where the problem lies.

Soon after John Taylor became CEO of Borealis, he launched a wide-

FIGURE 6.10

Decision-Driven Organizations Do Five Things Well

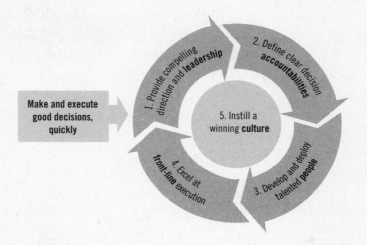

ranging process to determine the values by which the company would operate. People at the company agreed on three that you might find at any leading organization: responsibility, respect, and exceeding expectations. But the fourth was Borealis's own creation, the word *Nimblicity.*™ Combining nimbleness and simplicity, the word sent a message to all the company's units that organizational sluggishness and complexity should be eliminated wherever they might crop up.

12. Process Complexity

Where does complexity reside in your processes? What is that costing you?

St.George Bank, like others in Australia, experienced a slowdown in residential lending at one point, and so was developing a growth strategy for commercial banking. But the complexity of the bank's commercial credit processes was a major constraint on growth. Its systems for loan approval were largely decentralized. They treated all loan applications, large or small, in a similar way. A large fraction of applications had to be sent up the ladder to a central credit group. Then-CEO Gail Kelly and her team determined that this level of complexity was not inevitable—for example, they could create a "Fast Track" system for applications from existing customers that fell within certain risk parameters. That alone led to a 30 percent reduction in time spent by the lending officers. They also increased the amounts that a local lending officer could approve, resulting in a reduction of 50 percent or more in deals sent to the central credit group.

How can you identify such opportunities for process improvement? As at St.George Bank, process complexity can show up in any number of areas: on the production floor, in distribution networks, in interactions with customers, in back-office procedures. The key is to figure out where complexity is unavoidable—and where, by contrast, there are practices that can be put in place to reduce complexity while still delivering the products and services that customers want. A good way to get started is to use a tool called "process mapping." A process map uses pictorial diagrams to show the interactions between different steps in a process and the people or departments responsible for the steps. It enables the team to visualize and understand the whole process so that they can spot issues and opportunities for improvement, then address them through root-cause analysis. You want to map activities, inputs and outputs associated with each step, and wait times between steps.

One mortgage company, for example, found that its loan-turnaround time was twice the industry's best-practice time and that its loan-processing productivity was poor. A map of the loan-approval process revealed too many hand-offs (hence queues), too much wait time, and too much rework or redundancy (see the left-hand side of figure 6.11). A redesigned process—shown on the right-hand side of figure 6.11—cut the hours required for loan processing by 56 percent and total cost by 11 percent.

Successful streamlining of the processes revealed by such a map produces several mutually reinforcing benefits. It increases efficiency, allowing a company to reduce headcount and thereby lower its costs. It cuts down on errors and rework. It reduces cycle time, enabling the company to deliver the product or service to the customer significantly faster and

FIGURE 6.11

Mortgage Company Process Map

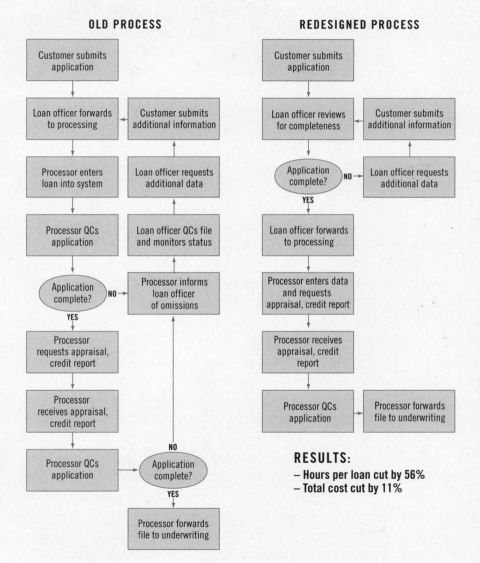

OLD PROCESS

- Customer submits application
- Loan officer forwards to processing
- Processor enters loan into system
- Processor QCs application
- Application complete? — NO → Processor informs loan officer of omissions
- YES
- Processor requests appraisal, credit report
- Processor receives appraisal, credit report
- Processor QCs application
- Application complete? — NO
- YES
- Processor forwards file to underwriting

- Customer submits additional information
- Loan officer requests additional data
- Loan officer QCs file and monitors status

REDESIGNED PROCESS

- Customer submits application
- Loan officer reviews for completeness
- Application complete? — NO → Loan officer requests additional data
- YES
- Loan officer forwards to processing
- Processor enters data and requests appraisal, credit report
- Processor receives appraisal, credit report
- Processor QCs application → Processor forwards file to underwriting

- Customer submits additional information

RESULTS:

– Hours per loan cut by 56%
– Total cost cut by 11%

thus enhancing customer loyalty. More-loyal customers are likely to order more, thereby generating growth and increasing the possibilities for still greater economies in production or service delivery. One Asian bank that we studied standardized and automated many of its loan-application procedures, and centralized back-office operations that had previously been located in its branches. The resulting simplification allowed the bank to reduce the time necessary to approve a loan by 32 to 40 percent. And even though the bank's overall headcount declined, branch personnel now had more time to focus on cross-selling and other methods of increasing revenue. Thanks to these moves, the bank was projecting a 5 percent to 11 percent increase in net interest income.

More ambitiously, you may want to explore a particular combination of lean-manufacturing and Six-Sigma techniques called "Lean Six Sigma," or LSS. Taken separately, these two philosophies and sets of techniques are tremendously powerful; they are capable of improving productivity and reducing defects by orders of magnitude. Applied independently, however, both are fraught with potential pitfalls. For example, companies sometimes train many of their people to be "black belts" and set them loose indiscriminately to fix processes, without considering which processes might be most important. LSS, by contrast, begins with a company's strategy and with identifying the processes that are central to that strategy. Effective LSS teams concentrate on identifying opportunities across a business's entire value chain, rather than in one particular silo, and focus on the largest opportunities for adding value. They are organized around critical metrics and the opportunities for dramatic improvements in those critical metrics.[11]

LSS also looks at information technology—a perennial source of process complexity at many companies—but not as a "silver bullet" that will somehow fix things all by itself. In fact, IT organizations often find themselves with byzantine systems that have developed over the years one layer at a time, with each successive "improvement" only adding to the complexity of the whole thing. The result can be devastating. Charles Schwab, for instance, found at one point that it was spending 18 percent of revenue on IT while three leading competitors were spending several percentage points less. The difference gave Schwab a cost disadvantage of hundreds of millions of dollars. Schwab also found that big IT projects were repeatedly taking longer and costing far more than expected.[12] Such difficulties can be fixed, as Schwab and others have found. But they first must be diagnosed. Compare your level of IT spending with that of competitors, and to your own historical levels. Interview people in your organization— including front-line employees—to determine whether IT is an unnecessary source of process complexity.

As you attack process complexity, remember our cautionary tales from chapter 5. The oil company we mentioned, for instance, had simplified process after process, but managers weren't seeing the expected benefits. Its process simplification was undermined by unnecessary complexity in the company's organization and decision-making procedures. So gather the data for all three of the must-have facts relating to simplicity, then determine the most fruitful point of attack.

CONDUCTING A PERFORMANCE-IMPROVEMENT DIAGNOSTIC IS A challenging task. To complete it, you must gather and analyze a lot of data. But its value extends well beyond simply showing you your point of departure. A complete diagnosis highlights the most important threats and opportunities you face and gives you an ability to assess the full-potential performance of your business. It thus lays the groundwork for mapping out your point of arrival and the road that will get you there.

IMPLICATIONS FOR THE GENERAL MANAGER

- Carry out a rigorous full-potential performance-improvement analysis of your business position using all the diagnostic tools of the twelve must-have facts. Figure 6.12 shows a simplified version. This diagnosis will examine both internal and external facts, and will require a sharp competitive focus. Try to complete the assessment of your point of departure in the first ninety days.

- Distill from the detailed analyses of the full-potential performance-improvement diagnosis the few critical areas that will provide the most potential improvement (cost? customers and segmentation? complexity? capabilities? and so on), and prioritize those areas based on impact and ease/risk of execution.

- Build consensus with all stakeholders on the true point of departure. Spell out the few critical action imperatives, the required urgency of change, and the likely resource commitments necessary to build and leverage your capabilities.

FIGURE 6.12

Twelve Must-Have Facts Help Define
the Points of Departure and Arrival

LAW 1 Costs and Prices Always Decline	LAW 2 Competitive Position Determines Your Options	LAW 3 Customers and Profit Pools Don't Stand Still	LAW 4 Simplicity Gets Results
1. Cost and price experience curve	**4.** Competitive position, winning business models	**7.** Right customer segments	**10.** Product/service complexity
2. Relative cost position, key levers	**5.** Market landscape, key trends	**8.** Customer retention and loyalty vs. competitors	**11.** Organization and decision-making complexity
3. Product line profitability	**6.** Key capability gaps	**9.** Profit-pool share and trends	**12.** Process complexity

**Accurately diagnose your point of departure.
Define a point of arrival based on specific goals.**

SEVEN

Where You're Going: Mapping Your Point of Arrival and Making a Plan

Good business leaders create a vision, articulate the vision, passionately own the vision, and relentlessly drive it to completion.

—JACK WELCH

WHAT DO WE MEAN BY "POINT OF ARRIVAL"?

When you accepted your position as general manager, you knew that your overall objective would be to arrive at an improved business situation as seen through the eyes of most or all of the relevant stakeholders—shareholders, customers, suppliers, senior management, employees, and community constituencies. But we use the term "point of arrival" in a specific way. Your point of arrival isn't some vague statement about improvement. Rather, the point of arrival is a set of *carefully defined, numerically specific goals* that can be accomplished in two years or three years or five years, whatever your time horizon may be. You may be a new manager or CEO, or you may be a longer-term leader facing an inflection point, a need to put the business on a new trajectory. But whatever your situation, your point of arrival should explicitly describe the performance of your organization at the point in the future that corresponds to your likely tenure.

Great managers have an intuitive understanding of the importance of spelling out a point of arrival: we heard all sorts of unprompted comments to that effect in our interviews. "We started off with a very clear sense of what we wanted to do," said Mitt Romney. "We wrote those things down." Jacques Nasser, who helped to revitalize Ford in the 1990s, said, "Part of the success was getting to a view of where we wanted to be as soon as we could. Communicating a vision of the future was very, very important." Elisabeth Babcock, who became CEO of the newly merged nonprofit Crittenton Women's Union in Boston, articulated it clearly:

> Perhaps the most important thing you can do strategically is to get that depiction of the "organization on the hill." What is the organization? In an optimal state, what would it be delivering in terms of market services? How would it be functioning relative to the environment? How would you have built on the core competencies to grow the organizational capacities that deliver those services and interact well with the environment in the first place?

Romney's three-year time frame was imposed on him by the Olympic schedule. Warren Knowlton set a three-year time frame in advance, because he wanted to return to the United States at the end of that time. You may not face the same kind of constraints, but you should nonetheless think in terms of a definite time horizon.

MAPPING YOUR POINT OF ARRIVAL

Crafting your point of arrival begins with the expectations of your stakeholders, so a first priority should be to interview and consult with them. They will all have opinions about what you should be focusing on and trying to achieve. Some of the ideas they give you will be ones you will learn from and adopt. Others you may want to de-emphasize or even reject. In the latter case you will need to set expectations accordingly.

Criteria for the Point of Arrival

Whatever the input you receive, you will want your point of arrival to measure up on at least three counts.

It must be compelling. It should convey a sense of urgency, of a burning platform, and it should include a set of initiatives big enough to address that urgent need. "You have to set really big, audacious goals so that people will reach out and change things," says Kevin Rollins, the CEO who led Dell's remarkable growth in the early 2000s before his departure in 2007. "If you set goals of 5 percent or 10 percent or some other small improvement, people don't change everything." Big improvements in Dell's already fast supply chain and rapid order-to-delivery process were critical to the company's continued growth and prosperity through the late 1990s and early 2000s. Otherwise, the company could have been dragged down by the high cost of obsolescent inventory, and it wouldn't have come down the experience curve as fast as it needed to. Bill McDermott, who became CEO of SAP Americas in 2002, announced at the time that the unit would be a $3 billion operation in 2005. "That gave us only a few short years to double the size of our business," he recalled. (SAP Americas hit the goal.) Like Dell and SAP Americas, some of the most successful companies have set goals ambitious enough to challenge many aspects of their business model and practices. It's a move that frequently leads to dramatically greater possibilities.

It must be motivational. The stakeholders in your business—particularly your management team, your employees, and your boss or your board—need to be excited about where you want to take the business. You want them to be active participants in the changes you'll be making. You want them to be enthusiastic supporters. So you'd better develop answers to some basic questions about your point of arrival. Is the new plan worth doing? Why? What will it mean for each of them, and for the business as a whole? In 2004, chief executive Kerry Killinger of Washington Mutual—the big banking firm known as WaMu—embarked on the latest in a series of five-year strategic plans. The objectives included better returns for shareholders, more opportunities for managers and employees, the ability to provide better service to customers, and other stakeholder benefits as well. But it wasn't just numbers on a spreadsheet. Killinger declared that WaMu aspired to be the "national leader in consumer and small-business banking." That kind of goal, to be the biggest or the best at something, is what fires up the troops.

People also respond to a noble purpose. In health care or pharmaceuticals, for instance, it might be to save thousands of lives. In any company it might include behaving in an ecologically responsible way. At Genzyme, says CEO Henri Termeer, the knowledge that the company's drugs represent a lifeline to critically ill patients is a powerful motivator for people at every level of the organization. For a start-up entrepreneur, a point of arrival capable of attracting and motivating investors and talented employees is an essential ingredient of a business plan. For example, Dr. Karl Ulrich, a professor at the University of Pennsylvania's Wharton School, sought a way to counteract the climate impact of driving his car. He studied existing methods of offsetting the carbon dioxide his car was emitting, but he grew frustrated by the high minimum-purchase requirements in the market for renewable energy contracts. So in October 2004 he gave his students $5,000 and challenged them to create an affordable carbon-offset program for drivers. The result was TerraPass, a Web-based enterprise that sells "passes" to consumers to counterbalance the carbon dioxide emissions from their driving. (Money from the passes funds renewable-energy programs.) The two-and-a-half-year-old company counts 60,000 customers at this writing, and has created such high-profile partnerships as Ford's Greener Miles program, which provides a link on Ford's Web site allowing car owners to purchase passes.

It must be realistic. It must make sense in terms of the four laws. By way of analogy, imagine for a moment that you and your spouse decide to take the family to a nice resort 500 miles away for a week's vacation. Assuming you can afford it, that's a realistic point of arrival, one that family members would think of as reasonable. The trip would probably be motivating, even exciting, to everybody. But if you then said that you planned to get to the resort on horseback, the plan would no longer be realistic—

you couldn't get there and back in the allotted time. A point of arrival for travel has to make sense in terms of the laws of physics. A point of arrival for a company has to make sense in terms of the laws of business.

What does that mean? It means that the point of arrival can't depend on raising prices on your existing products, unless something very specific is temporarily overwhelming the experience curve. It means that the strategy to reach the point of arrival must depend upon an analysis of relative market share and an assessment of how profit pools in the industry are moving. It means that a company can't simply plan on adding complexity—more new products, for instance—unless it can show that it remains properly balanced on the innovation fulcrum, and that the benefits will outweigh the costs.

So the point of arrival must specify the level of expected performance improvement, and the necessary change must be able to be accomplished in the given time frame. Knowlton had come to Morgan after leading turnarounds at Pilkington and Owens Corning. He knew what realistic performance standards were for industrial operations, and he set his expectations at Morgan to reflect them. Idris Jala at Malaysia Airlines said his company would return to profitability by 2008. That was a reasonable goal in a reasonable time frame.

One component of WaMu's five-year plan was a targeted increase in the number of households served by the company's retail bank. A specific innovation—WaMu Free Checking™—had demonstrated an ability to drive significant annual growth in retail households where it had been tested; it had also increased the bank's ability to sell additional services to these customers. A second component was the company's commitment to "manage for best-in-class productivity"—in other words, reducing costs while maintaining service levels, in keeping with the experience curve. In retail banking, for instance, WaMu was streamlining its middle- and back-office operations and optimizing labor costs. By the third quarter of 2006, it had achieved an 8.5 percent year-to-date reduction in retail staff since the first of the year while delivering top-tier customer satisfaction, behind Wachovia but ahead of Bank of America, JPMorgan Chase, and Wells Fargo.[1] Growth in market share, cost reduction, high customer satisfaction—the plan for retail banking made sense in terms of the four laws.

Formulating the Point of Arrival

A new chief should have a robust assessment of the point of departure within the first ninety days on the job so that she has a good sense of the business's strengths, weaknesses, threats, and opportunities. She should aim at having a well-formulated set of objectives by or before the 120-day mark.

It may help at this point to have an overview of the whole process. Though setting the point of arrival is the second step, ultimately it will be linked to the point of departure by a few critical action imperatives, each one leading to detailed action plans. You will then be mapping your success in reaching the point of arrival with just a few key metrics related to each law (see figure 7.1). Keep this map in mind as you set out to define your point of arrival.

Identify hypotheses. The first set of hypotheses about a point of arrival will likely emerge from the assessment of the point of departure itself—from the must-have facts you have gathered and the detailed performance-improvement diagnosis you have conducted. The new general manager may discover that the company needs to drive down procurement costs to improve its profitability. It may need to drive down prices to improve its competitive position in certain key products. Perhaps it needs to simplify its product line or acquire capabilities that it doesn't have. These hypotheses are the basis for another round of listening conversations with key executives, employees, customers, and others, for another review of internal reports and outside reports, and for another round of fact gathering. The ultimate goal is to build consensus with stakeholders and to set the appropriate expectations.

Knowlton, for example, came up with some preliminary objectives for Morgan Crucible from the answers to his initial questions. Morgan's costs were out of line and had not been coming down, so Knowlton's point of arrival would have to include cost reduction. Some of Morgan's business units operated in commodity markets with little or no pricing power, so his point of arrival would have to include fixing or divesting those units. The organization—nine unrelated business units, 200 businesses in eighty countries, a heavily staffed corporate office, a separate research-and-

FIGURE 7.1

Going from Point of Departure to Point of Arrival

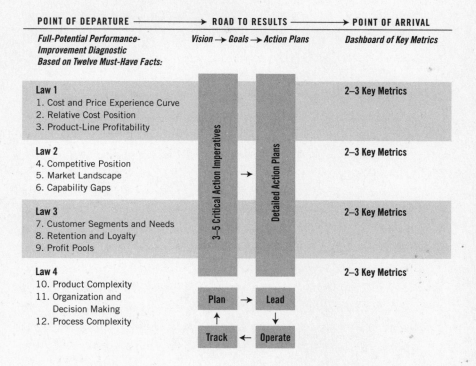

development facility inclined to focus mainly on long-term projects—was not only unnecessarily costly, it was far too complex. So his point of arrival would have to include organizational simplification.

Focus on key metrics. You should take what you learn in each of the four areas and identify the *two or three metrics* for each critical action imperative that will drive and define the performance that you are looking for. Note we said just two or three in each area! Remember that simplicity gets results. Just as you don't want an indiscriminate laundry list of questions to identify your point of departure, you can't use an indiscriminate laundry list of improvements to characterize your point of arrival. A compelling point of arrival should be simple and memorable. Every employee in the company should be able to describe it in no more time than it takes to ride six floors on an elevator.

Where costs and prices are concerned, for instance, you will want to set future targets for both, along with a projection for the slope of the experience curve. You may also want to target your cost position relative to your chief competitors'. Some years ago, Jim Haas took a job as chief of National Steel's service-center division. Labor costs were more than half of the division's costs, and Haas was able to sign contracts with his plants' unions that gave him roughly a five-dollar-an-hour labor-cost advantage over his competitors. Not surprisingly, the division grew rapidly. Later, when he was running the integrated steel operations at National, he set a three-year goal to move from the number-eight position in the American steel industry (measured by profit per ton) to number one. He achieved it exactly on schedule.

Where market position is concerned, you can set a future target for absolute and relative market share by segment. You have to project where your competitors will be as well—after all, you can't realistically project a growth in share without having an idea where it will come from. When Antonio Perez of Kodak launched the company's new ink-jet printer, he was attempting to move into a different profit pool and collapse a price umbrella. Bold moves such as this are difficult and unpredictable—but you can assume that his team produced the best estimates they could on how Hewlett-Packard and other competitors would respond, and how much market share Kodak might hope to take from them.

In general, you need to project where profit pools are moving, how large they are likely to be, and who will be competing for them. Lou Gerstner of IBM couldn't have invested the necessary dollars in building up IBM's Global Services unit without good estimates of how many customers there would be in this market, how much the average customer in different segments would be likely to spend, and how much margin IBM could expect to earn on delivering those services.

As for capabilities, you need to set targets for the complexity of your product line and business processes, as well as for the future structure and decision-making processes of your organization. Remember the comparison we drew between the Honda Accord, with its three styles and 484 possible configurations, and the 35,908 configurations available for the

Ford Fusion? If we were appointed general managers responsible for the Fusion, we might well set a point of arrival that included reducing the number of available permutations.

Modify the hypotheses through discussion and detailed analysis. The general manager formulates ideas and homes in on the key variables that will determine the point of arrival. She puts those variables together and develops a working hypothesis of where she wants to take the business. This is a preliminary hypothesis, sometimes called a "straw man": for the moment, it's no more than a plausible picture of the future.

Then comes the hard part. What does the rest of the team think? What does the corporate office or the board think? How about middle managers, employees, customers, suppliers? The general manager has to forge a consensus, and we use the word "forge" deliberately. It's like the process of tempering steel—it usually involves a good deal of heat, but the end product will be stronger than it was before. When there are differences of opinion, a critical step is often to ask the question, "What would have to be true for hypothesis A to be correct?" Then, "What analysis would demonstrate that the preliminary goals for the point of arrival are correct or not?" A couple of rounds of this kind of analytic questioning will often bring the group to consensus and set expectations correctly. Figure 7.2 shows some generic objectives and critical action imperatives that could emerge from these discussions.

Sometimes actual full consensus is appropriate. When he was CEO of Bain Capital, Mitt Romney wouldn't go forward with a project unless every one of the eighteen partners agreed. It was the same for Richard Crawford, the former chief of Cambridge Industries. "If I couldn't get my top management team to agree on something," he told us, "there was probably something wrong with it, and we didn't do it." Other times the CEO simply has to set the direction, and invite those who disagree to reconsider or leave the company. But no experienced general manager takes such a step without doing a lot of listening and analysis first.

Once the manager has established a consensus, the point of arrival should be clear. So, too, should the critical action imperatives. Internal stakeholders can begin to relate their individual jobs to the agreed-upon

FIGURE 7.2

Deriving Critical Action Imperatives From the Point of Departure

Action Imperatives That a Typical Company Might Set from Its Diagnostic:

Vision: Regain market leadership to become the most profitable company in our industry by aggressive cost management and superior value propositions in high-margin and growth segments

Goal: Increase business profits by 70% and ROA by 3 percentage points in three years

Costs and Prices	Competitive Position	Customers and Profit Pools	Complexity Management

• Reduce costs by $200 million to move **relative cost position** from 110% of the best competitor to 90%
 	
  – 90% cost experience-curve slope to 70%
	• Move from below the **ROA/RMS band** into the band
	
	  – Increase relative market share from 0.9 to 1.2
		• Move **share of high-profit segment** x from 40% to 60% with retention increase of three percentage points:
		
		  – Improve service
		  – Cut price selectively
		
		• Move **share of profit pool** from 40% of $2 billion to 50% of $2.8 billion
			• Cut **SKU complexity** from 100,000 to 2,000 with reduction of **organization layers** in SG&A* from five to three and **outsource** 20% of all G&A costs

*SG&A is selling, general, and administrative expenses

point of arrival. External stakeholders can begin to form realistic expectations of future performance and actions the organization will be taking. The company will know where it is going.

Point-of-Arrival Pitfalls

All this may sound easy. It isn't. In fact, many general managers make fundamental mistakes in determining their point of arrival. Usually the reason isn't hard to find: they have paid insufficient attention to one or more of the four laws or the twelve must-have facts. Here are some common ways in which managers violate each of the laws.

Violations of the first law. Remember the story of Allis-Chalmers and its competitors in chapter 2? Allis set a goal of building a turbine that could produce electricity for about $330 a megawatt. By the time it could do so, competitors were selling turbines that could generate power for a lot less. Allis's cost-reduction plans were not aggressive enough, given the experience curve. This is a common mistake. So, too, is the opposite error: cost targets that are too ambitious given the current position on the experience curve, and its slope. The experience curve is a powerful analytic tool that shows you how rapidly you can—and how rapidly you must— bring your costs down. You ignore it at your peril.

Violations of the second law. Many general managers like to set nice round financial targets: a 10 percent increase in revenues, a 20 percent increase in profits, and so on. That may be fine—but if the targets are inconsistent with the ROA/RMS band, your market position, and the strategies of your competitors, the likely result will be either wildly unrealistic goals or else that corporate swamp known as "satisfactory underperformance." Many managers fall into this trap. In repeated research studies, we have found that the growth plans of all the competitors in an industry add up to about double the likely industry growth rate. So most companies never hit their plans. The band defines what's possible in your industry. Your position on the band defines what's possible for your company. If you want financial results that are inconsistent with your position on the band, you have to figure out how to change your position.

One change is simply to move up the band—to gain share and increase profitability. But here's another potential pitfall: failing to determine explicitly where the share you gain will come from—which customers and which competitors. Perhaps the market is expanding, and you are poised to capture a disproportionate share of the overall growth. You should be able to explain why this is so, and how you intend to capture it. (Think of WaMu's free checking account, which had proven its capacity in this regard.) Or perhaps one of your competitors is weak, and you can poach some of its share, much as Toyota has poached share from General Motors. Your plan to gain share must itself be realistic—it must be based on a deep understanding of customer behavior, why customers will increasingly turn to you rather than to a competitor, and how a competitor might respond to your actions.

Violations of the third law. Shifting customer behavior and profit pools can undermine even big, seemingly successful companies. Montgomery Ward, for instance, was once a strong competitor of Sears in catalog sales and department stores. In the 1990s it set an ambitious point of arrival, embarking on a major program to expand the number of stores. But the program failed to take into account the fact that existing stores were already suffering, because more and more customers were taking their business to specialty retailers such as Best Buy and Circuit City. The expansion move failed, and Montgomery Ward filed for bankruptcy protection in 1997. If your point of arrival requires capabilities that you don't now have—a film company wanting to enter digital photography, for instance—it must also include a plan for acquiring those capabilities.

Violations of the fourth law. If your product line is too complex, your point of arrival shouldn't necessarily assume you can easily reduce costs—unless you take on the complexity challenge first. If your company can't make decisions effectively and carry them out, your point of arrival must include a plan to reduce decision-making complexity. Think back to Chrysler's wiring harness (chapter 5): until the decision-making process was fixed, the company was simply unable to reduce costs as much as it needed to. The process change was a necessary companion to the reduction of options complexity.

THERE ARE MANY MORE GENERIC PITFALLS AS WELL. A GENERAL manager can fail to communicate the point of arrival effectively. If you do not communicate a simple point of arrival with only three to five major cornerstones, your organization is likely to wind up confused and unfocused. Employees and other stakeholders in that situation won't understand where their company is headed, and won't know what they can do to help. A general manager can also fail to set goals that reflect the company's actual momentum, as revealed by the diagnosis. If your profit pool is shrinking, your proposed point of arrival can't be based on doing more of the same. A general manager can also map out a point of arrival that is simply too complex. At Morgan Crucible, all of Knowlton's moves could be boiled down to just three imperatives: reduce costs, change the portfolio to reduce the company's dependence on commodity businesses, and invest to gain share in industrial segments with higher growth and margins. At Chrysler, Hal Sperlich's turnaround plan similarly hinged on three imperatives: make cars that people wanted to buy, reduce costs massively, and reduce complexity. These are points of arrival that everyone—managers, employees, shareholders, board members—can understand and move toward.

CREATING A PERFORMANCE-IMPROVEMENT ACTION PLAN

Your diagnosis of the point of departure identifies where you can create new value. Your point of arrival sets the target—the vision of where your business will be a few years from now. Your next step is to define a road map—a plan—for getting from where you are now to where you want to be.

The Basics of an Effective Plan

We have already mentioned one essential characteristic of a plan that will work: it has a realistic time frame, a time frame that corresponds to the likely tenure of the general manager. In addition, an effective plan always has two seemingly contradictory characteristics.

On the one hand, it is simple. Like the point of arrival itself, the fundamentals of a plan are easily understandable. It contains three or four broad action imperatives, very rarely more. The specific action initiatives you will create from these imperatives obviously depend on your company's situation. As a rule of thumb, though, many leaders set one initiative relating to costs, one relating to customers, and one relating to organizational capabilities and structure. The action imperatives can then be rolled up into a set of overall financial goals.

On the other hand, the plan is highly detailed. As general manager, you have applied the full performance-improvement diagnostic. You know not only that costs need to come down 15 percent a year over the next three years, say, but also exactly which costs are out of line and which you will be able to reduce. You understand the levers you can pull to achieve the goals you have set, whatever they may be. You can now create a *performance-improvement action plan* that cascades the broad initiatives downward and outward all through the organization, so that managers and employees on the front lines know what they must do to contribute (see figure 7.3).

FIGURE 7.3

Action Plan Example

Zoom in on first bullet under Costs and Prices in Figure 7.2

Action imperative: Reduce costs by $200 million to move **relative cost position** from 110% of the best competitor to 90%

Initiatives	Resource Allocation and Capability Acquisition	Metrics and Interim Milestones	Contingency Plan Triggers and Details

• **Reduce Costs of Goods Sold by $XM**
 	
  – ***Manufacturing:*** *outsource manufacturing of product line X to third party in China*
 	
  – ***Purchasing:*** *Consolidate suppliers of raw materials X and Y and negotiate volume discounts*
	• **Resources required:**
	
	  – *Two 80% dedicated initiative leaders: Nicolas Smith for manufacturing and Angela Chou for purchasing*
	
	• **New capabilities required:**
	
	  – *Assessment of third-party manufacturers in China—new hire to set up and oversee all third-party manufacturers*
		• **Top metric: total COGS**
		
		• **Additional metrics:**
		
		  – *COGS as % of sales*
		  – *% of manufacturing capacity outsourced*
		  – *Raw materials costs*
		  – *Average volume discounts*
		  – *Number of suppliers*
		
		• **Milestones: Manufacturing**
		
		  – *By 3/30: create list of 3–5 third-party manufacturers*
		  – *By 6/30: select partner*
		  – *By 8/30: agree on detailed plan of production outsourcing*
		  – *By 12/30: move all production to China*
		
		• **Milestones: Purchasing**
		
		  – *By 3/30: evaluate all current suppliers, select top 10*
		  – *By 8/30: negotiate volume discounts*
		  – *By 10/30: finalize supplier consolidation*
			• **Manufacturing:**
			
			  – *Third-party provider's quality deteriorates →establish conditional contracts with #2 and #3 potential providers*
			
			  – *Distribution disruptions from China → increase safety stock for first 90 days of program implementation*
			
			• **Purchasing:**
			
			  – *One of suppliers goes out of business → incorporate financial monitoring of suppliers into ongoing partnership evaluation*

In the previous chapter, we described how Gerard Arpey and his team identified American Airlines's gaps versus the competition, and how they determined what was driving each of the gaps. Arpey's plan then mapped out which gaps they would attack first and how they would go about it.

Many of the targets required help from employees or the unions; others simply required concerted action on the part of management. To date, American Airlines has taken more than $5 billion out of its cost structure. It has returned to profitability in spite of continuing jet-fuel price increases and severe competition from low-cost carriers.

Other Key Elements of a Plan

General managers often map out the targets they're setting in a simple chart like that in figure 7.4. The chart summarizes the anticipated impact of the major areas of potential and their priority and allows managers to build their action plans accordingly.

Whatever the specifics of a company's plan may be, there are at least three elements that it must always include:

Resource allocation and capability acquisition that fit with the action

FIGURE 7.4

Performance-Improvement Diagnosis
Creates Targets for Full Potential

Double Profitability in the Next Three Years

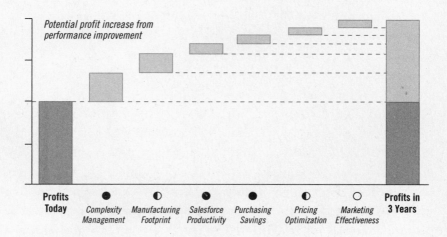

imperatives. A company that sets out to gain pricing flexibility through product differentiation can't then stint on R&D or brand development. Indeed, virtually every source of value targeted in the diagnostic process is likely to require both investment dollars and the development of one or more capabilities. If a company doesn't already possess the required capabilities, it will have to develop or acquire them.

Where is the money going to come from? Both tasks require a financial plan showing the source of these investments. Managers in a turnaround situation, such as Knowlton at Morgan Crucible or Brenneman at Continental, will have to bootstrap their finances, freeing up cash either from sale of assets or from cost cutting and complexity reduction. Jim Haas at National Steel realized that significant investment was required to improve his relative cost position, and that the company's resources would permit aggressive investment in only about 60 percent of its capacity. The remaining capacity would have to be ignored and ultimately retired. Relentless and systematic application of best demonstrated practices greatly improved Haas's costs and added to the cash pool required for these investments in new equipment and processes. But even if you're not in that kind of cash-tight situation, you naturally need to identify the sources of funds you will be using and the likely payback. Projections of revenue, earnings, and investment levels over the life of the plan will show whether it is financially viable.

Metrics and interim milestones. The small number of action imperatives should create a small number of key metrics, the very few operating variables that absolutely must be on target if the plan is to succeed. The plan should contain targets for these variables, not just for the point of arrival but for interim milestones along the way.

Metrics, too, will cascade down to lower levels of the organization as each one sets its own specific initiatives. Knowlton set a goal of reducing labor costs as a percent of revenue across the board. Individual business units could achieve this goal in various ways: by outsourcing more, by relocating to lower-cost countries, by increasing productivity in an existing plant, by changing the mix of products made and sold, or by some combination of measures. At SLOC, Romney knew how much revenue he needed to generate to meet the overall Olympics budget. Each revenue-generating division within the organization naturally had targets of its own that rolled up into the total.

Contingency-plan triggers and details. Idris Jala of Malaysia Airlines was careful to define his points of arrival and to map out a plan for getting there over a three-year period. The whole thing was contained in a forty-seven-page document that laid out objectives, plan, interim milestones, and so on. This is what he had to say about it:

> In this plan that we put forward, we arrive at three different points in each of the years. By the end of Year One we show how much money or how much improvement in the P&L we would make by the end of the year, then what our P&L would look like in Year Two and Year Three. Those are the points of arrival.
>
> But once you get down to execution, my own experience is this: more than 70 percent of what happens is totally different from what was considered in the plan . . . In the laboratory you cannot predict what responses will come from the competition. It's like a game of chess. If you sit down in a room and say, "Let me predict my sixteenth move," that's wrong. You can never predict your sixteenth move in a game of chess, because you never know what an opponent's going to do. And so at every point along the path, your next move has to depend on changes in responses to competition, changes in environment, changes in the capability of your staff, and so on.

So if things do go off track, you need to know what you are going to do. You need triggers that tell you when the plan has gone awry, and contingency plans that you can then put into effect. And if something appears that was wholly unexpected—an unanticipated move by a new competitor, for instance—you have to be sure that your information-gathering and decision-making capabilities will enable you to respond effectively. The four laws in this book will continue to be the essential guide to the options you have available for response.

Telstra's Point of Departure, Point of Arrival, and Plan

When Sol Trujillo became CEO of Telstra, Australia's largest telecommunications company, he faced serious challenges. The Australian government was in the process of selling Telstra to the public, but the company was still tightly regulated. Costs were on the rise. Revenues were declining, thanks largely to the erosion of Telstra's PSTN revenue—the revenue derived from traditional dial-tone telephone service. The company was heavily dependent on this and on other older products; in fact, only 2 percent of revenue was coming from products less than three years old. As Trujillo had seen in many other companies in the sector, Telstra suffered from a stifling lack of innovation and new ideas that could spark growth. Telstra's market share in key product categories was declining, and both revenues and margins were under extreme pressure. In the critical mobile-telephone market, for example, Telstra's share had steadily declined for over a decade. This pressure would continue into the future if nothing were done.

Trujillo was intent on defining what he calls "a path to winning" built around a clear understanding of how the company would be differentiated from its competitors. At the same time he wanted to quickly reset the company's cultural norms about speed of action. Long, drawn-out evaluations leading only to further analysis would be replaced with decisive actions based on the right facts.

Trujillo first launched a multipronged diagnosis using an approach like the one described in the previous chapter. The diagnostic process turned up some revelations. Across the entire company, for instance, Trujillo and his team discovered that complexity was a chief source of cost creep. Telstra had multiple wireless networks and multiple data networks. It had more than 300 different network platforms provided by a vast array of vendors. The level of complexity had been growing steadily over time, pushing up costs. Even in Telstra's mobile operation, there were three network platforms with multiple (and often incompatible) technologies. IT systems were similarly complex. To enter a multi-product order, the company acknowledged, a customer service representative might need to use as many as seven different systems and as many as eighty different screens. Completing such an order could take more than an hour.[2]

Telstra's divisions drilled down to establish their own points of departure. The Consumer division, for instance, charted the decline in its PSTN revenue, noting that it began in March 2004. Interviewing customers, the division's managers found a wish for simplicity, convenience, and service—benefits the customers felt they were not fully receiving, either from Telstra or from any of its competitors. The managers also found a tight link between customers' choice of carrier for their home phone service and their choice of provider for rapidly growing broadband Internet services. Meanwhile, the Business and Government division had recognized that its "traditional carriage" market share—the carrying of voice and data over proprietary networks—was declining, even while customers were exhibiting strong demand for IP telephony, wireless data solutions, and other advanced services. IP (Internet protocol) telephony alone was growing at an annual rate of 62 percent, though with much lower margins than the traditional legacy services. This division's customers increasingly sought a secure, reliable IP-based network with cost-effective bandwidth, new applications with rich functionality, and innovation.[3]

Based on this kind of research into customer needs and on their deep experience in the sector over many years, Trujillo and his team devised a visionary point of arrival for the entire company: "To give the customer a powerful, seamless user experience across all devices and all platforms in a 1-click, 1-touch, 1-screen way—whether that customer is an individual, small business, large business, or governmental agency."[4] In his first report to the investor community, four months after joining the company, he planted "stakes in the ground" and publicly committed to challenging targets for the following five years. The targets included overall revenue growth of 2.0 to 2.5 percent a year, and an absolute level of costs the same in 2010 as it was in 2006. The divisions established their own points of arrival in keeping with the overall vision. The Business and Government division, for instance, proposed to lead customer IP migration and transformation, build a "Telstra-only" suite of services and solutions, and differentiate on customer service and value creation.[5] Operations proposed to create a "single, integrated factory"[6] with low unit cost, rapid delivery of services, and a consistent customer experience, with jobs completed "right first time."

The road map for change and the metrics that would track progress are easiest to see at the divisional level. Operations planned to reduce the number of network platforms 60 percent in three years and 65 percent in five years. It would cut the number of IT systems by 75 percent in three years and 80 percent in five. It would invest more than A$10 billion to build the so-called Next Generation Network (including wireless and fixed), and more than A$1 billion in transforming the company's IT capability. It would reduce the capital-expenditure-to-sales ratio to 12 to 13 percent by FY 2010; reduce headcount by 6,000 to 8,000 over three years, and more than 10,000 over five; and contribute to a goal of more than $A3 billion a year in improved cash flow through cost savings and other initiatives.

The Consumer business unit's product-development and marketing plan for reaching its point of arrival, similarly, had four key points and corresponding metrics. One was to migrate customers to higher-value platforms—for example, at least 80 percent broadband in FY 2008, up from 41 percent in FY 2005. A second was to shift the customer mix, retaining existing customers while simultaneously acquiring more high-value customers and increasing the company's share of wallet through cross-selling and increased usage. One metric here was to be growth in average revenue per user, or ARPU. A third part of the plan: deliver on the power of integration. That meant, for instance, increasing the proportion of customers using multiple Telstra products (a goal of 60 percent, up from 47 percent). Finally, the division planned to drive adoption and penetration of new Telstra services. One relevant metric was growth in nonvoice ARPU, which the division proposed to double in three years.

In mid-2007, two years into Trujillo's five-year plan, Telstra's future was by no means assured. The new CEO had undertaken an immense task, and he faced opposition not just from competitors but from some politicians and regulators. But the company was meeting all the metrics laid out in that initial point-of-arrival plan two years prior, and he was going about his task in the right way, doing everything possible to ensure success.

YOU CAN SEE: WHEN YOU GET DOWN INTO THE NITTY-GRITTY OF an individual company's point of departure, point of arrival, and plan to get there, the details accumulate, and it's easy for an outsider to get lost. What makes it all understandable for the general manager responsible for improving the business is the four laws, the template based on them, and the simplicity of the path to success.

Once you have your plan in place, it's time to embark on the journey—the road to results—with the solid foundation you have laid. That is the subject of the next chapter.

IMPLICATIONS FOR THE GENERAL MANAGER

- Form your point of arrival on the basis of your point-of-departure diagnostic. It should be examined in light of the twelve must-have facts, and it should be consistent with the four laws. The point of arrival should be compelling, motivating, and realistic; it should match the likely job tenure of the general manager and the expectations of key stakeholders, with clear progress milestones in twelve to eighteen months. It will set the standards by which you are evaluated during your tenure.

- Establish strong consensus on your point of arrival with all stakeholders. Develop a simple, memorable structure for communicating and monitoring the point of arrival.

- Develop detailed action plans linked to and supporting three to five critical action imperatives, based on the twelve must-have facts and the in-depth performance-improvement diagnostic. The plan should include all the levers necessary to move performance in the direction you want to go, at the pace required by your point-of-arrival timeline.

- Use relatively few critical metrics to measure success—probably no more than eight to twelve metrics, under the three to five critical action imperatives. Typically, these will include key strategic, operational, and organizational measures.

EIGHT

The Road to Results

All truth passes through three stages. First, it is ridiculed. Second,
it is violently opposed. Third, it is accepted as self-evident.

—ARTHUR SCHOPENHAUER

THE FINAL STEP IS FREQUENTLY THE HARDEST. IT IS THE SUCCESS-
ful execution of the plan.

Many companies have foundered because they couldn't accomplish the
objectives laid out in a plan. Many otherwise insightful managers have accurately diagnosed their point of departure, have carefully mapped out
their point of arrival—and then have gotten lost on the journey. "Hundreds of studies examined the success rates of change initiatives that were
heavily dependent upon people," reported the Web site Workforce.com in
2003. "The results are sobering: most studies cited failure rates in the 80
percent to 90 percent range."[1] When survey respondents were presented
with the statement, "I have seen many change initiatives that have failed,"
close to 70 percent checked "Agree" or "Strongly agree."[2]

Managers often fail to bring about performance improvement because
there are so many ways to fail. The organization may not have the right

skills. The right people may not be in the right places. Change leaders may underestimate the importance of incentives, of communication, of monitoring progress. But the fundamental reason for failure is that people in an organization are often unaware of the need or urgency for performance-improving change and therefore prefer their accustomed ways of doing things. Some may actually work to undermine the leader's efforts. "Companies resist change—even the good ones—and most assuredly they resist mostly while conditions are favorable," says Fred Rowan, CEO of Carter's, the Atlanta-based children's clothing company. "They continue along the safest and soundest route." [3]

Despite the obstacles, at least one group of managers succeeds regularly at bringing about performance improvement. They don't win every time, by any means—in fact, according to one estimate they fail to recoup their initial investment close to 40 percent of the time. But they win often enough, and big enough, to earn considerable returns for their investors. We're referring, of course, to the managers employed by private-equity (PE) firms. PE firms in the top quartile have compiled a remarkable track record of profitability by buying companies, improving them, and then either reselling them or taking them public. [4] One consortium of firms bought Sealy Corp. in 1997 for $830 million. The group revamped the company's strategy and operations, then resold it in 2004 for a better-than-fivefold return on equity. Another consortium spent $2.6 billion in 2004 to buy Warner Music Group, even though the music industry at the time was beset by fierce competition, piracy, and uncertainty about the future. In less than two years the group had pared down Warner's roster of artists, promoted the most promising ones, made content more widely available on digital devices, and come out with new products, such as premium-price digital albums with bonus tracks. The moves boosted Warner's cash flow and earnings to the point where the buyout firms could take the company public at a price that implied they had tripled their original investment. [5]

What is the private-equity secret? [6] As many observers have pointed out, managers of private companies don't have to worry about meeting Wall Street's quarterly expectations. And they have active, involved owners, typically with a deep well of business expertise. But the most important secret may lie elsewhere. In nearly every case, successful private-equity managers do precisely what we're recommending in this book: they diagnose a point of departure, craft a point of arrival, and then rigorously execute a plan for getting there. As we write, CEO Gerald L. (Jerry) Storch is leading a turnaround of Toys "R" Us, which was acquired by a consortium of buyout firms in mid-2005. (Storch became CEO of Toys "R" Us in February 2006.) The turnaround was far from complete when we interviewed Storch, but he and his team were already successfully implementing a specific, detailed plan to increase sales, improve customer satisfaction, return the company to profitability, and position it for continued growth. Meanwhile, John Chidsey had become CEO of Burger King, the big fast-food chain, acquired by a private-equity consortium in December 2002. By mid-2007 Chidsey and his team had racked up fourteen straight quarters of same-store sales growth as well as the best level of consecutive (comparable operations) performance in more than a decade. We will relate in this chapter how Storch, Chidsey, and other leaders went about executing their plans.

One other thing: private-equity owners and managers always aim at achieving results within a well-defined time frame, typically no more than three years. Our colleague Stan Pace led a team that studied twenty-one of the most dramatic corporate transformations (both public and private) in the late 1980s and 1990s. "The most successful transformers we studied substantially completed their turnarounds in two years or less," Pace reported. "None took more than three years."[7] Get things done fast and you're more likely to see the kind of results that will make a real difference.

How can you take a page from the private-equity book and lead change successfully? How can you move as rapidly as possible from your point of departure to your point of arrival? How can you carry out the plan you have devised, ensuring that it unfolds the way it is supposed to—or at least as much as possible, given the likelihood that unforeseen events will affect it? It won't happen by itself. At Bain we like to say that successful managers "plot" change. It turns out that PLOT is a useful acronym for the steps involved. In keeping with our principle of process simplicity, there are only four central categories.

You can guess what the P in PLOT stands for: *Plan.* Planning, as we described it in the previous chapter, involves defining the points of departure and arrival and coming to consensus on both, then spelling out the critical few action imperatives that can move the organization from the one to the other. The present chapter is all about getting it done, and so focuses on the three other elements. *Lead* means getting people fired up and building a culture that supports change. *Operate* involves driving specific initiatives and holding people accountable—it's the day-to-day execution of the strategy. *Track* includes measuring performance and acting on the results (see figure 8.1). Master each of these and you will increase your odds of successfully navigating the road to results.

LEAD

Volumes have been written on leadership, and we don't propose to repeat all those lessons here. Rather, we want to home in on just one topic: how

FIGURE 8.1

Some of the Best Managers PLOT Their Own Story for Successful Change

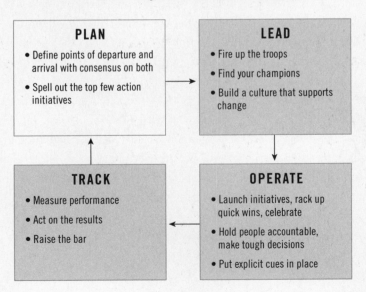

PLAN
- Define points of departure and arrival with consensus on both
- Spell out the top few action initiatives

LEAD
- Fire up the troops
- Find your champions
- Build a culture that supports change

TRACK
- Measure performance
- Act on the results
- Raise the bar

OPERATE
- Launch initiatives, rack up quick wins, celebrate
- Hold people accountable, make tough decisions
- Put explicit cues in place

leaders successfully move an organization from the point of departure to the point of arrival in a limited time frame.

This kind of leadership turns on two fundamental tasks: getting people on your side and pursuing your goal with the required sense of urgency. You need the active support and engagement of your boss or your board, your senior team, your middle managers, and your employees—often even your customers and suppliers. You need to align everyone around the mission and the critical few action imperatives you developed in the planning stage. You want people to care as much as you do about reaching the point of arrival. You want them to develop a passion for the mission ahead. "Here, there are 3,500 leaders, from the first line up to me," says Ralph Heath, president of Lockheed Martin Aeronautics. "Where I add value is in getting alignment. If I can get everyone aligned so that we are all working in one direction, then we succeed."

David Weidman of Celanese has his own slant on this task. "I believe in the 'Rule of the Revolutionary,'" he says. "The number of people you need to drive change in an organization equals the square root of the organization you are trying to change. In our company we have about 10,000 people, so I needed 100 revolutionaries to drive the change. From day one, my job was to go out and find those 100 people, bring them in, reward them, feed them, get their skill levels up, motivate and encourage them, move them forward, and help them to drive the organization. And we have had a singular focus on doing just that."

Fire Up the Troops

Why should people want to change? Why should anyone expect them to buy into a major shift in an organization's direction, given the natural human fear of the unknown? A leader has to build the case for performance improvement at this most fundamental level by crafting and communicating a powerful set of messages.

Define the burning platform. You have learned a lot already in the first months you have been leading the organization. You have produced a compelling performance-improvement diagnosis of the organization's situation, its point of departure. You have learned that something needs to be changed, and you can show exactly what it is. Maybe the organization is in a financial crisis, like Morgan Crucible or the Salt Lake Organizing Committee. Maybe it is underperforming and in danger of being overtaken by competitors, like Toys "R" Us or Burger King. Maybe it has been successful in the past but now faces a new set of challenges or opportunities, like the fitness-equipment company we described.

All this learning should generate an urgent set of messages, backed by the hard data from your diagnosis. Don't mince words: show people exactly why they can't continue with business as usual. *We're in danger of bankruptcy*, and here's why. *We are uncompetitive*, and here are the numbers. *We will be facing new competition*, and here's where it will be coming from. *Our customer needs and our profit pools are changing*, and here's how we can respond. *We have a new opportunity*—here's where it is, here is the size of the market, and these are the capabilities and resources we will require. When Chidsey joined Burger King—first as CFO and executive vice president, later as CEO—he and his team discovered some of the challenges that underlay the company's poor results. There were few new products in the company's pipeline. As many as one-third of its U.S. restaurants were in financial difficulty. Relations between the company and its franchisees were troubled. The company had little in the way of operational systems and metrics, hence no way of holding franchisees accountable for performance.

If you run a nonprofit, you can similarly identify and quantify the problem your organization is trying to solve. When Partners In Health and Socios En Salud went into a Peruvian community to attack drug-resistant tuberculosis, staffers literally counted prospective patients one by one. At the time, said Jim Yong Kim, "Peru had the best TB control program in the developing world. Yet there were all these people dying of drug-resistant forms of the disease. In our community we counted about fifty who were not doing well with the [conventional] programs." It's the same for any organization, including a government. David Cicilline, who was first elected mayor of Providence, Rhode Island, in 2002 (with 84 percent of the vote), could point to a crumbling infrastructure, poor city services, a budget deficit, and a legacy of corruption. (The previous mayor,

Vincent "Buddy" Cianci, had resigned after a conviction on racketeering charges.) Cicilline conducted a citizens' satisfaction survey early in his first term—"a really good way," he notes, "to get a baseline, to gauge what people's perceptions were about city services, crime, schools, and the infrastructure."

You can spell out the point of arrival with data as well. *We will be a top-quartile company. We will overtake competitor X. We will reduce the incidence of drug-resistant TB in this region by Y percent. We will have a balanced budget.* You need to convey not only the urgency of change today, but the need for better performance in the future. Even in business, the message should have an aspirational element—financial results alone are rarely enough. Being the best, pursuing excellence, making your customers' lives better—these are all powerful motivators, and it's your job to frame the point of arrival in a manner that gets everyone excited. In his budget address to the city council for fiscal 2008, Mayor Cicilline explained how he proposed to balance the budget—but he also spoke of a "new Providence," a "city that innovates, delivering more and more value for every dollar that comes in," a "government that can inspire faith and confidence again . . . that can be a force for positive change." As Hal Sperlich once said to us, "It is noble intent that inspires people to join you in the journey."

Communicate all the time—and with every tool at your disposal. You can't talk too much about performance improvement. You and the rest of your team need to be almost obsessive about achieving your goals and about getting others on board. You can use any number of methods—videotaped talks, plant and branch-office visits, newsletters, e-mails, in-person question-and-answer sessions, and of course the many avenues made possible by an intranet, such as blogs, chat rooms, and message boards.

Every CEO has his or her own techniques. Burger King's Chidsey records a biweekly voice mail—it was weekly at first—that is accessible to everyone in the company's global network. He sponsors eight to ten "Ops Excellence" conferences in the United States alone, each one attracting about 1,000 people in addition to an annual global convention. Jerry Storch of Toys "R" Us holds an all-hands meeting once a quarter—a couple of thousand people gather in the company's headquarters auditorium, others watch it on video in the cafeteria, still others dial in from the field. John Taylor, who led a resurgence of the Vienna-based plastics company Borealis, tours his company's facilities regularly. "In the first couple of years, I went to every location myself and gave the same presentation more than twenty times. I think you just have to communicate, communicate, communicate."

The goals of all this communication are simple. Everyone in the organization should be able to remember and repeat the three, four, or five major initiatives in the plan and understand why they make sense. People should become converts to the new vision—they should be able to articulate how what they do fits into achieving the objectives. Inspiration is catching. As more people commit to the new goals, others will climb on the bandwagon as well. Do things right, says Sol Trujillo of Telstra, "and your people then follow you, they'll believe in you, they will do whatever you need to do, like working seven days a week, 365 days out of the year. That's what happens here, because people for the first time have belief in leadership."

Adjust the message as change proceeds. At first you need to convey urgency. Later in the process, your job is to reinforce the message and to build confidence. Change unsettles people. They wonder whether they will still have a job, whether they will be able to change, whether they will like the new environment. You need to address those concerns even while you're insisting on your new priorities. Don't underestimate how fiercely people can cling to the old ways of doing things, even when an organization is in desperate straits. Warren Knowlton, for instance, recalls one company director who urged him not to cut overhead because the existing overhead level was "about right" for a company of Morgan Crucible's size—even though Morgan was in severe financial crisis.

Find Your "Rowers," and Eliminate the "Drillers"

Weidman calls them revolutionaries. Most organizations just call them champions. Whatever the name, they're the people who will row the boat alongside you and lead performance improvement throughout the organization. As Weidman suggests, you want to find them, cultivate them, and get them working together.

Build the core team. At the heart of this process is the core change team, the senior leaders entrusted with directing and overseeing the road to results. Who should be on it? CEOs hired from the outside to take over an organization often bring trusted lieutenants with them. There's a reason for that: the lieutenants have typically been through it all before, and they have no vested interest in maintaining the status quo. "People [in a company] are always protective of what they have done. They will justify what they have done. What you need are knowing eyes that can help you," says Trujillo. Lower-level general managers may not have the option of bringing people with them, but they need to find or hire a few people right away whom they can trust to serve on the core change team.

That task is difficult enough. But it's easy compared with making quick decisions about who in senior management should *not* be on the core change team. This can be one of the toughest tasks a new manager faces.

The fact is, people facing the prospect of change react differently. Some will be enthusiastic. They'll grab an oar and ask how they can help row the boat. But others will be down below decks, busily drilling holes in the bottom. They are the "drillers"—the people who are actively working to undermine you and sabotage your change efforts. And a third group—call them the "passengers"—will be prepared to go along for the ride, provided somebody else does the rowing. If you catch somebody drilling, or if you know who was responsible for serious performance failures in the past, you can just move those people out. But what about the passengers, the senior people whose performance is acceptable but who seem lukewarm about the new direction? Some can become rowers and some can't. How do you find out who is who?

The consensus among most CEOs we spoke with was that you may need to replace a significant fraction of the senior team, particularly if the company's performance has been poor. "I'm not aware of any major turnaround that has not involved a major change in people at the top," says Storch. Storch found, however, that there were plenty of capable people one level below the senior leaders, some of whom were ready for more responsibility. At Burger King, the private-equity sponsors made a point of bringing in a lot of fresh faces—including many people who came to the company from other industries. The advantage, Chidsey says, was that "there were no cliques, no factions, no history of 'Oh, he did this, or she did that.' " The fact that many came from outside of the industry meant that they had no preconceptions about how things ought to work, and that they often brought new perspectives. "Everybody had different skill sets, but they all found a way to plug in."

But some CEOs who took over an organization performing below expectations were encouraged by the people they found on the job. "You're always tempted to say, when a company is languishing, you must have not very good management," says John Lundgren, who became CEO of The Stanley Works in 2004. "But I was pleasantly surprised. When I started talking to people about in-depth diagnosis of the positions of our businesses, improved decision making with rigorous, fact-based monitoring, and coupling all of that with real accountability for results, that combination of ingredients was transforming. People you might have assumed to be below par were liberated, and they embraced the commitment to higher performance levels." Lundgren ended up replacing only a few members of his senior management team.

In making decisions about individuals there is no substitute for face-to-face communication. Have a candid discussion with everyone you have doubts about. Ask them, "Do you understand how different things are going to be? Do you buy into the new vision? Are you prepared to help row the boat vigorously?" Confronted like that, many doubters will select themselves out, particularly if they can do so without negative repercussions and with fair compensation. "I told my managers at the meeting we had in February 2003, 'If you don't want to be here, please tell me now and I'll pay your severance,' " said Knowlton. "I almost begged them to resign if they didn't want to be there." Several did choose to leave. Like Knowlton, you have to have a core team that you can depend on and trust. You can't tolerate mediocrity or a lukewarm attitude in your core group of leaders. If you do, you're sending a powerful message to the entire organization that you are not serious about the new direction and the pace of change required.

Sometimes, too, you can find ways to test people in action. Six weeks after Philip Teel took over as president of Northrop Grumman Ship Sys-

tems, the company's shipyard was hit—and devastated—by Hurricane Katrina. Suddenly Teel had a new point of departure on his hands. Major
parts of the facility needed to be repaired and rebuilt, even as work continued on as many regular projects as possible. Teel used the opportunity to
audition managers he felt might help lead the company's performance-
improvement program: he put them in charge of rebuilding projects. Some
turned in great performances, while others did not. But Teel now had a
better idea about which people he could count on to be the stars of his
company in the future. Many executives we spoke with used the technique
of grooming the new leading rowers by testing them first with a major
change-project assignment.

Create change teams throughout the organization. Below the core
change team are the many other teams responsible for carrying out the
critical initiatives in business units and functional departments.

The principles of effective team building have also been widely written
about elsewhere, so we'll review them only briefly. You want small, dedicated teams, with at least 25 percent of the members' time allocated to the
job at hand. You want people with a positive mindset and a can-do attitude. They should be well respected in the organization. You may need a
wide range of skills: depending on the mission, the skills required may
include cost management, financial knowledge, project-management expertise, procurement skills, or familiarity with information technology.
Teams need to operate without any sacred cows and with a commitment
to reliance on facts. They should have explicit objectives, with clearly assigned responsibilities and clear deadlines. They also should have whatever resources they need to get the job done. A written workplan can help
get everyone on the same page, and can serve as an early warning system
to identify potential roadblocks.

Effective general managers naturally put their own stamp on these precepts. Listen to Idris Jala, who describes how teams operate at Malaysia
Airlines. His change teams, he says, are called laboratories. "I might call a
few people in and say, 'I want a laboratory on increasing revenue.' I lock
them in a room for a month and a half or so. Their job is to figure out
how to fix it, how to move it, whatever the challenge is. They don't do anything else—it's a full-time job, they drop any existing activities to just

do this." The team stays at work until it has fulfilled its agreed-upon "exit criteria," that is, coming up with the specific steps needed for the indicated change. The laboratory, says Jala, "is not a job, it's a calling."

Build a Culture That Supports Performance Improvement

People in the organization should be thinking like business owners, assessing risks and assuming responsibilities without being asked. They should be motivated by the mission, proud of what they are achieving— and never fully satisfied with their progress. How do you support that kind of thought and action?

Use incentives. The single most important action that you can take is to change your incentive structure. Our research suggests that incentives are the most critical factor other than the quality of senior management in determining the success of a change effort.

If possible, link incentives directly to the critical action imperatives you're relying on to achieve your point of arrival. The Latin American airline TACA, for instance, undertook a restructuring program in 2001 that was designed first to reduce costs and then to improve service. The company changed executive compensation to tie in with these initiatives: base salaries were lowered, but the managers had an opportunity to make more than before if the company hit its operational and financial targets. As a result of this and other initiatives, TACA recovered from near-bankruptcy in 2001 to become one of the most profitable companies in the industry by 2003. In 2005, TACA expanded its incentive program to include the entire company, paying bonuses to every employee whenever it hit targets relating to on-time performance and customer loyalty (as measured by Net Promoter Scores).

Many senior executives are reluctant to change incentives too quickly. "It's people's job to do these tasks," they argue. "Why should I give extra rewards for what they should be doing anyway?" That's a mistake. Most of the successful general managers we studied made liberal and creative use of focused incentives to help drive the critical action imperatives of their plan. Incentives are one of the most powerful tools employed by private-equity firms. Usually, one of the very first changes private-equity firms implement after buying a company is to align incentives with the key imperatives for the business.

Both for-profit and nonprofit organizations need to remember that incentives aren't just about money. People respond to a variety of encouragements—promotion, praise, setting records, the chance to solve a social problem. They value symbolic rewards as well as more pay. Winning a competitive battle is frequently a powerful incentive. So is the attainment of an "impossible" goal like putting a man on the moon or eliminating drug-resistant TB. Genzyme, the biotech company, was the first to develop an effective treatment for Gaucher disease, an illness that can be fatal. The company's original product took years to develop. The product relied on cells derived from human placentas, and at first it took 22,000 placentas to provide material to treat just one patient for a year. "We overcame all these hurdles in order to save kids' lives," says CEO Henri Termeer, adding that the "passion" that characterizes Genzyme's culture can be traced to those challenging beginnings. The goal of saving children's lives whatever the difficulties has continued to be a powerful incentive for everyone in the organization.

Streamline the structure. Too many organizations grow fat over time. They initiate projects, add people and resources—and when the project is finished, the people and resources don't go away. More people generate more costs, more meetings, and more-muddled decision making. They always seem to be busy, perhaps because human beings are good at finding ways to keep themselves busy. These are the passengers who do not vitally contribute to the change effort.

Given that tendency toward bloat, outstanding leaders are often able to cut general and administrative costs between 10 percent and 30 percent. They reduce activities, redesign processes, and restructure the organization by eliminating layers and increasing spans. Former General Electric CEO Jack Welch put in place a test of what he called "productive G&A," or general and administrative expenses. "Check the phone logs," he told executives at the World Knowledge Forum in Seoul in 2005. "If the calls are coming in from the field [asking for help], your job is valuable. If the calls are going out, just gathering information, it may not be."

Immediate streamlining facilitates the performance-improvement process. For instance, we studied product development at one consumer-products company and discovered that several different people and functions—as many as five—believed they had final authority to make key decisions. Defining decision rights allowed the company to cut product-development time in half and at the same time to create more successful products. Some of those would-be decision makers could contribute input, agreement, or recommendations; some would actually perform the work. But only one person could be the final authority for any given decision.

Build capabilities. Companies undertaking major change need to rely on their strongest capabilities; they need to strengthen them and put them to work. Then they need to build or acquire capabilities that they lack, just as Genzyme did as it grew from start-up to well-established biotech company (see chapter 6).

At Emerson, for instance, then-CEO Chuck Knight realized early on that many of his businesses were in tough, commodity-like industries with increasingly aggressive low-cost global competitors. Understanding the first law, he saw that Emerson did not have strong enough capabilities in this area. So he launched a major initiative to create world-class—now legendary—cost-management capabilities, including an entire system and process for managing costs. Emerson has used this capability repeatedly in making successful acquisitions; it has been central to the company's success for many years. Danaher, a large industrial conglomerate headquartered in Washington, DC, has done something similar. It has acquired a large number of manufacturing companies and managed them according to what it calls the "Danaher Business System"—essentially, a set of capabilities related to cost control, tightly focused product development, and lean manufacturing. Over two decades Danaher has returned roughly 25 percent a year to shareholders.

When Chidsey came to Burger King, his team recognized that the company needed an unusual—and, they hoped, temporary—capability, namely the ability to structure workout plans for the nearly 3,000 restaurants that were in financial difficulty. Instead of creating an in-house department of workout specialists, they contracted the work out to independent teams. "Team members were experts at bankruptcy law, experts on how to deal with landlords and tax authorities, and so on," Chidsey explained. The teams cleaned up the system in just two years, closing restaurants that couldn't be fixed and restructuring the finances of many others.

Avoid the "Valley of Death"

Every performance-improvement program goes through phases. Let's say you are successful in laying out a vision and a compelling plan for change. Let's imagine, too, that people sign up for it. Now they will head out onto the battlefield with cries of enthusiasm. But before long, a reaction is likely to set in. Change is hard. Subordinates resist. The new ways of doing things are risky. The necessary resources may not be in place. People find it hard to make the transition from the old processes to the new ones. When that happens, some will begin to question the wisdom or feasibility of the vision.

This is an inflection point encountered by every major change effort, and it's precisely when most of them fail. They drop into the "Valley of Death" (see figure 8.2). People in most organizations have already seen this many times before, and so are cynical. They may begin referring to your

FIGURE 8.2

Leaders Can Help People Sustain Their Commitment to Change

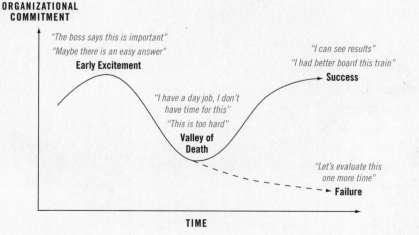

efforts as the "Program of the Month." They may tell one another, "This, too, will pass," accompanied by a knowing look or a rolling of the eyes.

This is the point that will test the leadership of your team the most. Listen closely to the objections, and seek out new perspectives. Check to be sure you have the consensus you need among your key people. But don't shrink from taking actions that reinforce your message. Remove people from their positions if they are obstructing the change. Visibly reward someone who has broken through the wall of resistance. Find success stories and hold them up as an ensign to the rest of the organization, particularly those that mark specific milestones in the plan. Finally, be sure to paint the vision of where you are going over and over again, so that the organization can taste success and renew its enthusiasm. The whole process will require enormous effort, and it will need the support of your entire core team. Do not flag. This is a time for maximum effort to avoid the pitfalls and traps so many change efforts fall into. If you are successful, the inflection point will turn upward, and the discretionary energy unleashed in the organization can be enormous. At that point, the change process should become self-sustaining.

OPERATE

To operate is to execute—to get things done. Here's an outline of the types of activities you'll need to focus on to make the changes happen.

Launch the Initiatives, Rack Up Quick Wins, and Celebrate

We have suggested that you pursue just three, four, or five action imperatives—no more. You may be wondering: how can you change a large organization by focusing on such a small number of priorities?

The answer is that you can't change an organization by focusing on a *large* number of priorities. Too many priorities are really no priorities at all. A small, targeted list of imperatives, by contrast, concentrates people's minds. It helps them understand where to put their efforts. It also allows you to focus your investments on just those objectives, rather than spreading funds like peanut butter throughout the organization. Differential resource allocation shows that you are putting your money where your mouth is. It reinforces the message that these three, four, or five imperatives are what really matter right now.

Then, too, an imperative can be a big, bold set of objectives that cascades throughout the organization, translating into a variety of specific initiatives and creating the possibility of substantial change everywhere. Look at Malaysia Airlines's turnaround plan. Idris Jala and his team laid out just five imperatives. One they called "Flying to win customers," meaning reconfiguring the airline's network and product portfolio to ensure that it could be a top-tier player in every market it served. A second was "Mastering operational excellence," which included both greater reliability and higher productivity. A third was "Financing and aligning the business on [the] P&L." This imperative involved creating a world-class finance organization "that ensures true financial accountability, transparency, and performance orientation in our business."

Jala's fourth imperative was "Unleashing talents and capabilities" by building a performance-oriented, cross-functional culture; and the fifth was "Winning coalitions," a reflection of the fact that a national airline is a political entity and needs support from the government as well as from other stakeholders.

These are big objectives, but look at how they cascade throughout the organization over time. Take the first imperative, flying to win customers, which spawned several specific initiatives. Malaysia Airlines would change its orientation to focus on leisure travelers first, business travelers second—"we will fly only where there are large attractive flows of leisure customers." It would shift from largely point-to-point routes to a hub-and-spoke system, with a major hub in Kuala Lumpur. Over the longer term it would move toward smaller aircraft with greater seat density, and it would focus on lowering its sales and marketing costs through greater reliance on the Internet. These goals established a context for many other objectives, such as assessing the profitability of individual routes and taking appropriate actions. The goals effectively created a series of marching orders for the relevant managers and employees.

John Taylor created something similar at Borealis, the plastics company. When he arrived in 2001, he found an organization that was losing money and was close to breaching its banking covenants. Its cost base was high, its strategy unclear, its focus on customers inadequate, and its safety record mediocre. Taylor promptly developed what he dubbed the "9Q Plan," a series of broad initiatives designed to improve performance over the next nine quarters. Taylor set targets for safety ("I simply don't want anyone to get hurt in an organization for which I am responsible—and I have learned that really safe plants give you very good financial results"). He established a goal of 11 percent after tax for return on capital employed. Other targets and corresponding initiatives were designed to improve productivity, alter the product mix, and bring the company closer to the customer.

The 9Q program became a "brand" within the organization, a widely understood symbol of the company's turnaround, with imperatives for every facility and every employee. A critical element of the program was the countdown: results against the targets were tracked and announced every quarter, and the "ticking clock" (nine, eight, seven . . .) kept the pressure on and reinforced the sense of urgency throughout the company. When Borealis achieved its 9Q objectives, the stage was set for a still-broader revamping of the company's overall strategy.

Find quick wins. Every plan needs to include "quick wins"—visible actions that are achievable within twelve to eighteen months or sooner, and that will build support for longer-term performance improvement. Knowlton's quick wins included rapid divestiture of business units that were not part of his long-term plan for Morgan Crucible. The sales bolstered the company's cash position and staved off the threat of insolvency; they also signaled the entire organization that this was no longer business as usual. Malaysia Airlines launched a series of annual "travel fairs," discount-sales campaigns that created buzz, rewarded customers, and generated millions of dollars in incremental net income after tax. Quick wins like these have an immediate financial impact. They also boost credibility and generate momentum.

Quick wins are doubly important when the long-term goals are particularly ambitious. Providence mayor Cicilline came into office with five major priorities: government integrity, strong neighborhoods, great schools, safe streets, and a dynamic economy. These were, and are, major issues, and significant improvements might take years. But some things the mayor could do right away, even as he was eliminating the budget deficit he had inherited. Under his objective of creating strong neighborhoods, for instance, he gathered data on services such as cleaning up the parks and tending to the city's trees. (The forestry department had a huge backlog of citizen requests for services on trees.) The data allowed Cicilline to analyze the city's shortcomings in these areas and make plans for more efficient use of personnel and equipment. Soon more trash cans were in place, the parks were being cleaned twice as often as before, and the backlog of untended trees had been eliminated.

Celebrate. Recognize and celebrate your achievements along the way. Successes foster a sense of accomplishment, signal that the organization can really achieve ambitious new objectives, and help dissolve resistance. They can be used as case studies, showing people how to achieve results. Individuals who have led successes and those who have contributed should be singled out for recognition and reward. "Celebrating victories along the way is an amazingly effective way to keep people engaged on the whole journey," write Jack and Suzy Welch. "Such small successes are chances to congratulate the team and boost spirits for the challenges ahead."[8]

In the 1990s, Kevin Ryan and his team led a turnaround of Wesley Jessen, a maker of specialty contact lenses, nearly tripling the company's revenue and growing net income to 8 percent of sales in just two years. Ryan, like our other CEOs, was a firm believer in a simple strategy. "We had four statements, seven words," he told our colleague Stan Pace. "They were: 'Build volume. Spend effectively. Be accountable. Cash.' This is what we all have to do." Another key to Ryan's success was celebration of successes: "a 'victory board' by the cafeteria celebrated new ad campaigns and sales achievements and displayed pictures of Hollywood movie stars wearing Wesley Jessen contacts in their movies."[9]

Many companies we know have successfully utilized best-demonstrated-practices techniques to create quick wins and celebrate successes. As Jim Haas of National Steel explains it:

Most people want to be—and want to look like—heroes to their peers. Getting them to share their best practices with appropriate recognition among their colleagues is about a hundred times more effective than only boring in on the areas with the worst practices and performance. That just makes people feel bad, and besides, they seldom have the total solution. But most departments have some best practice to share—even the "worst" performers. The key is getting them to showcase their best practice and to make as many heroes as you can early on in the process. This will eventually drive out the worst practices.

Don't get distracted. A corollary of focusing on just a few major initiatives is that you cannot do everything you might want to do. This was a recurrent theme among our interviewees. "I think the hardest part was not so much identifying the five core priorities," said Mayor Cicilline, "because I think they would be your core mission in most cities. The challenge was, What do you do with the other issues?" At Burger King, Chidsey was acutely aware of all the things he and his team couldn't do while they focused on key imperatives such as the new-product pipeline and franchisee relations. He knew the company needed a new broiler design. He knew that Burger King's restaurants were too expensive to build. Nearly all of the company's problems were in its U.S. network, so his team was unable to devote much attention to operations in Europe and elsewhere. His attitude? "Yes, I know that's important, but we can get to that later." And in fact the company did get to these concerns later, once the more urgent problems had been resolved.

Hold People Accountable, and Make the Tough Decisions

Another recurrent theme among our interviewees was the lack of accountability they found in the organizations they took over. People were allowed to get away with underperformance. Metrics and procedures used to gauge performance were poor or nonexistent. Toys "R" Us was a prime example. "There were no good measurements or performance standards," Jerry Storch told us. "People didn't receive regular performance reviews."

Use fact-based accountability. Holding people accountable doesn't have to mean yelling at them. Instead, establish a nonnegotiable process for overseeing the process of change. It should include clear plans of action linked to the critical imperatives, with frequent review and immediate resolution of issues when necessary by the team in charge. If something doesn't happen, the team confronts it directly—no avoiding reality or hoping for miracles. The approach should be one of solving problems, not punishing. A rigorous, fact-based assessment can identify the reasons for failure. The team can then develop a plan of action to recover the lost ground. Jürgen von Kuczkowski, former CEO of Vodafone Germany, described just such a process when we spoke with him. The company had a special task force for customer satisfaction, both external and internal. The results came in every month (later, every quarter), and the team sat down to examine them. Negative results generated no recriminations, just a plan of action to fix them.

At Malaysia Airlines, Jala has developed an interesting system for ensuring accountability. Wherever possible, he creates mini–profit-and-loss statements (P&Ls) with one person responsible for each. Each route, for instance, might have its own P&L. (In some of the Shell divisions that he ran before joining the airline, each customer had its own P&L.) "Once you start to 'personalize' the P&L in this manner," he says, "you transfer the responsibilities and accountabilities down the line. You get many CEOs in the company—so it's not just the fellow at the top who is worried."

Monthly meetings at the airline review these mini-P&Ls, and allow teams working on each initiative to report exactly what they have done and what its effect will be on the overall P&L. The meetings create accountability not just to the boss but to peers: "You can't have one guy saying, 'You know, I keep on not doing anything.' He can't keep saying that because his colleagues will ask him the question, 'Why?' " Weekly meetings of the management team serve as interim checkpoints, and Jala himself monitors results closely. In 2006, for example, the airline's cash flow was a pressing issue. The laboratory team on cash flow broke down projected improvement by activity—sales of specific assets, better borrowing terms, efforts to generate more revenue per passenger, and so on—and assigned responsibility for each one. Jala himself tracked their progress in minute detail, firing off e-mails when someone fell behind. At 5:30 p.m. every day, he got a report on exactly how much cash the airline had in every bank account all over the world.

Work with the passengers, get rid of the drillers. Over time, you will inevitably encounter opposition. The best thing is to confront opponents with open dialogue, once again using facts and data rather than emotion to make your case. Be sure the organizational structure isn't somehow facilitating opposition, for example by keeping one department siloed and away from the field of play. And be sure that the incentives are aligned properly so that people are rewarded for the right actions.

Even in the best of circumstances, though, not everyone will be pulling their oar. If they're passengers, they need extra attention. Usually, other rowers can help develop the passengers to the point where they pick up an oar. This is a critical part of your organizational-development efforts, and you can marshal all the training, incentive, and performance-assessment tools your organization has at its disposal. Your top rowers must take on the task of coaching and developing the passengers, or else determining that they will not make it as a part of the new team.

If you find more drillers, however, they obviously need to go, right now, regardless of where they may be in the organization. Managers and employees who are trying to change need to see that unsupportive or destructive colleagues will face stark consequences. Nothing is so demoralizing, after the healthy debate has taken place and the course has been set, as breaking your back to make an initiative happen, then seeing that someone who has been working at cross-purposes gets off scot-free.

Richard Crawford of Cambridge Industries explains this need bluntly and graphically:

> You have to make sure that everybody understands you mean what you say, that the rules are changing. You'll always get somebody that is mucking up what you want—that wants to stay with the old ways and in many ways may try to undermine you. The first thing you've got to do is [fire] the guy. You've got to get rid of him. So that everybody else will say, "Hey, it really has changed. He really does expect us to do what he said he did."

[In our company] nobody's going to be mad at you if you make a mistake, but when you violate the fundamentals of what's best for the business, then you are not going to be here.

John Taylor replaced his CFO and HR director early on. At Borealis, he said, "This had never really been done before. It caused some shock waves." Mayor Cicilline dismissed three top officials in the city's department of communications when he found that the department had no accounting for cell phones, city vehicles, spending, or overtime.

Nearly every CEO we spoke with made a similar point. One said, "Rowers make more rowers out of passengers. But drillers make holes."

Put Explicit Cues in Place

As general manager, you give off dozens of cues to your managers and employees every day, and not just by what you say but by what you do. You meet with one person and not with another. You work on topic A rather than topic B. Your calendar reflects your priorities: it indicates what you feel is worth your time. When you are trying to improve a business, only one thing is worth your time: activities that help you reach your point of arrival. If you focus only on those things, others in the organization will focus only on them as well. You will be sending the right message, day in and day out, to the people you're depending on to help you. Attending too many Rotary Club lunches or executive conferences/golf trips may send the wrong message to your organization.

There are other cues you can give as well. The people who worked at Morgan Crucible's headquarters both before and after Warren Knowlton became CEO noticed some differences. Under Knowlton's leadership, the staff was now in open-plan offices ("so that people would have to communicate with each other"). Internal boards, each of which met regularly, were eliminated. Knowlton and his team called meetings whenever they needed to talk about issues, rather than keeping to a schedule of meetings every six weeks. Meetings lasted ninety minutes rather than five or six hours. The cafeteria was closed, as we noted earlier. Knowlton gave the women who worked in the cafeteria £250 apiece out of his own pocket (and a handwritten note thanking them for their hard work) in addition to their normal severance payments from the company. ("It wasn't their fault we screwed up," he said.) Every one of these actions was a cue: things are going to be different around here.

As part of his campaign to repair relationships with Burger King's franchisees, John Chidsey emphasized to his staff that franchisees were the customers, and were to be referred to as such. (Burger King's ultimate consumers were "guests" or "end users.") "Our customer is the franchisee," he said to us. "We are here to give them better tools, better equipment, better training. It literally reached the point where I would fine people a dollar for every time they talked about the end user as the customer." Chidsey also began doing things like taking top-performing franchisees to the Masters Tournament or the Super Bowl—gestures that were unheard of in the company up to that point. Again, these were all cues about the importance of franchisee relationships in a business that was 90 percent conducted through franchised restaurants.

You can also use explicit cues to focus attention on one particular change initiative. A classic example took place in the 1990s at American Standard, the New Jersey–based manufacturer of plumbing fixtures, air-conditioning systems, and automotive products. Then-CEO Mano Kampouris had launched an improvement initiative aimed at doubling inventory turns, with the goal of liberating substantial amounts of cash and reducing costs. He used a set of principles known as Demand Flow® technology, which are similar to Lean Six Sigma techniques. Teams scrutinized every activity and cost element with the principal goal of reducing cycle times, eliminating waste and idle time in the manufacturing and distribution processes, and improving customer order-to-delivery times (fill rates).

Kampouris had little lapel pins made up, in the shape of a target with the letters TNT—for "Twice Net Turns"—printed over the bull's-eye. Employees wore them. Visitors, too. At times, if visitors forgot to wear their pins, they would be reminded by employees who saw them. Of course, it wasn't just the pins. Every employee also went through rigorous training programs in the principles of Demand Flow technology. There were signs throughout the buildings showing the TNT symbols and tracking progress against the targets. American Standard achieved its inventory goals; in fact, some divisions had close to zero net working capital, with inventory turns in the mid-to-high teens, a level unheard of at the time in heavy manufacturing businesses. Many companies visited American Standard to find out how they were achieving such unprecedented levels of performance—visits that were highly motivating to the entire organization.

Later, Kampouris mounted a similar campaign to increase net earnings ("Twice Net Earnings," or TNE) through organic growth and international expansion. That worked too. Never underestimate the power of cues.

TRACK

What's measured is managed. It's a cliché, but it's true. Great managers assume that they will track key indicators relentlessly—and that everyone else in the organization will, too. At De Beers Consolidated Mines, every employee can see production figures as well as other key metrics on his or her computer. The scoreboard is color coded: red, for instance, indicates that the organization is behind its target. Why include production figures even for office workers? "Everyone in this organization must understand we need to produce diamonds to stay in business," says managing director David Noko. "When people walk in, they know you are counting the very thing that brings you revenue."

Measure Performance

You, of course, want to measure the three or four key indicators that will lead you to your point of arrival. These are your Killer ABC metrics, and a dashboard on every executive's desk should show them.

Create well-structured dashboards. Your car's dashboard doesn't show everything you might possibly want to know about your vehicle's operation, only the important things. A business dashboard is the same. The ideal is a simple page that you as general manager can look at regularly to determine where you are on your road to results. Like Noko, you may want to color-code or shade it to indicate what's on track and what isn't. But it should include only the handful of metrics that matter to achieving your goals—basic indicators such as net profit, relative market share, quality and cost performance, and customer-service levels (see figure 8.3).

To be sure, it's always tempting to add more metrics. But doing so is almost always counterproductive. Instead, structure a cascade of metrics so that everything the organization measures flows into the critical few that show up on your dashboard. Individuals will then have their own goals and metrics, and they should learn how theirs roll up into the overall indicators for the entire organization. If cash is one of the key corporate measures, for instance, then days sales outstanding will be a critical metric for the relevant people in the finance department. With this approach, a single page can tell you most of what you need to know about your performance. If performance is not where you want it to be, you will be able to drill down and uncover the problem areas.

The right measurements by themselves can help drive performance. When Bill McDermott became CEO of SAP Americas, he began to track the sales reps' performance for every quarter instead of for the year. That abruptly altered the reps' traditional approach of counting on a big fourth quarter to pull them through the year. He also expected the reps' pipeline to total three times their quota on a rolling basis, quarter by quarter, and half of the pipeline had to be assigned to one of SAP's implementation partners, such as IBM Global Services. These two measurement changes helped boost the reps' performance substantially.[10]

FIGURE 8.3

Example Dashboard Built on Four Strategic Cornerstones

CUT COSTS TO COMPETE	GIVE CUSTOMERS WHAT THEY VALUE	PULL TOGETHER, WIN TOGETHER	BUILD FINANCIAL FOUNDATION FOR THE FUTURE
Competitive variable cost structure	*Profitable geographies and segments*	*World-class labor management*	*Sustainable profitability, viability*
● Operational excellence	● Network optimization	◐ Communications	● Revenue growth
○ Capability sourcing	● Attractive value proposition by segment	○ Culture, trust	◐ Expense management
◐ Labor relief (rate, rules, scope)	◐ Product upgrades	○ Aligned incentives and partnership	◐ Balance sheet restructuring

Key: ● = Ahead of Target   ◐ = On Track   ○ = Behind Target

If done well, metrics will cascade throughout the organization and will be linked to an individual owner to ensure accountability. That person may be a senior executive, the head of a business unit or functional department, an operations manager, the worker on the line, or the rep in front of the customer. Success by each accountable owner will lead to the overall success of the enterprise.

Act on the Results

It should go without saying: the purpose of measurement is to facilitate appropriate action. Depending on what the metrics reveal, you may need to take three different kinds of action.

Bank success (and financial results). Winston Churchill once said, "However beautiful the strategy, you should occasionally look at the results." If your interim goals are being achieved and the numbers are on track, you need to make sure that you are consolidating and institutionalizing the gains. Too often, things have a way of slipping. The gain in market share may not last when a competitor counterattacks. The cost improvements slip away as raw-materials prices rise. There are many other such leaks. So you will want to monitor the progress and the current momentum on the variables you are tracking for signs of slippage. And you should update the budgets and the short-term targets with the newly achieved performance levels as the new baseline.

Competing interests and complacency can sometimes interfere with hitting the milestones. One clothing company, for instance, set a target of increasing its gross margin, and a sourcing team achieved a 15 percent savings on fabric costs. The designers then decided that they wanted to upgrade the trim on some product lines, and the marketers wanted to cut the price of the premium brand to increase sales. Neither of these was part of the company's strategic plan, and the general manager had to veto the proposals to maintain the improvements in gross margin.

Trigger contingency plans. If your organization doesn't hit its performance milestones, you should know when to trigger your contingency plans.

Chuck Knight at Emerson always required his managers to have contingency plans in place in case of a downturn in the market. They could thus take prompt corrective action if their businesses were in danger of missing the targets established in the planning process. As it happened, it was Knight's successor, David Farr, who missed the company's single biggest performance target and had to respond accordingly.

When Farr took over in October 2000, Emerson had a remarkable and possibly unparalleled track record: forty-three consecutive years of annual increases in earnings and earnings per share. At first the string seemed likely to continue, as Farr's first two quarters brought some of the best results in the company's history. But then Farr noticed trouble in the metrics he was tracking. "The monthly presidents' operating reports and other indicators revealed the onset of a sharp downturn. Orders declined rapidly and customer shipment requests were being pushed out. The bottom fell out of the telecommunications equipment market, and demand throughout our businesses worldwide began to soften and decline—an extremely unusual and unlikely occurrence."

Farr monitored the situation and decided he had to take actions "far beyond those already under way." But what should be done? Maybe he and his team could keep the earnings string going by, for example, delaying or reducing investments. But they quickly decided that doing so would harm the long-term prospects of the company. Emerson needed to invest in emerging markets such as China, India, Eastern Europe, and Russia. It needed to continue investing in technology as the company shifted to a more sophisticated mix of products. So Farr and the team developed new plans for the following two years. They would take a charge of $377 million against earnings in 2001. They would restructure the company, including a shift in Emerson's asset base and business makeup. "Relying on the plans and disciplines of the management process, we rationalized current operations, built new facilities in low-cost locations, and accelerated some new-product development and engineering programs and projects while terminating others," Farr later wrote. Emerson divested ten divisions and made several acquisitions. It repositioned key executives. "Everyone knew that we were on a journey involving significant changes to Emerson's total cost structure and global competitive position."

The results? Emerson remained profitable, and its stock price generally outperformed competitive benchmarks. "Best of all, after economic conditions began to pick up in the late summer of 2003, we've been growing rapidly—as is evident from our recent very strong performance." [11]

Raising the Bar: The Carter's Story

And what do you do if you achieve your point of arrival—or if you see the numbers tracking so well that you know you'll hit your goals ahead of schedule? Reset the bar, higher. Focus on a new set of challenges. Take your point of arrival as your new point of departure, and repeat the whole process.

Most general managers don't get a chance to do this. If they are successful, they move on to a better job. If they are unsuccessful, they just move on. A lucky few do get the chance. Fred Rowan and his entire senior management team at Carter's have been together for close to fifteen years at this writing, and have taken the company from one set of challenges and opportunities to another. In our experience this is a rare tenure for a successful management team. The group has truly built a full-potential culture; its accomplishments show that performance improvement at successful companies is a never-ending process.

Rowan became CEO of Carter's in 1992. At that point the company was in a classic turnaround situation. Sales and profits were down. Warehouses were stuffed with unsold inventory, costs were escalating, and new competitors were encroaching on Carter's turf. "We were the last fully integrated company of our kind in the United States," Rowan said to our colleague Chris Zook, "with plants that made yarn, plants that did cutting and sewing, and even an embroidery plant. Our systems were mostly manual. We were facing competitors producing offshore, with lean product lines, fast cycle times, and newer information systems. The business was near death operationally." [12]

In the first few years Rowan and his team put Carter's back on its feet. They reduced inventory. They got costs under control and put the company on a firm financial footing. That first phase lasted two to three years. Then they raised the bar. In the next phase they revamped Carter's product line, bringing out new products while significantly reducing the number of SKUs. They also developed a "mainstream" sales channel—department stores such as Kohl's, JCPenney, and Sears—that the company had previously stayed away from. That phase, too, lasted about three years.

In 1997 Rowan once more raised the bar: now he focused on revamping and expanding Carter's retail stores. In hindsight, Rowan says he wishes he had been more aggressive on moving production overseas in that period as well: "We weren't bold enough in those years." From 1999 to 2002, however, Carter's took on that challenge. It closed its domestic plants and opened up sourcing in China and elsewhere. These moves prepared it to move into the discount retail channel with a new brand for Target. It introduced the brand in December 1999 and rolled it out in January 2000. When Wal-Mart approached Carter's, it was ready for the retailing giant. From 2002 to 2005 the company ramped up its business with Wal-Mart.

In 2005 Rowan saw yet another new opportunity. OshKosh B'Gosh, another leading children's clothing company, was up for sale, and Carter's bought it, supported by Berkshire Partners, which at the time was Carter's private-equity sponsor. But OshKosh needed improvement. Its product line was too complex, its brand diluted. Many of its retail stores were losing money, and its product costs were too high. As Rowan and the team began to turn OshKosh around, the process forced them to reexamine Carter's, because the brands had to be positioned with each other in a complementary way. Carter's would be "soft and emotional," they decided, OshKosh "active and rugged." They designed the product and the packaging accordingly. "If you can't tell right away whether a child is wearing *Carter's* or *OshKosh*," the company said, "we're not doing our job."

Rowan has led Carter's to a resounding success. Sales have grown steadily, from $227 million in 1992 to $1.34 billion in 2006, roughly a 13 percent compound annual growth rate. Earnings before interest and taxes have grown from $6 million to $165 million over the same time frame, a 28 percent growth rate.[13] Shareholder value has increased by a factor of fifteen since Rowan took over, and by a factor of 9.5 just since the company's 2003 IPO. Yet Rowan continues to change Carter's—and continues to hold it to ever-rising standards. In its 2006 annual report—a year when the company's sales grew 20 percent and adjusted earnings 24 percent—Carter's bluntly gave itself a grade of C in some of its operations and an overall performance grade of B. "We were disappointed with Carter's 5 percent [retail] sales growth," the report said, referring to growth in Carter's own retail stores. "We changed too many things too quickly." With OshKosh, "we were overly optimistic and projected having better product in place for our Fall 2006 line." In 2007, Carter's was continuing to work on the OshKosh division. It was revitalizing its brand strategy for both divisions, renewing its product lines, and again reinventing its retail operations.

We suspect that Fred Rowan would feel at home with the messages of this chapter. He knows how to focus on a few critical imperatives, for example. The slogan "Trust the power of fewer things" appears all over the company, and is repeated daily by managers in one context or another. He also understands the importance of inspiring the troops and tracking progress. "I probably spend a third of my time communicating with my managers about our plans and reviewing progress," he says. "The entire senior management team has meetings every Tuesday and Wednesday to review what happened last week with all of our key customers and every distribution channel, the status of our delivery performance, and the progress we have made on product designs and brand enhancements for the consumer, since these are the lifeblood of our business." Rowan also understands what change entails. When he launched a major initiative a few years ago to "elevate the Carter's brand" in the minds of consumers, he made a major commitment of financial and human resources; the action imperatives materially changed the priorities of every single department in the company and reinforced the message that winning the consumers' hearts and minds (and share of wallet) was one of the cornerstones of the new point of arrival.

Rowan, in short, has reinvented Carter's repeatedly. His point of arrival has always become a new point of departure. Rowan summarized his approach for us:

We have always held ourselves to a higher performance standard, and we are never satisfied for very long with what we have achieved in the past—there is always another hill to climb, and that is the wellspring of our passion and motivation. Customers and consumers are more demanding now than ever before, and we must continue to focus aggressively on our effectiveness in meeting their needs and our efficiency in doing so to stay ahead of our competitors. We will not accept anything less than full-potential performance.

If you can successfully steer your organization down its road to results, your point of arrival can be a new starting point. You can raise the bar again and again, just as Carter's has done several times in the last fifteen years.

MAKING THE HANDOFF

Churchill offers a good deal of wisdom for this chapter: "Success," he said, "is never final." Even Fred Rowan will have to retire some day—and when he does he will face the challenge that other general managers are likely to face after only a few years on the job: handing the organization off to a successor.

Given the brevity of most general managers' tenure, management transitions are happening all the time, and so play an essential role in determining an organization's long-term success. A study by the firm Booz Allen Hamilton found that transitions often lead to a drop in stock-market performance—0.8 percent below average for planned successions and 12.6 percent below average for forced successions.[14] A CEO can do a great job during his tenure, but if he fails at setting his successor up to succeed, he won't leave much of a legacy.

Don't underestimate the value of such a legacy. Of course it can be tempting to hope that your successor doesn't quite measure up to you; the contrast, you might think, will make you look better. But it doesn't work that way. If your successor fails, your own reputation will be tarnished. People will ask questions: did you manage the business to make yourself look good, meanwhile hollowing it out and leaving your successor with an empty sack? "With increasing regularity, executives are being called back by their former companies to resume the chief executive's job," wrote Kenneth W. Freeman, former CEO of Quest Diagnostics. "But think twice be-

THE ROAD TO RESULTS

fore you do it. It means not only that your successor failed, but that you did, too—at succession planning."[15]

If the business continues to grow and prosper after your departure, by contrast, your portrait will continue to hang in the lobby. You can take pride in knowing that you are continuing to contribute to shareholder value and rewarding careers for employees. A seamless handoff can enable a company to continue its growth trajectory with scarcely a blip on Wall Street. The 2006 transition at PepsiCo from Steven Reinemund to Indra K. Nooyi, for instance, was remarkably smooth, and the stock even rose slightly. As Walter Lippmann once wrote, "The final test of a leader is that he leaves behind in other men the conviction and the will to carry on."

But management transitions are often problematic. As we noted in chapter 1, about 40 percent of CEOs seem to last less than two years on average. Other senior executives and general managers often have an equally short tenure.

Why should this be? On the face of things, you would expect most new CEOs to succeed. Individuals chosen to lead a company invariably have exceptional abilities and a long list of accomplishments. If they didn't, they would never make the short list of candidates. If they come from outside a company, they are typically nominated and vetted by sophisticated, highly competent executive search firms. If they are insiders, they have performed well for a period of years under close scrutiny by their superiors. All new CEOs, whether insiders or outsiders, are ultimately selected by outgoing chief executives and by the board members they will be reporting to— savvy and experienced business leaders every one. Yet many of these new CEOs fail to deliver what was expected of them. We suspect that the failure rates of general managers below the level of CEO are more or less comparable. The evidence we reviewed in chapter 1, indeed, suggests that general managers are turning over even faster than CEOs.

Most of the writing and thinking on management succession focuses on two solutions to this puzzle. One is the process of choosing successors. In the case of CEOs, for instance, analysts have pointed out that nearly half of large companies have no meaningful succession plan. "Even those that have plans aren't happy with them," observed Ram Charan in *Harvard*

Business Review. "The Corporate Leadership Council (CLC), a human-resource research organization, surveyed 276 large companies last year and found that only 20 percent of responding HR executives were satisfied with their top-management succession processes."[16]

A second factor singled out for attention is the personality and skills of the prospective leader. Boards, people in the field point out, often focus on the wrong traits and ignore more important ones. "In our experience . . . CEOs, presidents, executive vice presidents, and other top-level people often fall into the trap of making decisions about candidates based on lopsided or distorted information," write Melvin Sorcher and James Brant, two consultants who specialize in helping companies make such judgments. "Frequently, they fall prey to the 'halo effect': overvaluing certain attributes while undervaluing others."[17]

We believe that both these factors are important: companies do need better succession planning, and they do need to learn to make better judgments about candidates than they seem to do now. But if you read the above comments carefully, the focus is on the attributes of the leader who is brought in. Our belief is that these attributes are necessary but not sufficient. We think a different kind of variable is equally important.

An outgoing CEO who understands the four laws—and has used them to establish a point of departure, a point of arrival, and a road to results—leaves her successor with a huge advantage. The entire organization has learned to operate in a particular way. People understand the experience curve and have the data to tell the new leader where the organization stands on it. They know their market position, and they are familiar with assessing and tracking their industry's profit pools. They have probably already attacked complexity in product line, processes, and organization—and they are likely to know how to continue reducing it.

When a new leader takes over in this environment, the old point of arrival becomes his point of departure. He doesn't have to start from scratch gathering the twelve must-have facts; he only has to update the data. He will find it easier to build consensus around a full-potential diagnosis and a new point of arrival. He will find it easier to map out and communicate a road to results. In short, he is set up to succeed. For the new CEO, it's the difference between taking a job in a country where you speak the language and one where you don't. You can get up to speed—and get the organization up to speed—a lot faster.

Warren Knowlton transformed Morgan Crucible in about three and a half years. If his predecessor had understood the four laws and even just gathered the data for a point of departure diagnosis, he told us, he could have accomplished what he did in half the time. Knowlton wasn't going to make the same mistake in handing the reins to his successor. He recruited a new CFO, Mark Robertshaw, about two years before he himself expected to leave the company, and he specifically sought out an individual who "had top-rate business skills and a broad perspective about what was needed to grow the bottom line." Working closely with the board, he then created a new position combining the CFO and COO roles and appointed Robertshaw to fill it. "I made sure that my successor and I worked on critical yet discrete objectives—and where the two came together, that we had a common front." When Knowlton announced his retirement, the board appointed Robertshaw as CEO. Robertshaw has continued to lead the company in strong performance since then: Morgan Crucible enjoyed more than 11 percent top-line growth in 2006 with a 33 percent increase in annual pretax profit. In mid-2007 the stock hit 318 pence, an increase of 21 percent from the maximum it reached under Knowlton.

The importance of speaking the same language is borne out by the fact that new CEOs who are insiders do better, on average, than new CEOs who are outsiders. In North America, 55 percent of all outside CEOs who left their jobs in 2003 were asked to resign by their boards. The comparable figure for insiders was 34 percent. In Europe, the figures were 70 percent for outsiders, 55 percent for insiders.[18] Imagine now if the insider is schooled in the four laws and the journey we have suggested in this book. She can hit the ground running. One reason for PepsiCo's smooth transition was that Nooyi, who had been president and CFO of the company for more than five years before becoming CEO, had played a critical role in PepsiCo's strategic moves throughout Reinemund's tenure. "She has been very involved with every major decision PepsiCo has made over the past five-plus years and therefore we expect this transition to be very smooth," wrote one analyst.[19]

NOW WE OURSELVES MUST MAKE A DIFFERENT KIND OF HANDOFF: we have said what we wanted to say in this book, and we hope you will take our message and apply it in your organization. We think it will help you become a great manager and improve your organization's performance.

Once more, we want to put this message in context. These four laws are some of the key fundamentals of business. They reveal patterns and regularities that you must understand if you are to be effective. The diagnosis of your point of departure and the mapping out of a point of arrival and a road to results are how you put your understanding of the laws to work. The process shows you how to gather the data you need and craft a strategy that will get you where you are going.

We have no illusions that all of business can somehow be boiled down to these laws and precepts. Business is one of the most intricate endeavors on earth—one reason why it is so fascinating to study and so rewarding to pursue. Our own plan of attack requires that you gather immense amounts of data and that you dive deeply into the particular points of analysis that are most important to your business. But there's still plenty of surface that we haven't even scratched. The books about leadership and about the attributes of great companies have much to teach us. So do those that map out cutting-edge new ideas. And so do the specialized books that plunge into the details of sales and marketing, say, or mergers and acquisitions. You need many kinds of ideas and information beyond what we have been able to lay out in one volume.

But there are a few things we want you to take away from this book. Just being a good leader is not enough. You can be a wonderful leader, the kind of person that people naturally want to follow—but if you don't develop a compelling view of where you're starting from and where you're going early in your tenure, you won't accomplish much. You may simply run out of time. Leading an organization that has been successful in the past isn't enough, either. The world is changing too fast. Look at the chief executives of IBM who preceded Lou Gerstner. They inherited and ran a company that had been the envy of the world, a paragon of technological innovation and managerial excellence. But by the time Gerstner got there, IBM was mired in a swamp of underperformance.

We believe the four laws provide the essential grounding you need to lead a company or any other organization effectively. They will help you avoid pitfalls and drive performance improvement. The laws are the basics of business; they are the equivalent of dribbling, passing, and shooting in basketball or soccer. As you master them, thinking about them will become second nature. As you develop a gut-level understanding of your point of departure and a vision of your point of arrival, you will be able to communicate it in a two-minute conversation. And as you design your road to results, you will be ensuring that you have put in place the necessary conditions for your organization to move ahead. None of this is easy. But if you do all of it well, your odds of success will rise dramatically. You will face the challenge of the breakthrough imperative, and you will master it.

> Every day you make progress. Every step may be fruitful. Yet there will stretch out before you an ever-lengthening, ever-ascending, ever-improving path. You know you will never get to the end of the journey. But this, so far from discouraging, only adds to the joy and glory of the climb.
>
> —WINSTON CHURCHILL

IMPLICATIONS FOR THE GENERAL MANAGER

- Plan: be sure you have defined your points of arrival and departure, build consensus around both, and reinforce the few critical initiatives that will get you from one to the other during your tenure.

- Lead: inspire the troops, align the leadership around the critical action imperatives, and build a culture that supports change.

- Operate: drive initiatives and quick wins and celebrate successes. Hold people rigorously accountable, and put explicit cues in place to reinforce your message. Put incentives in place that reinforce your key imperatives and richly reward performance.

- Track: measure your performance with dashboards, and act on the results—bank your successes, trigger your contingency plans when necessary, and raise the bar if you achieve your point of arrival.

- Prepare the handoff to your successor. Setting a point of arrival that conforms to the four laws and is realistic, compelling, and motivational may be the most important legacy you leave.

Research Methodology

This book is based on data from focused research, surveys, interviews, and analyses. The studies and methods are summarized in this appendix.

ADDITIONAL RESEARCH BASED ON THE *PROFIT FROM THE CORE* DATABASE

Purpose

To determine whether the CEOs of companies defined as sustained value creators (SVCs) were a significant and systematic factor in determining their companies' performance.

Method

In preparation for writing his first book, *Profit from the Core*, our colleague Chris Zook compiled a database for Bain & Company of 1,854 public companies in the G8 economies with sales over $500 million. The database, maintained and updated, was used most recently by Zook in his latest book, *Unstoppable*, and now contains 1,804 companies. Of these, only 202 qualify as SVCs. As Zook defines them, SVCs are companies with

1995 sales more than US$500 million; compound annual growth rates greater than 5.5 percent for revenue and profit in the years 1995 through 2005; and shareholder return greater than zero over the same period.

Focusing on these 202 companies, we first researched publicly available CEO start dates and departure dates in the years from 1995 to 2005. A total of 413 CEOs led those 202 companies during the period. Next, we examined stock-price performance compared with the relevant in-country index over the span of each CEO's tenure (or to December 2005, if that came first). On average, we found that the SVC CEOs outperformed their market index by a ratio of three to one.

Our team then investigated whether there were meaningful differences in stock price *during* a CEO's tenure. We found that for the first six months of a CEO's tenure, the SVCs' stock performance on average tracked the broader index very closely, at a ratio of 1.1 to 1.0. Stock performance then crept up steadily under the same CEO's leadership, requiring six years to outperform the broader index on average by two to one. It took the full average CEO tenure of nine years for the companies to outperform by three to one.

RESEARCH ON CEO DEPARTURES

Purpose

To identify whether CEOs leaving their company for performance-related reasons had apparently not adhered to one of the four laws.

Method

We analyzed data from Challenger, Gray & Christmas, an executive out-placement firm that tracks CEO departures.[1] Of 1,478 total CEO departures from U.S. companies in 2006, we randomly selected 225 for further study. Of these, 38 percent were deemed to be related to the CEO's performance (including disagreements with the board). That figure was comparable to the rate found in a similar study conducted by the consulting firm Booz Allen Hamilton.[2] Booz Allen found that 32 percent of a sample of

357 departures of CEOs who left their jobs in 2006 were performance related or due to disagreements with the board. (Other reasons for departures included mergers, regular transitions such as planned retirements,
health issues, and legal issues or wrongdoing.)

We then examined press articles, expert interviews, company Web
sites, and other public sources to analyze each of the performance-related
departures in greater depth. In 91 percent of the cases we found that CEOs
departing for performance-related reasons had not followed at least one of
the four laws described in this book, or had not taken actions consistent
with the laws. This sample has a 95 percent confidence level that the results
are accurate to plus or minus 10 percentage points.

INTERVIEWS WITH CEOS AND GENERAL MANAGERS

Purpose

To gather the wisdom, advice, and lessons learned from a cross-section of
the most consistently successful general managers of the last couple of
decades.

Method

We developed a long list of managers who had created substantial performance improvement in their organizations, including heads of nonprofits
and the mayor of Providence, Rhode Island. We compiled much of this list
by polling Bain partners who headed our offices or industry practices
about appropriate contacts in their geographies. The full list of interviewees follows.

Gerard Arpey, chairman and CEO, AMR Corp.
Elisabeth Babcock, CEO, Crittenton Women's Union
Greg Brenneman, CEO, Quiznos; former president and COO, Continental
    Airlines; former CEO, Burger King
John Chidsey, CEO, Burger King
David Cicilline, mayor, Providence, Rhode Island

Richard Crawford, CEO, The CrawfordGroup; former chairman, Cambridge
    Industries
Paul Fulton, retired president, Sara Lee Corp., Hanes
Pier Francesco Guarguaglini, chairman and CEO, Finmeccanica S.p.A.
Jim Haas, retired president, National Steel
Ralph Heath, executive vice president and COO,
    Lockheed Martin Aeronautics
Idris Jala, CEO, Malaysia Airlines
Mano Kampouris, retired CEO, American Standard
Jim Keyes, chairman and CEO, Blockbuster; former CEO, 7-Eleven Stores
Jim Yong Kim, cofounder, Partners In Health
Warren Knowlton, CEO, Graham Packaging; former CEO, Morgan Crucible
Wendy Kopp, founder and CEO, Teach For America
Kathleen Ligocki, former CEO, Tower Automotive; former president,
    Ford of Mexico
George Lorch, retired CEO, Armstrong
John Lundgren, chairman and CEO, The Stanley Works
Bill McDermott, president and CEO, SAP Americas and Asia Pacific Japan
Jacques Nasser, former CEO, Ford Motor
David Noko, managing director, De Beers Consolidated Mines
Kevin Rollins, former CEO, Dell
Mitt Romney, former CEO, Salt Lake Organizing Committee
Fred Rowan, CEO, Carter's
Gabe Schmergel, retired CEO, Genetics Institute
Hal Sperlich, former president, Chrysler
Gerald Storch, chairman and CEO, Toys "R" Us
John Taylor, CEO, Borealis
Philip Teel, corporate vice president and president,
    Northrop Grumman Ship Systems
Henri Termeer, chairman and CEO, Genzyme
Sol Trujillo, CEO, Telstra
Sunny Verghese, group managing director and CEO, Olam International
Jürgen von Kuczkowski, former CEO, Vodafone Germany
Bill Walczak, CEO, Codman Square Health Center
David Weidman, chairman and CEO, Celanese

Mike White, vice chairman, PepsiCo International
Meg Whitman, president and CEO, eBay

SURVEYS OF EXECUTIVES

Purpose

To develop quantitative evidence complementing the qualitative interviews. Our goal was to substantiate some of the key findings with more
comprehensive information.

Methods

1. A survey in January 2006 by Bain & Company, in partnership with
eRewards, of executives. Responses were received from 183 CEOs, chief
operating officers, and business-unit presidents from companies with
more than $500 million in annual sales. This detailed performance-
improvement survey covered a broad range of industries in North America. It assessed the respondents' usage of key performance-improvement
tools, and it asked their opinions on a variety of issues facing CEOs
today.

2. A survey in January 2005 by Bain & Company, in partnership with
the Economist Intelligence Unit. Responses were received from 960 executives internationally across industries. This survey was part of Bain's
multiyear research since 1993 on management tools and trends; it was
supplemented with follow-up interviews on the circumstances under
which various tools are most likely to produce results. One of the findings
was that 68 percent of executives globally believe that excessive complexity is raising costs and hindering growth. Among Asian executives, the
figure is 81 percent.

ANALYSIS OF PERFORMANCE IMPROVEMENT BY OTHER COMPANIES

Purpose

To examine the decisions and actions underlying substantial performance improvement at successful companies, and, conversely, to discover what had contributed to the underperformance of struggling or bankrupt businesses.

Method

We screened the top 1,000 publicly traded companies from public sources to find companies that had achieved or failed to achieve substantial performance improvement. For companies that passed the screen (outpaced the market overall and their respective industry; performance improvement correlated with CEO tenure), we did extensive research to examine CEO decisions and actions underlying substantial performance improvement. We supplemented this with examples from our own and other Bain partners' experience. For each company, we used one or more of the following sources to highlight specific examples:

- Company sources, including internal and external presentations

- Articles written about the company in business publications such as *Fortune, BusinessWeek, Forbes,* the *Wall Street Journal,* the *Economist,* and *Harvard Business Review*, in addition to industry and trade publications

- Books written about the company or the industry by leaders or outsiders

- Annual reports and financials

- Interviews with leaders, employees, ex-employees, analysts, private equity contacts, and so on

STOCK-PRICE INDICES FOR THE POSITIVE EXAMPLES USED IN THIS BOOK

Purpose

To document the stock-price performance of interviewees and positive examples chosen for this book.

Method

As described in the SVC research earlier in this appendix, for each positive example found in the book, we analyzed how stock price performed compared with the relevant in-country index over the span of a given general manager's tenure. On average, we found that the general managers that we interviewed and the other positive examples we researched for this book outperformed their market index by five to one during their tenure to date.

RESEARCH ON THE POWER OF RELATIVE MARKET SHARE

Purpose

To determine the overall power of the ROA/RMS chart and the power of the second law.

Method

Our work began with a review of the PIMS database, which has consistently shown that companies with greater market share across all industries have higher returns than companies with lower market share, as discussed in chapter 3. But the experience curve suggests that the key driver should be relative market share (RMS). So we did a detailed analysis of the relative market share and shareholder-return performance of 185 companies in thirty-three industries. We arrayed them against their true competitors using the correctly defined business, taking into account cost, customer, and competitor sharing. These data showed that companies with an RMS greater than 2.5 times that of their largest competitor earned, on average, a 28.5 percent return on capital, and that aggregations of companies in RMS groupings (greater than 2.5X, 1.3 to 2.4X, 0.6 to 1.2X, 0.3 to 0.6X, and less than 0.3X) fell neatly into an ROA/RMS band with those under 0.3X earning just 3.8 percent on capital on average, well below their cost of that capital. In fact, companies with the highest relative market share earned returns in excess of their cost of capital approximately 80 percent of the time. Those at the low end exceeded their cost of capital approximately 20 percent of the time.

RESEARCH ON THE IMPACT OF COMPLEXITY

Purpose

To determine whether complexity is correlated with positive or negative company performance.

Method

We examined 110 companies in seventeen industries, including both business-to-business and business-to-consumer: aerospace, airlines, automobile, cellular manufacturing, cellular service, chemicals, computer hardware, cosmetics, credit cards, fast food, medical equipment, mining/construction, mortgages, mutual funds, pharmaceutical, steel, and tires. We prioritized the complexity metric most relevant for each industry using three main criteria: value-chain analysis on where complexity shows up in an industry's operations; customer perceptions of complexity in each industry; and the availability of public data. For example, for fast-food restaurants, the complexity metric is the number of entrees on the menu. We researched the top six to nine companies within each industry where financials were publicly available. Figure A1.1 shows the actual data for a few of these industries: mutual funds, cosmetics, and automotive.

Having collected complexity data for all 110 companies and financials for the years 2000 to 2005, we used a multivariable linear regression model

FIGURE A1.1

Less Complex Businesses Grow More Quickly and Make More Money

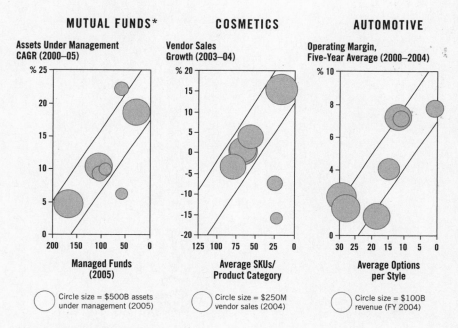

MUTUAL FUNDS*	COSMETICS	AUTOMOTIVE
Assets Under Management CAGR (2000–05)	Vendor Sales Growth (2003–04)	Operating Margin, Five-Year Average (2000–2004)
Managed Funds (2005)	Average SKUs/ Product Category	Average Options per Style
Circle size = $500B assets under management (2005)	Circle size = $250M vendor sales (2004)	Circle size = $100B revenue (FY 2004)

*Source: Company Web sites and financials
Top seven mutual funds companies in U.S. focusing on funds management as core business

to test the effect of complexity and size on revenue growth, triangulating through three methodologies. The findings of all three models were statistically significant.

As a brief statistics refresher, p-value is the probability that the result is due to chance rather than the hypothesis tested (when p is less than 0.05, the effect is statistically significant, translating to less than 5 percent likelihood that the effect is due to chance rather than the tested hypothesis). R^2 is the amount of variability in the outcome explained by all the predictors tested; it varies from 0 percent to 100 percent, where a higher R^2 indicates predictors with high explanatory power and accuracy (for example, $R^2 = .87$ means 87 percent of revenue growth is explained by the model). The coefficient measures how much of the outcome is explained by that predictor. The unstandardized coefficient indicates for every unit increase in predictor (for example, complexity), how much the outcome (revenue growth), will change by that coefficient amount.

- Model A: Complexity, size, and revenue growth measured in deciles; revenue growth measured across industries. A constant was included in the regression. Complexity coefficient = −0.24, $p<.001$, $R^2=.41$. Low-complexity companies grow 1.3 times faster than average-complexity companies.

- Model B: Complexity, size, and revenue growth measured in standardized scores; revenue growth measured within industry. A constant was included in the regression. Complexity coefficient = −0.34, $p<.001$, $R^2=.11$. Low-complexity companies grow 1.5 times faster than average-complexity companies.

- Model C: Complexity, size, and revenue growth measured in deciles; revenue growth measured across industries. A constant was not included in the regression. Complexity coefficient = −0.24, $p<.001$, $R^2=.87$. Low-complexity companies grow 1.5 times faster than average-complexity companies.

Overall, less complex companies grow 1.3 to 1.5 times faster than their average competitors. Average companies miss out on the possibility of 30 percent to 50 percent faster revenue growth. Complexity has nearly eight times more predictive power for growth than relative size, suggesting that low complexity is part of the pattern for a successful business.

Experience Curves

We have written this appendix to provide managers and their teams with brief guidelines for creating experience curves. We have also summarized our perspectives on a few special situations that often need to be considered.

GUIDELINES FOR CREATING AN EXPERIENCE CURVE

The experience curve, as described in chapter 2, shows how unit prices and costs generally decline as experience accumulates. The first step in creating such a curve is gathering the necessary data and determining the right "unit of experience." Often the unit of experience is straightforward—square feet of carpet for a carpet manufacturer, for example. But if costs and prices seem to be rising over time, it may be because you are neglecting what customers really value and thus not looking at the proper unit of experience. People who buy tires, for instance, aren't just buying a tire; they are buying a ride on a set of tires. If a company improves tires so that they deliver more miles per tire, the price of the tire may rise but the price per mile driven will decline. The experience curve in this case should reflect the price per mile driven.

Ideally, you would collect data going all the way back to the first year of experience. That's often impossible, of course, particularly for products that have been around for centuries. So go back as far as you can, and collect data from the earliest year possible. Then estimate prior years' production. We rely on a simple formula for this task. The formula is derived from a mathematical algorithm used to calculate the sum of a geometric series with a finite beginning. It assumes a constant growth rate, which is often not the case, so if you are able to get data on actual growth rates you should adjust accordingly. But for most industries you can get a reasonable estimate of prior experience as follows:

Total experience prior to year 1 = (2/3) ×
(volume in year 1/CAGR), where CAGR is the compound
annual growth rate of volume from year 1 to the latest year

Let's imagine, for example, that widgets were made before year 2000, but that no one collected production data prior to that year. There were 100 widgets produced in the year 2000 and 240 produced in the year 2005. So the compound annual growth rate for that period is 19.1 percent. The formula shows the following:

Total experience prior to year 2000 =
(2/3) × (100/0.191) = about 350 widgets

It's always wise to reality-check your calculations through your own and other expert estimates. In our example—after evaluating how long widgets have been made, evaluating historic growth rates (using tools like the S curve), and talking with experts—we would accept 350 as a reasonable estimate for total experience before year 2000. This means that accumulated experience at the end of year 2000 would be 350 + 100 = 450 widgets.

Companies also accumulate benefits from experience within and across industries. When it entered the bottled-water market, for example, PepsiCo brought beverage experience in sales, marketing, distribution, and other areas. To estimate how much of that expertise is relevant to the new business, you need to determine the percentage of costs that are shared. In the case of PepsiCo, everything but some portion of the cost of goods sold would be shared—packaging, technology, distribution, machinery, and so on. So you would count a high percentage of all beverage production as PepsiCo's previous bottled-water experience. In the case of Wal-Mart's entry into the grocery business, the proportion would be somewhat less. The company could leverage its experience in distribution, scale, and floor space, but sections like the produce department would be new to it, and it would have to acquire or develop the relevant expertise over time.

Once you have collected the raw price and cost data to match the experience time period, you need to correct for inflation, so that your unit price and cost data are in constant terms. If you don't have deflators readily at hand, you can use easy-to-find online calculators. In the United States, for example, the National Aeronautics and Space Administration (NASA) Web site offers a gross domestic product (GDP) inflation calculator that can equalize costs for any year from 1940 to 2009. It can be found at http://cost.jsc.nasa.gov/inflateGDP.html.

The next analytic step is running a regression. You can do this easily in Excel. The dependent variable is the natural log of inflation-adjusted prices or costs. The independent variable is the natural log of accumulated experience. Putting the variables into a log scale converts the curve into a straight line, which makes analysis and interpretation easier (see figure A2.1). As a short statistics refresher, you'll need to check that the R^2 is sensible, where an R^2 closer to 1 suggests that the regression equation has greater explanatory power (that is, it predicts the dependent variable with greater accuracy). For example, $R^2 = 0.6$ can be interpreted that approximately 60 percent of variation is explained by the regression. You may also want to go further to ensure that the regression is statistically significant, or whether it could be described by chance. You do this by looking at the p-value. If the p-value is less than .05, then the regression helps explain the dependent variable. If it's bigger than .05, the reverse is true—the regression could possibly be described by chance and may not help.

The final calculation is the slope of the experience curve. "Slope" in this context is different from the conventional regression-line slope, which is calculated as the change in Y over the change in X. The slope of the experience curve is defined as 1 minus the rate of price or cost decline for

FIGURE A2.1

The Curve Is Converted to a Natural Log Scale, Enabling Predictive Regression Calculations

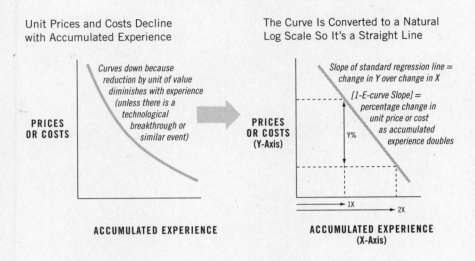

Unit Prices and Costs Decline with Accumulated Experience

The Curve Is Converted to a Natural Log Scale So It's a Straight Line

Curves down because reduction by unit of value diminishes with experience (unless there is a technological breakthrough or similar event)

PRICES OR COSTS

PRICES OR COSTS (Y-Axis)

Slope of standard regression line = change in Y over change in X

[1-E-curve Slope] = percentage change in unit price or cost as accumulated experience doubles

Y%

1X   2X

ACCUMULATED EXPERIENCE

ACCUMULATED EXPERIENCE (X-Axis)

every doubling of accumulated experience. For example, say your regression outputs are: X-coefficient = 0.174 and Y-intercept = 3.848. Then the slope = EXP [LN(2)* regression line slope] = EXP [.693* 0.174] = .89 = 89 percent. Once you have reality-checked your answers, you're ready to plot the data and regression lines.

Interpreting the experience curves can require drilling into more layers of data to understand the insights. For example, cost components may have different trends. In the aircraft oxygen mask example in figure A2.2, labor costs have been coming down very rapidly (almost 50 percent reduction every doubling of experience). However, given the low relative importance of labor to overall costs, it will now make a much bigger difference to focus efforts on reducing materials costs and overheads.

SPECIAL SITUATIONS

There are four major categories of special situations for experience curves:

FIGURE A2.2

Drilling Into Cost-Component Trends Diagnoses Biggest Sources of Value

Aircraft Oxygen Mask Example

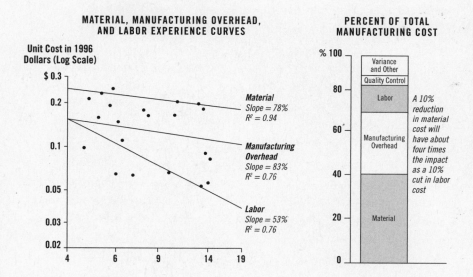

MATERIAL, MANUFACTURING OVERHEAD, AND LABOR EXPERIENCE CURVES

Unit Cost in 1996 Dollars (Log Scale)

Material
Slope = 78%
$R^2 = 0.94$

Manufacturing Overhead
Slope = 83%
$R^2 = 0.76$

Labor
Slope = 53%
$R^2 = 0.76$

PERCENT OF TOTAL MANUFACTURING COST

Variance and Other
Quality Control
Labor
Manufacturing Overhead
Material

A 10% reduction in material cost will have about four times the impact as a 10% cut in labor cost

Products or Services with Intangible or Subjective Value

In some industries, it is difficult to calculate the value a customer is receiving in the same way you would calculate something like tire cost per mile driven. An example is software. When customers buy Quicken from Intuit, say, they are buying productivity improvements (it takes less time to write checks or make payments), a better way of organizing financial information, and help in retrieving their data for tax or budget purposes. They may buy an annual upgrade without a discounted price because they continue to perceive that the value to them in productivity improvement is worth more than the cost of the software. But that value is likely to be different for different consumers, and it is difficult to measure. The same can hold true in many other industries, including information services, credit cards, and insurance. In all of these situations it can be difficult to determine the right unit of value. Suppose, for example, a particular provider does not offer the lowest overall costs. But suppose it does offer additional services or enhancements (including prestige driven by brand building) that the customer values. So the value received by the customer per dollar spent is high relative to the customer's other options. In these cases, it may be difficult to draw a price experience curve that captures the entire bundle of offerings using a completely objective unit of value.

However, the underlying components of cost should still follow an experience curve. For example, Intuit may be able to track lines of code developed per programmer over time. In every case, unit costs should be improving as experience increases. Often, too, price can be disaggregated by noting the enhancements that have been made to the product. For example, car prices over the last several decades have been rising in real terms at a rate of slightly more than 1 percent a year. But a car today is not the same as a car from thirty or forty years ago. Today's car includes safety features, along with many items that were once considered luxury options and are now usually standard (air conditioning, power windows, antilock brakes, and so on). If you disaggregate the components of price and perform apples-to-apples product comparisons, you can usually estimate a price experience curve.

External Factors, Including Patents, Regulations, etc.

These can form long-term price umbrellas. A patented drug, for instance, may not be easily challenged until its patent expires. Nevertheless, companies in this situation should still manage their costs down the experience curve. Research on patent expiration in the U.S. pharmaceutical industry, for instance, has shown that as more generic-drug manufacturers enter the market, the prices of generic drugs fall dramatically. If one generics company enters the market, the price of the drug averages 60 percent of the branded equivalent. If twenty generics companies are in the market, the price drops to only 20 percent of the branded drug.[1] As manufacturers of generics enter the market, both branded-drug and generic-drug prices fall. The companies that have managed costs along the experience curve will have profits to reinvest in, for example, new-product development.

Very Mature Industries and "High-Road" Categories

In some industries, experience doubles infrequently. For example, when we charted butter, we determined that at current growth rates it will take about twenty-eight years to double the experience of butter production. Corn, wheat, many other sorts of food products, clothing, basic machinery, and so on will fall into this category. Even if companies in these categories manage their costs aggressively, the annual cost reduction may be small. For example, if it takes twenty-eight years to double production and the slope of the experience curve is 68 percent (see the experience curve for butter in chapter 2), the annual price reductions for a company on the curve are likely to be just a little more than 1 percent. In this kind of environment, enhancements to service, quality, or brand building may serve to differentiate the product more than price alone. So companies naturally focus their energy on such enhancements, and attempt to create value for the customer through service, quality, or prestige. We call these "high-road" strategies.

In general, a high-road strategy can increase the profits of everyone at the high end of a market. The largest player still should have the highest potential profits because it should be coming down the cost experience curve fastest, but the overall price curve is higher. However, because the consumer values things other than just price, smaller companies can often make outsized returns by finding niche segments of customers who perceive high value in a certain product configuration. For example, consumer-electronics devices have come down a steep experience curve, but there are still segments of customers emotionally attached to vacuum-tube products for reasons of nostalgia or perceived warmth and clarity of sound. These customers value different attributes than the mass market and can afford high-end audio equipment (otherwise known as "price-no-object" equipment). Still, the market leader in this segment can earn higher returns because its costs should be lowest.

More detail on high-road strategies can be found in the article "Your Brand's Best Strategy," by Vijay Vishwanath and Jonathan Mark in *Harvard Business Review*, May–June 1997.

Depleting Natural Resources, Including Oil

In general, as resources begin to grow scarce, prices will rise until they hit the experience curve of a substitute. Customers then switch. Ethanol and other fuels are more expensive than oil today, but they're on their own experience curve and eventually will be viable substitutes. In some cases, using substitutes will require new machinery or processes (engines that can use ethanol, for instance). These, too, will have to come down experience curves so that the system costs of using the substitute are lower than the system costs of using the depleting resource. For products with high cyclicality, or with big demand-and-supply imbalances, the right approach is sometimes to look at the experience curve for value-added costs (labor,

FIGURE A2.3

Oil Exploration and Development Spend per Barrel Has Declined Over Time

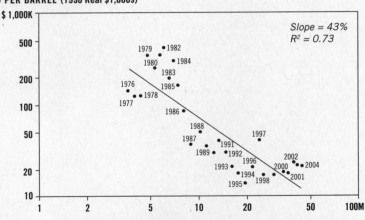

Note: COE is barrels of crude oil equivalent.

U.S. gross additions to proved reserves of crude oil, natural gas, and natural gas liquids are for U.S. total industry reserve additions. Expenditures adjusted for average depth of exploratory wells (crude oil, natural gas, and dry holes).

Source: EIA "Annual Energy Review," 2005

manufacturing, sales and marketing, and so on), instead of raw-material inputs like petroleum.

In the case of oil, the fact of a cartel controlling a depleting resource has kept prices artificially high for long periods. Yet the experience curve continues to apply. Even though oil is harder to find and companies must drill deeper, exploration and development costs are coming down. In fact, drilling spend per barrel of cumulative reserve additions per well is on a steep experience curve as shown in figure A2.3. (The analysis in the figure focused on total U.S.-based oil and natural gas production as reported by the Energy Information Administration. We compared expenditures on exploration and development with gross additions to cumulative reserve additions per well. The expenditures were adjusted for average well depth for crude oil, natural gas, and dry hole wells, where depth has increased over time. The barrels of crude oil equivalent [COE] were adjusted for number of wells, which have decreased over time.)

FIGURE A2.4

Ethanol and Electric Cars Have Downward Slope

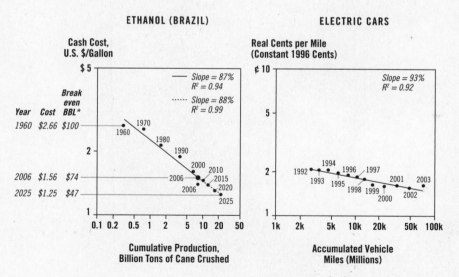

*Without subsidies, refers to the break-even price of a barrel of oil above which ethanol will make money.

Sources: Department of Transportation (NTS), Department of Energy (EIA), National Biodiesel Board, Bloomberg, Brazil Ministry of Agriculture, Bain estimates

So oil companies are continuing to improve their efficiency. What about the cost to consumers of oil substitutes? Our research has shown that the price per gallon of ethanol in Brazil (for ethanol made from cane sugar) has declined steadily as cumulative production of sugar has increased. Similarly, electric cars show a slight downward slope for price per mile to consumers, with a high R^2, also shown in figure A2.4. As major automakers and governments continue to pour money into research on hybrid and electric vehicles, prices to consumers should continue to decline.

Similarly, given that energy use could shift more to electricity, we asked what was happening to electricity generation costs. In 2003, coal and nuclear accounted for the vast bulk of electricity generated in the United States, at 57 percent and 23 percent, respectively. Much smaller amounts came from natural gas (15 percent), petroleum (3 percent), biomass (around 1 percent), and solar (less than 1 percent). After a big spike around the 1970s oil crisis, coal prices have come down a consistent experience

FIGURE A2.5

Electricity Prices from Coal Declining (Strong Trend Since 1978), Biomass Also Declining

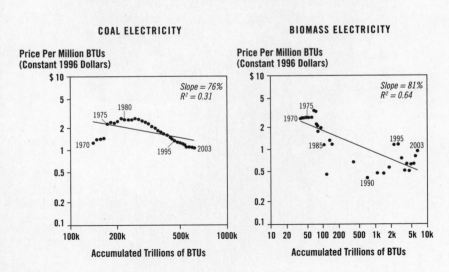

curve. While still a small source of electricity, biomass has generally been declining in price since the 1970s (see figure A2.5).

Over time, when oil supplies are depleted (significantly far in the future, given the rate at which OPEC countries are drawing down their proven reserves), these other forms of energy will become more viable, especially as they continue down their own experience curves.

The Full-Potential Performance-Improvement Diagnostic

This appendix maps out graphically what we call a "full-potential performance-improvement diagnostic." It boils down the analysis presented in chapter 6 into a series of charts that focus on your objectives for each piece of analysis, the questions you will ask, the data you will need, and the steps involved in assessing and using the data.

The performance-improvement diagnostic is a tool you can use to develop a comprehensive, data-driven assessment of your point of departure. It shows you in detail where your organization is today, so that you can identify threats to your current performance and opportunities for improvement. It highlights gaps between your own company's performance and full-potential performance along all the relevant business dimensions. The diagnostic process is grounded in the four laws and based explicitly on the twelve must-have facts (see figure A3.1). It thus reflects our fundamental views about what is important for performance improvement.

FIGURE A3.1

Defining Your Points of Departure and Arrival
Requires Twelve Must-Have Facts

LAW 1 Costs and Prices Always Decline	LAW 2 Competitive Position Determines Your Options	LAW 3 Customers and Profit Pools Don't Stand Still	LAW 4 Simplicity Gets Results
1. How does your cost slope compare to those of competitors? What is the slope of price changes in your industry right now and how does your cost curve compare?	**4.** Where do you and your competitors fall on the ROA/RMS chart? How are the leaders making money, and what is their approach? What is the full potential of your business position?	**7.** Which are the biggest, fastest-growing, and most profitable customer segments? How well do you meet customer needs relative to competitors and substitutes?	**10.** How complex are your products or service offerings, and what is that degree of complexity costing you? Where is your innovation fulcrum? What are the Killer ABCs in your business?
2. What are your costs compared with competitors'? Who is most efficient and effective in priority areas? Where can you improve most relative to others?	**5.** How big is your market? Which parts are growing fastest? Where are you gaining or losing share?	**8.** What proportion of customers are you retaining? How do your NPS ratings track against competitors'?	**11.** How complex is your decision making and organization relative to competitors'? What is the impact of this complexity?
3. Which of your products or services are making money (or not), and why?	**6.** What are the few capabilities that are creating a competitive advantage for you? Which are missing and are therefore holding you back, and which ones need to be strengthened or acquired?	**9.** How much of the profit pool do you have today? How is the profit pool likely to change in the future? What are the opportunities and threats?	**12.** Where does complexity reside in your processes? What is that costing you?

Before we get to the diagnostic tool itself, here are some answers to the most common questions we encounter.

When should I do it?

General managers should undertake and complete a performance-improvement diagnostic process within the first ninety to 120 days after taking on a new role as head of an organization. You may also want to perform one whenever you are about to launch a broad turnaround or major change initiative. Significant performance improvement never comes easily, but it is far more likely to occur when it begins with a solid base of facts that everyone can see, understand, and agree on. The diagnostic, in effect, lays the groundwork for the difficult process of change.

Who else needs to be involved?

Depending on the nature of your organization, you should involve all your direct reports, heads of functional departments, or both. You want to include all the key players for two reasons. One is to ensure that you get the right data—that no significant category is inadvertently overlooked or omitted. The other is to begin the process of building consensus on the need for change. People who are themselves involved in collecting the data that shows the need for improvement are more likely to buy in to the process. As we noted in chapter 6, David Weidman's direct reports at Celanese were startled to discover the extent to which the company was underperforming its peers. They could see clearly that Celanese needed to boost its performance simply to keep up with competitors.

Building consensus on the data also provides the foundation for determining your point of arrival and the three to five critical action imperatives that will get you there. It's easier for everyone to see where you might want to go when they understand where the organization is starting from. By highlighting critical performance gaps, the diagnostic is likely to help everyone understand where the most important levers for improvement can be found.

What data will I need, and where should I look for it?

Broadly speaking, you will need five categories of data:

- *Revenue and cost data* from your internal financial reporting systems

- *Industry data*, including market size, growth, profitability, customer segments, and so on, culled from analyst reports, trade publications, and the like

- *Competitor data*, including sales, costs, strategies, and so on, from competitors' annual reports, analyst reports, and industry experts

- *Customer data*, including customer segments, the needs and preferences of each segment, customer retention, ratings of your company's performance versus competitors on key dimensions, and Net Promoter Scores (NPS). This information can come from your own marketing research and customer surveys as well as from third-party research.

- *Organization data*, including the structure of the organization, spans and layers, decision-making processes, and capabilities, from your direct reports and functional-department heads.

How can I best use this appendix?

The appendix includes generic templates for each of the twelve must-have facts, along with guidelines on how to use each one. One caution: note that word "generic." These templates provide a guide for your effort, but ultimately the outputs must be customized for your business. There are unique aspects of your industry that need to be accounted for, and you will face specific actions by competitors that will require you to dig more deeply into particular areas. For each must-have fact, we have listed some additional tools that you can use if you do decide to drive to greater levels of detail. While we have not provided detailed descriptions of all these tools, you should be able to locate information on them in various business publications. You will want to adapt the diagnostic as necessary to develop a robust understanding of your point of departure in the context of your business and industry.

THE TWELVE MUST-HAVE FACTS

1. Experience Curves

Goal. The initial objectives here are to construct 1. an industry-wide price experience curve; 2. your own overall cost experience curve; and 3. if possible, cost experience curves for your chief competitors. Once you have your own overall cost curve in hand, you can construct experience curves

FIGURE A3.2

**① How Does Your Cost Slope Compare with Those of Competitors'?
What Is the Slope of Price Changes in Your Industry
Right Now and How Does Your Cost Curve Compare?**

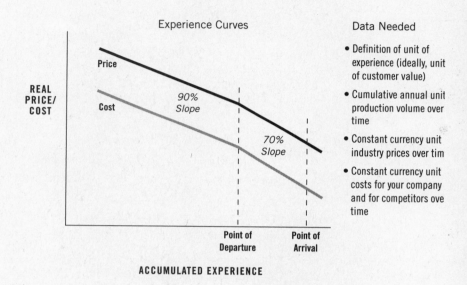

Experience Curves

Data Needed

- Definition of unit of experience (ideally, unit of customer value)
- Cumulative annual unit production volume over time
- Constant currency unit industry prices over tim
- Constant currency unit costs for your company and for competitors ove time

for every major cost element, including labor, overhead, and outsourced materials and services (see figure A3.2).

Approach. Please refer to appendix 2, which shows how to construct experience curves.

Additional tools. The tools you will be using to manage to the experience curve are those of general cost management, outlined in the following section.

2. Relative Cost Position Analysis

Goal. The objective of relative cost position (RCP) analysis is to determine a company's practical full-potential cost position based on a comparison of *unit* costs with those of its competitors (see figure A3.3). Of course, you may need to adjust the comparison for differences in your business.

FIGURE A3.3

❷ What Are Your Costs Compared with Competitors?
Who Is Most Efficient and Effective in Priority Areas?
Where Can You Improve Most Relative to Others?

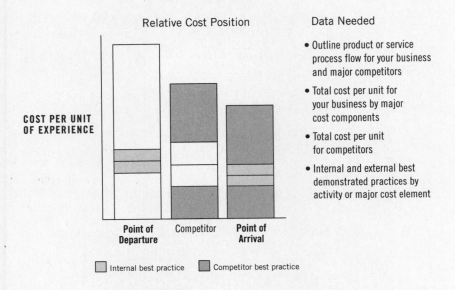

RCP analysis helps to answer both strategic and tactical questions. Strategically, it can help you understand where your competitors have their biggest cost advantage; what is driving their profitability; and how much flexibility they might have in a competitive battle. Tactically, it helps determine where to focus your cost-reduction efforts (on labor? on raw materials? on overhead costs?) and which cost elements might decrease significantly with an increase in scale and experience. It also helps you understand which cost elements might benefit from different business practices.

Approach. You can approach an RCP analysis in two ways, bottom-up or top-down; ideally, you would undertake both, so that you are confident of your data. A *top-down* approach compares competitors' overall cost structure with your own at the macro level. A *bottom-up* approach, by contrast, begins with gathering primary data on each major cost element for yourself and your key competitors. You then triangulate, using cost data from multiple sources to reinforce and confirm your hypotheses. You must define key process and business-practice differences for major cost elements, assess the impact of these differences, and then test the conclusions against overall financial data (see figure A3.4).

Relative cost position analysis works best when you develop a target based on *best demonstrated practices*. That is, you build up a hypothetical cost position based on the "best of the best" by taking the lowest-cost provider's costs in each step of the value chain. The total will add up to lower costs than those of any one company in the industry but will represent an aspirational cost position. This helps you take into account the fact that while you improve, your competitors will be improving, too—so your targets must be more aggressive than where your lowest-cost competitor is today. You can then determine how far you can realistically improve against that aspirational benchmark.

FIGURE A3.4

Relative Cost Position Analysis Involves Five Major Steps

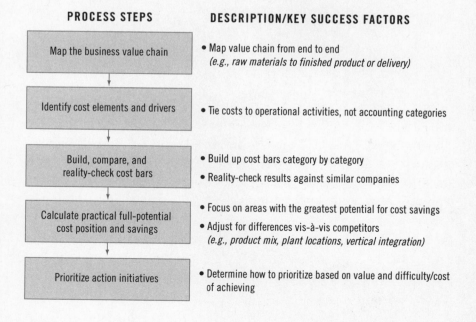

PROCESS STEPS	DESCRIPTION/KEY SUCCESS FACTORS
Map the business value chain	• Map value chain from end to end (e.g., raw materials to finished product or delivery)
Identify cost elements and drivers	• Tie costs to operational activities, not accounting categories
Build, compare, and reality-check cost bars	• Build up cost bars category by category • Reality-check results against similar companies
Calculate practical full-potential cost position and savings	• Focus on areas with the greatest potential for cost savings • Adjust for differences vis-à-vis competitors (e.g., product mix, plant locations, vertical integration)
Prioritize action initiatives	• Determine how to prioritize based on value and difficulty/cost of achieving

The key is to carry the process through to its conclusion: calculating your own full-potential cost position and savings, and determining the action imperatives.

Additional tools. Benchmarking against best demonstrated practices will give you an idea of the performance gap you face. The tools for implementation of your plan include a wide variety of cost-management and cost-reduction tools:

- **Supply chain:** supply-chain strategy, demand planning, inventory and order management, distribution management

- **Manufacturing:** manufacturing strategy, manufacturing footprint, plant improvement, Lean Six Sigma (LSS), outsourcing

- **Procurement:** supplier strategy, purchasing-cost reduction, vendor-performance management, supplier negotiation, organization and process improvement

- **SG&A:** overhead optimization (for example, finance, HR, IT, legal); salesforce productivity

- **CAPEX management:** CAPEX management and budgeting, working-capital management, real estate optimization

3. Product-Line Profitability Analysis

Goal. Product-line profitability (PLP) analysis is a diagnostic tool that helps you determine the true profitability of each product in a multi-product portfolio (see figure A3.5). You can use it to answer a variety of questions about product lines. Where should we focus our cost-reduction efforts? How can we optimize pricing? Which product lines should we drop? On which should we focus our research-and-development efforts? Where should we change sales incentives?

Approach. PLP requires going beyond conventional accounting, so you can't always just take the data from existing financial reports (see figure A3.6). There are three critical differences:

FIGURE A3.5

❸ Which of Your Products or Services Are Making Money (or Not), and Why?

Product-Line Profitability

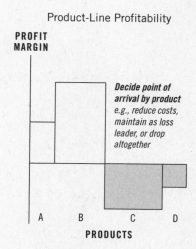

PROFIT
MARGIN

Decide point of arrival by product e.g., reduce costs, maintain as loss leader, or drop altogether

A   B   C   D

PRODUCTS

Bar Width = Revenue
Bar Area = Profit

Data Needed

• Direct costs for each product (materials, direct labor, packaging, etc.)

• Indirect costs for each product (logistics, selling, G&A, etc.)

• Major activities performed and cost drivers for each activity to allocate costs

• **Cost collection.** Typical accounting systems collect costs by function, such as R&D or advertising. PLP analysis requires collecting costs by product.

• **Cost assigned to products.** Accounting systems assign costs to product as cost of goods sold (COGS), which typically includes only direct labor and materials. PLP analysis includes all costs, including indirect.

• **Cost allocation method.** Accounting systems allocate costs according to the rules and standards of accounting (standard costing). PLP analysis determines activity-based cost drivers—cubic feet for warehouse labor, for example, or person-hours for delivery labor—and assigns costs to activities (activity-based costing). Of course, you must always be aware of and take into account fixed costs that would not go away if you eliminated some products. The key is to understand what the costs are and how they behave under different scenarios.

Additional tools. Activity-based costing, product-portfolio analysis.

FIGURE A3.6

Product-Line Profitability Involves Six Major Steps

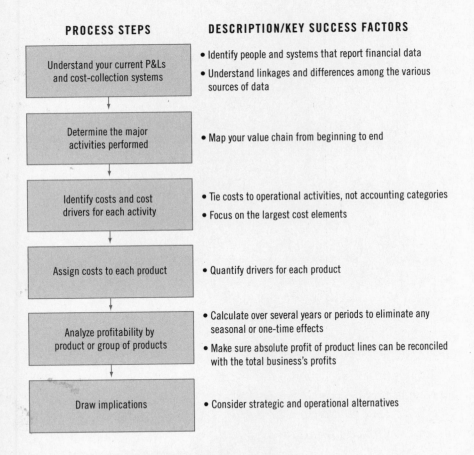

PROCESS STEPS	DESCRIPTION/KEY SUCCESS FACTORS
Understand your current P&Ls and cost-collection systems	• Identify people and systems that report financial data • Understand linkages and differences among the various sources of data
Determine the major activities performed	• Map your value chain from beginning to end
Identify costs and cost drivers for each activity	• Tie costs to operational activities, not accounting categories • Focus on the largest cost elements
Assign costs to each product	• Quantify drivers for each product
Analyze profitability by product or group of products	• Calculate over several years or periods to eliminate any seasonal or one-time effects • Make sure absolute profit of product lines can be reconciled with the total business's profits
Draw implications	• Consider strategic and operational alternatives

4. Return on Assets/Relative Market Share

Goal. The chart showing return on assets versus relative market share (ROA/RMS) can be used to diagnose operational underperformance and

FIGURE A3.7

❹ Where Do You and Your Competitors Fall on the ROA/RMS Chart? How Are the Leaders Making Money, and What Is Their Approach? What Is the Full Potential of Your Business Position?

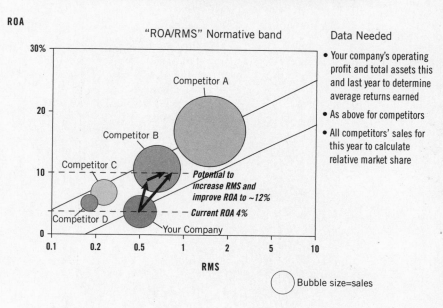

assess strategic opportunities and challenges (see figure A3.7). It can also provide an estimate of potential synergies available from a merger, and it can highlight inaccurate or changing business definitions in ways that can help drive winning strategies. Some companies will want to chart their ROA/RMS performance over a complete business cycle, so managers in these cases will have to compile at least five years' worth of data.

The logic underlying this chart is that companies with greater RMS have the potential to earn higher profits because of their greater accumulated experience, the lower cost position it permits, and the ability to reinvest more in R&D and customer enhancements. Research has shown that relative market share is a more powerful predictor of business performance than absolute market share; and return on assets is a better measure than (for instance) return on sales, since it takes into account the variation in asset intensity in different industries.

Approach. There are five critical steps in creating an ROA/RMS chart, shown in figure A3.8.

Additional tools. Another diagnostic tool for this step is a clear definition of your business's core. The implementation tools include strategic tools such as core full potential, adjacency mapping, core redefinition, and high-road strategies such as brand management. Companies will also want to determine and evaluate merger-and-acquisition strategies in light of this analysis.

FIGURE A3.8

ROA/RMS Involves Five Major Steps

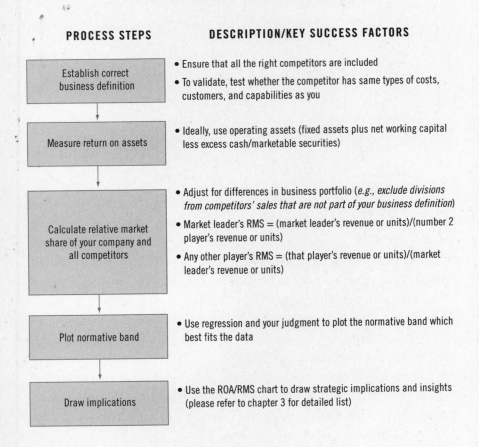

PROCESS STEPS   DESCRIPTION/KEY SUCCESS FACTORS

Establish correct business definition
- Ensure that all the right competitors are included
- To validate, test whether the competitor has same types of costs, customers, and capabilities as you

Measure return on assets
- Ideally, use operating assets (fixed assets plus net working capital less excess cash/marketable securities)

Calculate relative market share of your company and all competitors
- Adjust for differences in business portfolio (*e.g., exclude divisions from competitors' sales that are not part of your business definition*)
- Market leader's RMS = (market leader's revenue or units)/(number 2 player's revenue or units)
- Any other player's RMS = (that player's revenue or units)/(market leader's revenue or units)

Plot normative band
- Use regression and your judgment to plot the normative band which best fits the data

Draw implications
- Use the ROA/RMS chart to draw strategic implications and insights (please refer to chapter 3 for detailed list)

FIGURE A3.9

⑤ How Big Is Your Market? Which Parts Are Growing Fastest? Where Are You Gaining/Losing Share?

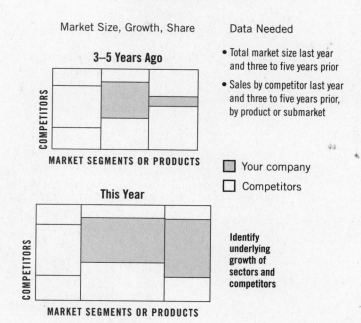

Market Size, Growth, Share

3–5 Years Ago

COMPETITORS

MARKET SEGMENTS OR PRODUCTS

This Year

COMPETITORS

MARKET SEGMENTS OR PRODUCTS

Data Needed

- Total market size last year and three to five years prior
- Sales by competitor last year and three to five years prior, by product or submarket

▨ Your company

☐ Competitors

Identify underlying growth of sectors and competitors

5. Market Size, Growth, and Share Analysis

Goal. A market map is a good starting point for diagnosing market growth rates and your competitive position in the market (see figure A3.9). It shows 1. the total size of the market; 2. key market segments and the size of each one; 3. market share of competitors in each segment; 4. areas of growth; and 5. areas where you are underperforming or overperforming.

Approach. There are four steps to creating a market map, as shown in figure A3.10.

Additional tools. Additional diagnostic tools for market analysis include core definition, market share and loss analysis, the S curve, and value chain mapping. Implementation tools include the same strategic tools mentioned under section 4.

FIGURE A3.10

Market Size, Growth, and Share Analysis Involves Four Major Steps

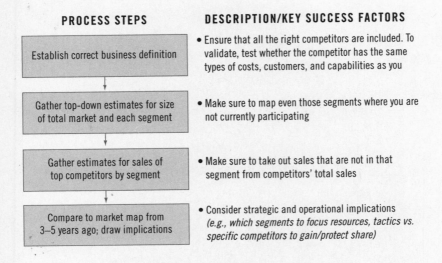

PROCESS STEPS

Establish correct business definition

Gather top-down estimates for size of total market and each segment

Gather estimates for sales of top competitors by segment

Compare to market map from 3–5 years ago; draw implications

DESCRIPTION/KEY SUCCESS FACTORS

• Ensure that all the right competitors are included. To validate, test whether the competitor has the same types of costs, customers, and capabilities as you

• Make sure to map even those segments where you are not currently participating

• Make sure to take out sales that are not in that segment from competitors' total sales

• Consider strategic and operational implications (*e.g., which segments to focus resources, tactics vs. specific competitors to gain/protect share*)

6. Capabilities Analysis

Goal. The goal of capabilities analysis is to develop a fact-based assessment of your capabilities, as viewed by your customers, your suppliers, and your employees (see figure A3.11). The analysis can be used to answer questions such as: Which capabilities truly differentiate us from the competition in the eyes of these stakeholders? Where do we have the biggest gaps in our capabilities? Chris Zook, in his book *Unstoppable*, shows how many companies have found "hidden assets" that allow them to develop new capabilities and thus redefine their core business.

Combined with an analysis of profit pools and changing customer needs, capabilities analysis allows you to determine which capabilities you need to invest in most aggressively to defend against possible harmful shifts in the profit pool, or which can be leveraged to increase your share of your own profit pool. It helps you assess how you can meet the most important needs of your customers better than the competition. It also helps you determine which capabilities might need to be outsourced.

FIGURE A3.11

⑥ What Are the Few Capabilities That Are Creating a Competitive Advantage for You? Which Are Missing and Which Ones Need to Be Strengthened or Acquired?

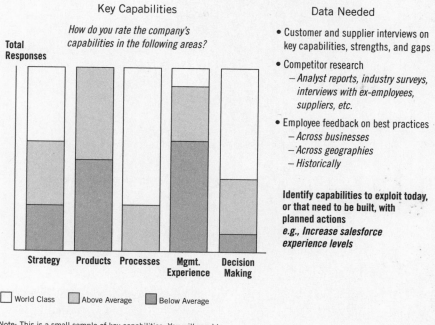

Key Capabilities

How do you rate the company's capabilities in the following areas?

Total Responses

Strategy   Products   Processes   Mgmt. Experience   Decision Making

☐ World Class   ▨ Above Average   ■ Below Average

Data Needed

- Customer and supplier interviews on key capabilities, strengths, and gaps
- Competitor research
  - *Analyst reports, industry surveys, interviews with ex-employees, suppliers, etc.*
- Employee feedback on best practices
  - *Across businesses*
  - *Across geographies*
  - *Historically*

Identify capabilities to exploit today, or that need to be built, with planned actions
e.g., Increase salesforce experience levels

Note: This is a small sample of key capabilities. You will need to determine which ones are most relevant to your organization.

Approach. Creating a capabilities rating chart involves four key steps, shown in figure A3.12.

Additional tools. In conducting a capabilities analysis, you might want to supplement the tool described above with additional in-depth assessments of your capabilities on the following dimensions: organizational effectiveness, R&D effectiveness, marketing mix effectiveness, strategic and tactical pricing, salesforce effectiveness, channel management, IT, and talent assessment. Implementation tools include everything that falls under the heading of capability sourcing covered in chapter 6.

FIGURE A3.12

Capabilities Analysis Involves Four Major Steps

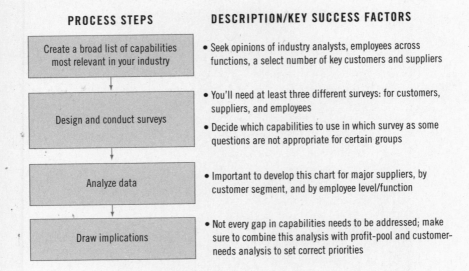

PROCESS STEPS	DESCRIPTION/KEY SUCCESS FACTORS
Create a broad list of capabilities most relevant in your industry	• Seek opinions of industry analysts, employees across functions, a select number of key customers and suppliers
Design and conduct surveys	• You'll need at least three different surveys: for customers, suppliers, and employees • Decide which capabilities to use in which survey as some questions are not appropriate for certain groups
Analyze data	• Important to develop this chart for major suppliers, by customer segment, and by employee level/function
Draw implications	• Not every gap in capabilities needs to be addressed; make sure to combine this analysis with profit-pool and customer-needs analysis to set correct priorities

7.1. Customer Segments Analysis

Goal. The goal of customer segments analysis is to identify the most attractive segments of a company's customer base (existing or potential), by comparing segments' size, growth, and profitability (see figure A3.13). The analysis helps show you how you can increase your growth and position on the ROA/RMS chart. It also helps you answer the question, "Which segments should we be targeting?"—though to answer this question fully, you will need to take into account your ability as compared with competitors to meet the customer segments' needs.

There are many different ways of segmenting a population. It can be based on demographics, behaviors, beliefs, needs, or the occasion of use of a product. What you are looking for is a segmentation that really defines the way a customer chooses one product over another. For example, many families may have a sports car and a minivan (and maybe an economy sedan) in their garage. They actually belong to three segments. The sports car is for the middle-aged husband, the minivan for the soccer mom, and

FIGURE A3.13

**⑦ Part 1: Which Are the Biggest,
Fastest-Growing, and Most Profitable Customer Segments?**

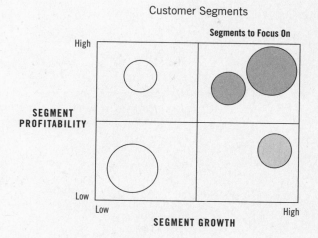

Circle size represents $ millions spend

the economy sedan for the teenage daughter. In this case, the segmentation is based on needs. One food company found an important customer segment composed of people who liked toppings on their ice cream, and was able to charge a premium for those toppings. This segmentation is based on occasion of use. Chocolate syrup is a commodity when used for baking, but a premium product for the ice cream lover segment. Consumers segment themselves out based on when and how they use the product, and some segments are more attractive and provide better returns.

Approach. This is a four-step process, as shown in figure A3.14.

FIGURE A3.14

Customer Segments Analysis Involves Four Major Steps

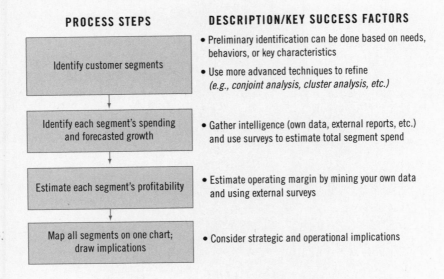

PROCESS STEPS

- Identify customer segments
- Identify each segment's spending and forecasted growth
- Estimate each segment's profitability
- Map all segments on one chart; draw implications

DESCRIPTION/KEY SUCCESS FACTORS

- Preliminary identification can be done based on needs, behaviors, or key characteristics
- Use more advanced techniques to refine (e.g., conjoint analysis, cluster analysis, etc.)

- Gather intelligence (own data, external reports, etc.) and use surveys to estimate total segment spend

- Estimate operating margin by mining your own data and using external surveys

- Consider strategic and operational implications

7.2. Segment Needs and Performance (SNAP) Analysis

Goal. The SNAP chart shows you the importance of different purchasing criteria to your customers (see figure A3.15). It also reveals how customers rate both you and your competitors against those criteria. Using the chart, you can see at a glance what different customer segments find important, what their perception is of your offerings, and how that compares with their perception of your competitors. You can identify the biggest gaps between the importance of a given criterion and your performance, and you can spot where you may be overinvesting or underinvesting in meeting specific customer needs. This analysis should be performed for every major customer segment so that you can see the differences in how purchasing criteria and performance vary by segment.

If possible, you should compare the chart with a similar one with data from two or three years ago. The comparison will suggest where customer needs have been changing, and what these changes may signal about potential shifts in profit pools.

FIGURE A3.15

⑦ Part 2: How Well Do You Meet Customer Needs Relative to Competitors and Substitutes?

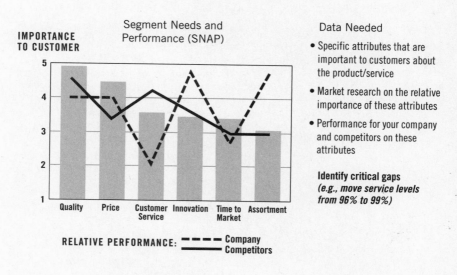

Segment Needs and Performance (SNAP)

IMPORTANCE TO CUSTOMER

Data Needed

• Specific attributes that are important to customers about the product/service

• Market research on the relative importance of these attributes

• Performance for your company and competitors on these attributes

Identify critical gaps (e.g., move service levels from 96% to 99%)

RELATIVE PERFORMANCE: ---- Company ⎯⎯ Competitors

Approach. To create a SNAP chart, carry out five steps, as shown in figure A3.16.

Additional tools. Customer segmentation tools that you can use in the diagnostic phase include analysis of lifetime customer value, conjoint and cluster analysis, CHAID (chi-square automatic interaction detector), and perceptual mapping. Other tools, such as customer ethnographic research and "voice of the customer" qualitative surveys, can be used to determine customer needs. Customer migration analysis and the revenue sieve will help you complete your diagnosis. For implementation, you need to focus both on customer acquisition and on the development of your customer value proposition. The latter includes analyzing the customer experience and assessing the effectiveness of your marketing mix, where the marketing mix includes product management and innovation, pricing strategy (tactical, strategic, and price customization), and sales-channel management (channel, salesforce, and store or brand strategy).

FIGURE A3.16

SNAP Analysis Involves Five Major Steps

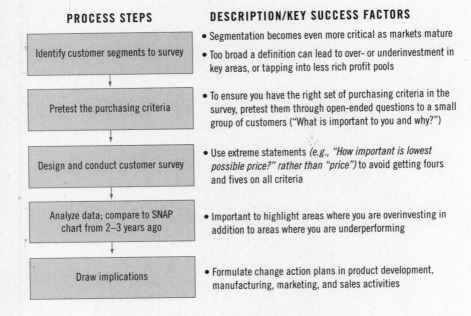

PROCESS STEPS	DESCRIPTION/KEY SUCCESS FACTORS
Identify customer segments to survey	• Segmentation becomes even more critical as markets mature • Too broad a definition can lead to over- or underinvestment in key areas, or tapping into less rich profit pools
Pretest the purchasing criteria	• To ensure you have the right set of purchasing criteria in the survey, pretest them through open-ended questions to a small group of customers ("What is important to you and why?")
Design and conduct customer survey	• Use extreme statements *(e.g., "How important is lowest possible price?" rather than "price")* to avoid getting fours and fives on all criteria
Analyze data; compare to SNAP chart from 2–3 years ago	• Important to highlight areas where you are overinvesting in addition to areas where you are underperforming
Draw implications	• Formulate change action plans in product development, manufacturing, marketing, and sales activities

8.1. Customer Retention Analysis

Goal. The objective of customer retention analysis is to establish a baseline (see figure A3.17). What proportion of your customers in each of your segments are you retaining? Then you can begin to assess the impact of retaining (or not retaining) specific segments, and you can analyze the root causes of customer defection. It is particularly important to analyze defectors. It turns out that satisfaction is usually built on a broad foundation of customer touch points and product attributes. But when a customer stops using your product, he can usually tell you exactly why with just one or two reasons. So it is much easier to determine why customers are leaving than why they are staying. If you can eliminate the reasons for defection, you will end up retaining more of your customers. The ideal is zero defections.

Approach. There are four basic steps (see figure A3.18); for more details,

FIGURE A3.17

⑧ Part 1: What Proportion of Customers Are You Retaining?

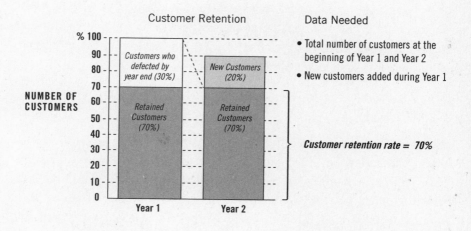

Customer Retention   Data Needed

% 100
90 Customers who
80 defected by   New Customers
    year end (30%)   (20%)
70
NUMBER OF 60
CUSTOMERS 50 Retained   Retained
    Customers   Customers
40   (70%)   (70%)
30
20
10
0
    Year 1   Year 2

• Total number of customers at the beginning of Year 1 and Year 2
• New customers added during Year 1

Customer retention rate = 70%

FIGURE A3.18

Customer Retention Involves Four Major Steps

PROCESS STEPS	DESCRIPTION/KEY SUCCESS FACTORS
Define "the customer"	• Choose definition of "the customer" that is actionable and has available data *(e.g., for a bank "the customer" can be a single account, an individual, or a household)*
Define "retention"	• For example, for a supermarket, it could be minimum $100 monthly spend for twelve consecutive months • For insurance, it could be annual policy renewal
Calculate retention rate	• RR = (Customers in Year 1) − (Customers in Year 2 − New Customers)/Customers in Year 1
Perform root cause analysis and draw implications	• Determine root causes of defection (interview/survey your defectors) • Consider strategic and operational ways to increase retention in most attractive segments

see the book *The Loyalty Effect*, by Fred Reichheld. You will also want to analyze this based not only on numbers of customers, but by level of spending. Are you losing your highest-spending (and most profitable) customers? Are customers whom you retain increasing their spend with you over time? This was a key insight for American Express. It was adding many customers each year, but the real growth came from the increased spending of its best customers.

8.2. NPS Analysis

Goal. Net Promoter Score, or NPS, gives you a simple, powerful way to track your ability to retain customers (see figure A3.19). The metric is based on one simple question: "How likely is it that you would recommend our company (or product or service) to a friend or colleague?" Respondents answer on a zero-to-ten scale, where zero means "extremely unlikely" and ten means "extremely likely." Those who give you a nine or a ten are "promoters"; they are likely to spend more with you, increase their

FIGURE A3.19

⑧ Part 2: How Does Your NPS Rating Track Against Competitors?

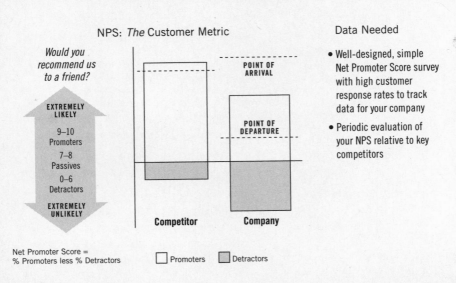

spending over time, and spread positive word of mouth. The eights and sevens are called "passives," while anybody scoring you six or below is a "detractor." NPS is simply the proportion of promoters minus the proportion of detractors.

There are many reasons to implement a regular measurement of NPS. It drives customer-centric decision making throughout the organization. It allows you to empower frontline employees to meet customer needs, and it establishes clear accountability for improvement. It helps you understand which practices turn people into promoters and which create detractors. NPS is most powerful when it is tracked over time by segment, and when it is compared with competitors' scores. Done right, it inculcates a kind of "NPS discipline" within an organization—a set of processes that keeps everyone focused on driving customer loyalty.

The retention metric mentioned earlier is useful for determining ways to reduce the number of detractors. NPS adds an additional dimension

FIGURE A3.20

NPS Involves Five Major Steps

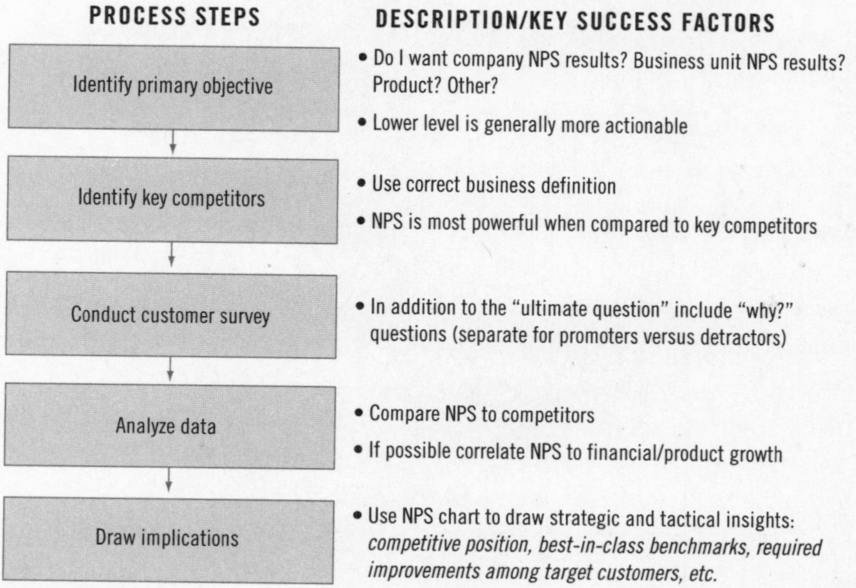

PROCESS STEPS	DESCRIPTION/KEY SUCCESS FACTORS
Identify primary objective	• Do I want company NPS results? Business unit NPS results? Product? Other? • Lower level is generally more actionable
Identify key competitors	• Use correct business definition • NPS is most powerful when compared to key competitors
Conduct customer survey	• In addition to the "ultimate question" include "why?" questions (separate for promoters versus detractors)
Analyze data	• Compare NPS to competitors • If possible correlate NPS to financial/product growth
Draw implications	• Use NPS chart to draw strategic and tactical insights: *competitive position, best-in-class benchmarks, required improvements among target customers, etc.*

that focuses the organization on creating promoters. There is a big difference between, on the one hand, eliminating the poor performance that is driving customers away, and on the other hand, developing attributes of your product or service offering that truly delight customers. It is the latter that will lead them to promote your product to their friends and neighbors. If you can do this, you will greatly enhance your potential for gaining market share.

Approach. Creating an NPS chart is a simple five-step process (see figure A3.20). But this is only the beginning of creating an NPS discipline. For a detailed discussion, see the book *The Ultimate Question*, by Fred Reichheld.

Additional tools. Tools to help you diagnose customer retention and loyalty include in-depth analyses of the key drivers (through customer surveys), root-cause analytic trees that identify the reasons for defection, and analysis of your share of wallet and how it is trending over time. Implementation tools include customer value-proposition development (discussed under section 7) and a variety of tools that are specifically designed to increase retention and loyalty. In the latter category are customer-relationship management (CRM), the creation of an NPS culture, and specific initiatives such as early-engagement programs, "save the sale" programs, loyalty and rewards programs, service recovery plans, and "zero defections" programs.

9. Profit-Pool Analysis

Goal. The objective of this analysis is to map total profits earned in your industry at all points along the value chain. This kind of map answers the basic question about an industry: where and how are companies making money? The pattern of profit concentration is often very different from the pattern of revenue concentration. Mapping profit pools over time also helps to answer questions about the evolution of the industry: Why did profit pools form where they did? How have they changed over time? Are the forces that created or shifted the pools likely to change?

A general manager who understands profit pools can often identify new sources of profits in low-margin industries; can chart acquisition and

FIGURE A3.21

❾ How Much of the Profit Pool Do You Have Today? How Is It Likely to Change in the Future? What Are Opportunities and Threats?

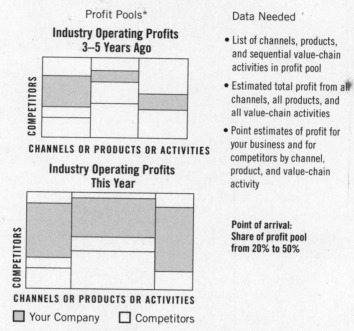

Profit Pools*

Industry Operating Profits 3–5 Years Ago

COMPETITORS

CHANNELS OR PRODUCTS OR ACTIVITIES

Industry Operating Profits This Year

COMPETITORS

CHANNELS OR PRODUCTS OR ACTIVITIES

☐ Your Company   ☐ Competitors

Data Needed

• List of channels, products, and sequential value-chain activities in profit pool

• Estimated total profit from all channels, all products, and all value-chain activities

• Point estimates of profit for your business and for competitors by channel, product, and value-chain activity

Point of arrival: Share of profit pool from 20% to 50%

*An alternative way to create a profit pool map is to show sales by segment on the X axis and percent operating margin on the Y axis.

expansion strategies; can make good decisions about which customers to pursue and which channels to use; and can guide product, pricing, and operating decisions effectively. This chart can be compiled either as shown in figure A3.21, with a rectangular box indicating total dollars of profits, or as shown in chapter 4, with the Y axis representing profit percentage, and the X axis showing sales dollars. Both are useful, but they have slightly different implications. The version in chapter 4, showing profit percentage, can help you understand where you are likely to get a good return on investment by pursuing that particular pool. The chart here, showing total profits, will help you understand where you and all key competitors par-

FIGURE A3.22

Profit-Pool Analysis Involves Four Major Steps

PROCESS STEPS	DESCRIPTION/KEY SUCCESS FACTORS
Map your business's value chain	• Map value chain from end to end (e.g., raw materials to finished product or delivery) • Go beyond traditional definitions to look at your business from the perspective of your customers, suppliers, and competitors
Estimate the size of your profit pool	• Initially, focus on the biggest pieces of the profit pool, such as the biggest companies or the companies that account for a large portion of industry profits • Use operating profit (vs. net or gross)
Reality-check your estimates	• Compare the estimates of total profit pool (top-down approach) with the estimates for each value-chain activity (bottom-up approach) • Collect additional data if necessary
Draw implications	• Use profit-pool map to draw strategic and tactical insights: *new sources of profit, acquisition and expansion strategies, customer segments/channels to pursue, adjustments to product, pricing, and operating decisions*

ticipate. It makes it easier to see relative movement among competitors and to spot trends that represent either threats or opportunities.

Approach. Creating a profit-pool map involves four steps, shown in figure A3.22.

Additional tools. The diagnostic tools for augmenting profit-pool analysis include SWOT analysis (strengths, weaknesses, opportunities, and threats), along with analysis of competitors, customer needs (see section 7), suppliers, and the governmental/regulatory environment. Scenario planning, adjacencies mapping, and value-chain mapping (including power shifts among the key players) are also helpful. For implementation, you can use war games and real-options analysis as well as many of the tools mentioned in other sections of this appendix.

🔟 How Complex Are Your Products or Service Offerings, and What Is That Degree of Complexity Costing You? Where Is Your Innovation Fulcrum? What Are the Killer ABCs in Your Business?

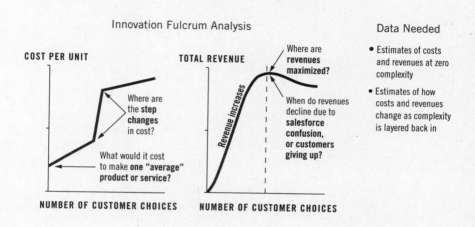

Innovation Fulcrum Analysis

10. Innovation Fulcrum ("Model T") Analysis

Goal. The objective of zero-base complexity analysis is to find your *innovation fulcrum*, the point where products or services meet customer needs with the lowest possible level of complexity (see figure A3.23).

This can be a significant challenge, partly because conventional management accounting systems and analysis focus only on the incremental costs of complexity. The Model T approach, by contrast, addresses the total systems cost of complexity. It begins by asking you to determine the cost of one single representative product, as if that were your company's only offering. Then you add variation back into the mix, and track the effects of increasing complexity on your costs as well as the true impact on revenues. As we pointed out in chapter 5, eliminating unnecessary complexity or postponing complexity until later in the value chain have been shown to increase profits.

FIGURE A3.24

Innovation Fulcrum Analysis ("Model T Analysis") Involves Four Major Steps

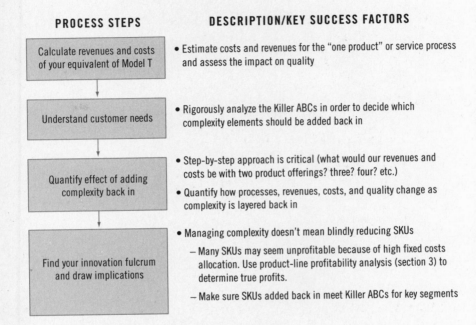

PROCESS STEPS

Calculate revenues and costs of your equivalent of Model T

Understand customer needs

Quantify effect of adding complexity back in

Find your innovation fulcrum and draw implications

DESCRIPTION/KEY SUCCESS FACTORS

- Estimate costs and revenues for the "one product" or service process and assess the impact on quality

- Rigorously analyze the Killer ABCs in order to decide which complexity elements should be added back in

- Step-by-step approach is critical (what would our revenues and costs be with two product offerings? three? four? etc.)
- Quantify how processes, revenues, costs, and quality change as complexity is layered back in

- Managing complexity doesn't mean blindly reducing SKUs
  - Many SKUs may seem unprofitable because of high fixed costs allocation. Use product-line profitability analysis (section 3) to determine true profits.
  - Make sure SKUs added back in meet Killer ABCs for key segments

A Model T analysis can be used to answer questions such as how many products or services we should have, which SKUs we might be able to eliminate, and which we might manage differently. It should also show you how much complexity is costing you. That is a good starting point for asking whether you understand the root causes of complexity, and whether you have the capabilities necessary to manage complexity effectively.

Approach. The zero-based complexity analysis involves four steps, shown in figure A3.24.

Additional tools. For implementation, use product complexity management with focused product development and innovation tactics.

FIGURE A3.25

⑪ Part 1: How Complex Is Your Decision Making Relative to Competitors?
What Is the Impact of This Complexity?

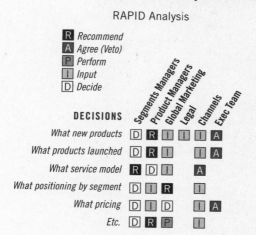

RAPID Analysis

R Recommend
A Agree (Veto)
P Perform
I Input
D Decide

DECISIONS

	Segments Managers	Product Managers	Global Marketing	Legal	Channels	Exec Team
What new products	D	R	I	I	I	A
What products launched	D	R	I		I	A
What service model	R	D	I		A	
What positioning by segment	D	I	R		I	
What pricing	D	I	D		I	A
Etc.	D	R	P		I	

Data Needed

• List of top decisions
• Opinions from different levels/ departments on who holds various decision rights (RAPID)
• Evaluation of impact on organization of current decision-making processes

11.1. RAPID Analysis

Goal. The objective of RAPID analysis is to improve decision-making processes by codifying individuals' roles in decisions.

RAPID is a loose acronym for the five key roles in a decision: recommend, input, agree, decide, and perform. Recommenders gather and assess the relevant facts and obtain input from the appropriate people. Those who provide the input can offer facts and judgment about the best course of action. Those who must agree must approve the recommendation; they have veto power. One person has the D—the ability to decide. And those who perform are responsible for carrying out the decision (see figure A3.25).

RAPID focuses attention on how critical decisions should be made; it provides a degree of analytical rigor in an area that most organizations never examine at all. Streamlining decision making reduces costs. It increases an organization's nimbleness by reducing labor time, meeting time, and time spent revisiting decisions or determining who should be making

FIGURE A3.26

RAPID Involves Four Major Steps

PROCESS STEPS	DESCRIPTION/KEY SUCCESS FACTORS
Establish key processes and decisions	• First establish core business processes *(e.g., develop products, manage brands, etc.)* • Then determine key management processes within each business process *(e.g., for managing brands → packaging, pricing, promotion, etc.)*
Design the organization "superstructure"	• Develop a basic outline or superstructure of the organization *(e.g., How many levels? What process/functional heads? Organized regionally or globally or by product, and so on).* • The RAPID method is applied to each decision with the context of the superstructure
Define decision accountabilities	• Put in place guiding principles about how decisions should be made *(e.g., end-to-end process should be visible in all top decisions)* • There's only one D, one R; can be multiple I and P; use A sparingly
Design the organization	• Determine the roles at various levels • Define the scope of each job • Identify the right person for each job (and tailor the job to the individual)

them. It helps to encourage focused management behavior, eliminate redundant analyses, and ensure accountability.

Approach. Conducting a RAPID analysis involves four steps (see figure A3.26; for more detail, see the article "Who Has the D?" by Paul Rogers and Marcia Blenko, *Harvard Business Review*, January 2006).

11.2. Spans-and-Layers Analysis

Goal. Spans-and-layers analysis is a tool used to analyze overhead. It shows the number of direct reports per manager (spans) and the number of management levels between the CEO and frontline employees (layers). Applying the analysis enables a company to lower overhead costs, reduce complexity in the organization, simplify decision making, and increase

FIGURE A3.27

⑪ Part 2: How Complex Is Your Organization Relative to Competitors? What Is the Impact of This Complexity? (high-level view)

Spans-and-Layers Analysis

LAYERS	CURRENT ORGANIZATION	CURRENT SPAN	TARGET SPAN OF CONTROL
1	CEO	12.0	12
2		6.8	10
3		5.9	10
4		5.9	10
5		6.7	12
6		8.3	12
7		9.9	15
8		7.8	15
9		5.0	15
	AVERAGE	8.3	13.3

Data Needed

• Comprehensive organizational chart showing number of layers and departments/divisions

• Organizational chart for each level showing total number of direct reports

FIGURE A3.28

(detailed view)

Spans-and-Layers Analysis

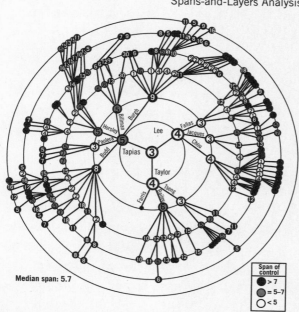

Median span: 5.7

Span of control
● > 7
◐ = 5–7
○ < 5

Data Needed

• Comprehensive organizational chart showing number of layers and departments/divisions

• Organizational chart for each level showing total number of direct reports

FIGURE A3.29

Spans-and-Layers Analysis Involves Four Major Steps

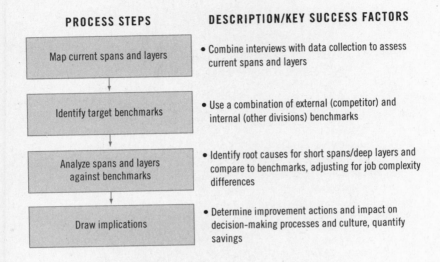

PROCESS STEPS | DESCRIPTION/KEY SUCCESS FACTORS

Map current spans and layers
- Combine interviews with data collection to assess current spans and layers

Identify target benchmarks
- Use a combination of external (competitor) and internal (other divisions) benchmarks

Analyze spans and layers against benchmarks
- Identify root causes for short spans/deep layers and compare to benchmarks, adjusting for job complexity differences

Draw implications
- Determine improvement actions and impact on decision-making processes and culture, quantify savings

the level of accountability and innovation. Figure A3.27 shows a high-level view of one organization's spans and layers; figure A3.28 turns up the magnification, and allows you to see exactly how many people report to individual managers in one unit.

Approach. There are four steps involved, as shown in figure A3.29.

Additional tools. Tools for implementation include vision and priority setting, organizational design (decision roles, structure, and processes), and key performance indicators (KPIs).

12. Process Mapping

Goal. The purpose of process mapping is to highlight issues and opportunities for improvement in business processes (see figure A3.30). It is also used to identify root causes of performance gaps, such as suboptimal steps, process disconnects, and bottlenecks. Addressing the issues uncovered by performance mapping can help reduce process complexity; improve ca-

FIGURE A3.30

⓬ Where Does Complexity Reside in Your Processes?
What Is That Costing You?

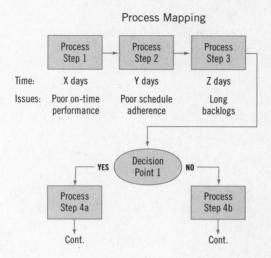

Process Mapping

Data Needed

- Map of key processes,
  step by step

- Estimates of time required
  for each process step and
  key issues involved

- Evaluation of impact on
  organization of current
  processes

pacity utilization; lower customer response time; shorten time to market, and reduce errors, rework, and scrap rates.

Approach. Building a process map involves just three steps as shown in figure A3.31.

Additional tools. Tools for implementation include business process redesign and Lean Six Sigma.

SUMMARY

Using the full-potential performance-improvement diagnostic entails gathering and analyzing a lot of data. But when it is complete you will have not only a thorough, fact-based assessment of where you are now, you will also have many good ideas about what needs improvement and what tools can be applied to generate that improvement. Figure A3.32 sums up the diagnostic process and the tools, as framed by the four laws and the twelve must-have facts.

FIGURE A3.31

Process Mapping Involves Three Major Steps

PROCESS STEPS	DESCRIPTION/KEY SUCCESS FACTORS
Plan process map	• Identify scope *(e.g., entire organization vs. one division; level of detail, etc.)* • Understand process elements *(e.g., facility walk-through; conversations with employees)* • Determine metrics *(e.g., handoffs, setups, etc.)*
Build process map	• Outline activities at high level • Define start, stop, and wait points • Document each step
Identify opportunities	• Understand performance gaps • Perform detailed root-cause analysis of issues

FIGURE A3.32

Summary: Performance-Improvement Diagnostic and Implementation Tools

DIAGNOSTIC TOOLS | **IMPLEMENTATION TOOLS**

LAW		Diagnostic	Implementation
LAW 1	1. Experience curve	Experience curve	Cost management
	2. Relative cost position	Relative cost position	Cost management
	3. Product-line profitability	Product-line profitability	Product portfolio management
LAW 2	4. Competitive positioning	ROA/RMS | Core definition	Growth strategy | High road/low road | M&A
	5. Market analysis	Market analysis	Growth strategy | High road/low road | M&A
	6. Capabilities	Capabilities assessment	Capabilities sourcing
LAW 3	7. Customer segments and needs	Customer segmentation | Customer needs/SNAP analysis	Cust. value propost. dev't | Cust. acquisition | Cust. retention & NPS culture
	8. Retention and loyalty	Retention & loyalty dignosis | NPS survey	Cust. value propost. dev't | Cust. acquisition | Cust. retention & NPS culture
	9. Profit pools	Profit-pool mapping | SWOT analysis | Scenario planning	Real options | War games | + other tools referenced
LAW 4	10. Product complexity	Model T diagnostic	Complexity management | Product dev't & innovation
	11. Org. and decision-making complexity	Organization diagnostic	Org. design | Vision & prior. | Metrics & incntv
	12. Process complexity	Process mapping	Bus. process redesign | Lean Six Sigma

Notes

CHAPTER 1: THE TWO KEYS TO BREAKTHROUGH RESULTS

1 Nanette Byrnes and David Kiley, "CEOs: Hello, You Must Be Going," *BusinessWeek*, February 12, 2007.
2 The outplacement firm of Challenger, Gray & Christmas issues regular press releases on the tenure of departing CEOs, based on the firm's proprietary data. The data here is derived from the firm's reports for June 27, 2002, and January 8, 2007.
3 "CEOs: Hello, You Must Be Going."
4 Boston: Harvard Business School Press, 2001, 2004, and 2007, respectively.
5 See Phil Rosenzweig, *The Halo Effect . . . and the Eight Other Business Delusions That Deceive Managers* (New York: Free Press, 2007).

CHAPTER 2: FIRST LAW: COSTS AND PRICES ALWAYS DECLINE

1 Winfred B. Hirschmann, "Profit from the Learning Curve," *Harvard Business Review*, January–February 1964, 125–126.
2 See appendix 2 for a discussion of the difference between the conventional slope of a curve and this definition of slope.
3 Experience prior to 1970 was calculated using real GDP growth rate (rather than production CAGR) without the two-thirds adjustment factor. This was done because of the extremely long history of production. The use of a precise growth rate also eliminated the need to use the two-thirds adjustment factor (see appendix 2).
4 Charles F. Knight with Davis Dyer, *Performance Without Compromise: How Emerson Consistently Achieves Winning Results* (Boston: Harvard Business School Press, 2005), 3. Knight's book provides detailed descriptions of how Emerson achieved its impressive results. For an earlier (and shorter) summary of the management process, see Charles F. Knight, "Emerson

Electric: Consistent Profits, Consistently," *Harvard Business Review*, January–February 1992.

5 Data taken from Knight, *Performance Without Compromise*, chapter 4, "Operational Excellence," 87–119.

6 Paul Calthrop, "Higher Net Price—Or Bust," *Harvard Business Review*, May 2007.

7 The price curve for a barrel of West Texas crude in the period 1946–2005 has a slope of 130 percent.

8 Radial tires accounted for a majority of tires sold in the United States in 1980. By 2000, virtually all tires sold in the U.S. market were radials.

9 This is the case in many parts of the health care industry: new technologies and treatments have been driving prices up, but they are providing benefits unavailable in the past. Health care, however, is also affected by a variety of other factors that mitigate the effects of the experience curve. For instance, hospitals may find that their attempts to cut costs are undermined by insurance-company and Medicare reimbursement practices (see "A Novel Plan Helps Hospital Wean Itself Off Pricey Tests," *Wall Street Journal*, January 12, 2007). And companies that produce patented lifesaving or life-enhancing drugs may find that they are not forced by competition to reduce costs or prices during the life of the patent. See appendix 2.

10 Retrieved from the Web site http://www.swapa.org/, accessed October 4, 2007.

11 For more information on capability sourcing, see Mark Gottfredson, Rudy Puryear, and Stephen Phillips, "Strategic Sourcing: From Periphery to the Core," *Harvard Business Review*, February 2005.

12 Bruce D. Henderson, "The Experience Curve Reviewed: History," in Carl W. Stern and Michael S. Deimler, eds., *The Boston Consulting Group on Strategy* (Hoboken, N.J.: John Wiley & Sons, 2006).

13 The minimill, which used scrap steel for its raw material and an electric-arc furnace for processing, was a classic disruptive innovation as described by Harvard Business School professor Clayton M. Christensen in his book *The Innovator's Dilemma* (Boston: Harvard Business School Press, 1997). Its initial products were of relatively low quality. They had only a limited market. But they were far less expensive than the products of the big integrated steel companies such as U.S. Steel.

CHAPTER 3: SECOND LAW: COMPETITIVE POSITION DETERMINES YOUR OPTIONS

1 See David Harding and Sam Rovit, *Mastering the Merger: Four Critical Decisions That Make or Break the Deal* (Boston: Harvard Business School Press, 2004), 3 and appendix.

2 ROI is defined in PIMS as profit before interest and taxes as a percentage of operating assets employed (working capital plus net property, plant, and equipment).

3 See Chris Zook with James Allen, *Profit from the Core* (Boston: Harvard Business School Press, 2001), 43.

4 This study was conducted by Bain teams under the direction of Mark Gottfredson.

5 Philip H. Dougherty, "AGB Would Play David to Nielsen Goliath," *New York Times*, March 16, 1988.

6 In 2005, AGB Group companies merged with Nielsen Media Research. The company mar-

kets its services outside the United States under the brand name AGB Nielsen Media Research.

7 Adrian J. Slywotzky with Karl Weber, *The Upside: The 7 Strategies for Turning Big Threats into Growth Breakthroughs* (New York: Crown Business, 2007), 105.

8 See Katie Hafner, "At Netflix, Victory for Voices over Keystrokes," *New York Times*, August 16, 2007.

9 In one study, we and our colleagues found that "winning" brands—brands that grow faster than their category each year—were 41 percent more likely than nonwinners to be innovators.

10 Slywotzky, *The Upside*, 187–188.

11 Darrell Rigby and Chris Zook, "Open-Market Innovation," *Harvard Business Review*, October 2002.

12 Louise Lee, "Dell: Color It Competitive," *BusinessWeek*, June 26, 2007.

13 Vijay Vishwanath and Jonathan Mark, "Your Brand's Best Strategy," *Harvard Business Review*, May–June 1997.

14 Department stores are an example. Premium stores such as Neiman-Marcus, Saks Fifth Avenue, and Nordstrom fall into one band, while traditional department stores such as Macy's, Dillard's, and JCPenney fall into another. Premium firms that are successful in creating a sustainable advantage often find that they can maintain higher margins because there is a significant segment of customers that prefers premium products and service.

15 We calculated the RMS of PlayStation for 1994 as follows: according to its Web site, Sony Computer Entertainment sold 300,000 units that year. The average price per unit, provided to us by the company, was 39,800 yen, or about $390. That works out to total sales of roughly $117 million. Nintendo sales for the same year were reported by a Barclays de Zoete Wedd Research report in March 1995 as $600 million. The ratio of Sony sales to Nintendo sales is 0.19.

16 Matt Richtel, "Nintendo's Wii, Radiating Fun, Is Eclipsing Sony Machine," *New York Times*, January 31, 2007.

17 David Welch, "Staying Paranoid at Toyota," *BusinessWeek*, July 2, 2007.

18 Carol Emert, "Little-known S.F. Firm Specializes in Complex Buyouts; 3 Partners Hunt Where Other Investment Firms Fear to Tread," *San Francisco Chronicle*, June 2, 2002.

CHAPTER 4: THIRD LAW: CUSTOMERS AND PROFIT POOLS DON'T STAND STILL

1 Orit Gadiesh and James L. Gilbert, "Profit Pools: A Fresh Look at Strategy," *Harvard Business Review*, May–June 1998.

2 "Profit Pools: A Fresh Look at Strategy."

3 Jim Carlton, "While Housing Withers, 'Green' Materials Bloom," *Wall Street Journal*, February 21, 2007.

4 In 1979, Hanes was acquired by Consolidated Foods Corp., which later changed its name to Sara Lee. Sara Lee then spun off Hanes as a separately traded public company in 2006. Hanes still makes L'eggs, although women don't wear pantyhose as frequently as they once did.

5 Southwest and other upstart airlines were largely responsible for driving airfares down

the experience curve. Between 1978 and 1996, the average change in real fares was as follows:

- −14.7 percent in routes not served by new entrants
- −30.5 percent in routes served by new entrants but not by Southwest Airlines
- −47.2 percent in routes served by Southwest Airlines but not by other new entrants
- −54.3 percent in routes served by both Southwest Airlines and other new entrants
- −32.2 percent in all routes.

See Steven A. Morrison and Clifford Winston, "Regulatory Reform of U.S. Intercity Transportation," in José A. Gómez-Ibáñez, William B. Tye, and Clifford Winston, eds., *Essays in Transportation Economics and Policy: A Handbook in Honor of John R. Meyer* (Washington, DC: Brookings Institution Press, 1999).

6 Data from annual reports to shareholders.

7 See David B. Yoffie and Michael Slind, "Apple Computer, 2006," Harvard Business School Case No. 9-706-496, April 12, 2006.

8 Slywotzky, *The Upside*, 168.

9 Amol Sharma, Nick Wingfield, and Li Yuan, "How Steve Jobs Played Hardball in iPhone Birth," *Wall Street Journal*, February 17, 2007.

10 Sarah Lacy, "How P&G Conquered Carpet," *BusinessWeek*, September 23, 2005.

11 See his books *The Loyalty Effect* (Boston: Harvard Business School Press, 2001) and *Loyalty Rules* (Boston: Harvard Business School Press, 2003).

12 If you're not familiar with the concept, we urge you to read Reichheld's latest book, *The Ultimate Question* (Boston: Harvard Business School Press, 2006).

13 On perceptual mapping, see Prof. Robert J. Dolan, "Perceptual Mapping: A Manager's Guide," Harvard Business School Case No. 9-590-121, July 5, 1990; on CHAID, see Darrell Rigby and Vijay Vishwanath, "Localization: the Revolution in Consumer Markets," *Harvard Business Review*, April 2006; on discrete choice, see Eric Almquist, Martin Kon, and Wolfgang Bock, "Economics' Gift to Marketing," *Mercer Management Journal* 15 (2003), available at http://www.marketingpower.com/content/economics%20gift%20to%20marketing%20final.pdf, accessed October 4, 2007.

14 Reichheld, *The Ultimate Question*, 163.

15 Diane Brady, "The Immelt Revolution," *BusinessWeek*, March 28, 2005.

16 Jeff Cares and Jim Miskel, "Take Your Third Move First," *Harvard Business Review*, March 2007.

17 See Mark Gottfredson, Rudy Puryear, and Stephen Phillips, "Strategic Sourcing: From Periphery to the Core," *Harvard Business Review*, February 2005.

18 Peter Cornelius, Alexander Van de Putte, and Mattia Romani, "Three Decades of Scenario Planning in Shell," *California Management Review*, Fall 2005, 93.

19 A full discussion of this technique is beyond the scope of this book. See, for example, Alexander B. van Putten and Ian C. MacMillan, "Making Real Options Really Work," *Harvard Business Review*, December 2004, and Tom Copeland and Peter Tufano, "A Real-World Way to Manage Real Options," *Harvard Business Review*, March 2004.

CHAPTER 5: FOURTH LAW: SIMPLICITY GETS RESULTS

1 James Knowles, *The Legends of King Arthur and His Knights*, Project Gutenberg eBook, http://www.gutenberg.org/etext/12753, accessed June 28, 2004.

2 George A. Miller, "The Magical Number Seven, Plus or Minus Two: Some Limits on Our Capacity for Processing Information," http://www.musanim.com/miller1956, accessed October 10, 2007.

3 See Nelson Cowan, "The Magical Number 4 in Short-Term Memory," *Behavioral and Brain Sciences* 24 (February 2001): 87–114. "The preponderance of evidence . . . suggests a mean memory capacity in adults of 3 to 5 chunks, whereas individual scores appear to range more widely from about 2 up to about 6 chunks."

4 See the Web site http://www.crest.com/products/toothpastes.jsp, accessed October 10, 2007.

5 For an extended discussion of the ramifications of choice, see Barry Schwartz, *The Paradox of Choice: Why More Is Less* (New York: Harper Perennial, 2005).

6 Chris Anderson, *The Long Tail: Why the Future of Business Is Selling Less of More* (New York: Hyperion, 2006).

7 Parts of this section appeared in different form in Mark Gottfredson and Keith Aspinall, "Innovation vs. Complexity: What Is Too Much of a Good Thing?" *Harvard Business Review*, November 2005.

8 Kathleen Eisenhardt and Donald Sull, "Strategy as Simple Rules," *Harvard Business Review*, January 2001.

9 This account draws heavily on Greg Brenneman, "Right Away and All at Once: How We Saved Continental," *Harvard Business Review*, September–October 1998.

10 Linda Tischler, "The Beauty of Simplicity," *Fast Company*, November 2005.

11 Deborah Ball, "Spoiling the Recipe: Flavor Experiment for KitKat Leaves Nestlé with a Bad Taste," *Wall Street Journal*, July 6, 2006.

12 Robert O. Work, "Naval Transformation and the Littoral Combat Ship" (Washington, DC: Center for Strategic and Budgetary Assessments, February 2004).

13 Paul Rogers and Marcia Blenko, "Who Has the D? How Clear Decision Roles Enhance Organizational Performance," *Harvard Business Review*, January 2006.

14 Jack Welch and Suzy Welch, "Ideas—The Welch Way: Lay Off the Layers; the More Layers in a Business, the More Spin, Meddling, and Worst of All, Delays," *BusinessWeek*, June 25, 2007.

15 Ricardo Arruda and Benjamin Ensor, "The March Toward Insurance Claims Automation," Forrester Research, February 8, 2007.

CHAPTER 6: WHERE YOU'RE STARTING FROM: DIAGNOSING YOUR POINT OF DEPARTURE

1 Harry Phillips, Williams de Broë, http://www.wdebroe.com/default.aspx, accessed on February 20, 2006.

2 See Mitt Romney with Timothy Robinson, *Turnaround: Crisis, Leadership, and the Olympic Games* (Washington, DC: Regnery, 2004), chapter 3.

3 *Turnaround*, 376–77.

4 Small hospitals were defined as having less than 100 beds, medium as 100 to 300 beds, and large as more than 300 beds. Small hospitals made up 48 percent of the market, medium 36 percent, and large 16 percent.

5 This is non-GAAP operating income, excluding amortization of intangibles, intellectual property research and development, and other one-time charges.

6 Mark Gottfredson, Rudy Puryear, and Stephen Phillips, "Strategic Sourcing: From the Periphery to the Core," *Harvard Business Review*, February 2005.

7 Rob Markey, John Ott, and Gerard du Toit, "Winning New Customers Using Loyalty-Based Segmentation," *Strategy & Leadership*, 35:3 (2007): 32–37.

8 *Turnaround*, 117–121.

9 Betsy Morris, "Charles Schwab's Big Challenge," *Fortune*, May 30, 2005.

10 See Paul Rogers and Marcia Blenko, "Who Has the D? How Clear Decision Roles Enhance Organizational Performance," *Harvard Business Review*, January 2006.

11 See Klaus Neuhaus and Peter Guarraia, "Want More from Lean Six Sigma?," *Harvard Management Update*, December 2004.

12 See David Shpilberg, Steve Berez, Rudy Puryear, and Sachin Shah, "Avoiding the Alignment Trap in Information Technology," *MIT Sloan Management Review*, Fall 2007.

CHAPTER 7: WHERE YOU'RE GOING: MAPPING YOUR POINT OF ARRIVAL AND MAKING A PLAN

1 See Steve Rotella, "Strategic Plan Execution," Presentation to Investor Day, September 6 and 7, 2006, http://media.corporate-ir.net/media_files/irol/10/101159/presentations/Rotella_090506.pdf.

2 See "Slide Presentation by Chief Operations Officer," Telstra Web site http://www.telstra.com.au/abouttelstra/investor/presentations.cfm.

3 See "Slide Presentation by GMD Telstra Business & Government," Telstra Web site http://www.telstra.com.au/abouttelstra/investor/presentations.cfm.

4 See "Outcome of Strategy Review, CEO Slides," Telstra Web site http://www.telstra.com.au/abouttelstra/investor/presentations.cfm.

5 See "Slide Presentation by GMD Telstra Business & Government."

6 See "Slide Presentation by Chief Operations Officer."

CHAPTER 8: THE ROAD TO RESULTS

1 See Robert W. Rogers, Richard S. Wellins, and Daryl R. Conner, "The Power of Realization," a white paper by Development Dimensions International, Inc.; http://www.ddiworld.com/pdf/ddi_realization_whitepaper.pdf, accessed October 12, 2007.

2 *Taking Stock*, survey by the Change Management Toolbook, February 2005, http://www.change-management-toolbook.com/res/Reports.html, accessed October 12, 2007.

3 "Carter's and OshKosh: The Changing Landscape of Branding and the Business of Design," *Leaders Magazine*, April–May–June 2006.

4 In the thirty-five years between 1969 and 2006, the returns for the bottom quartile of U.S. buyout funds were all negative. So we are not saying that private equity by itself ensures high returns. But the top performers' record has been remarkable. In that same thirty-five-year time period, top-quartile funds enjoyed internal rates of return of 36 percent, with some earning triple digits. By comparison, the top-quartile companies that were part of the S&P 500 as of year-end 2006 generated annual shareholder returns of 28 percent on average, from the time they went public. See Orit Gadiesh and Hugh MacArthur, *Memo to the CEO: Lessons from Private Equity Any Company Can Use* (Boston: Harvard Business School Press, 2008).

5 For more on these deals, see Chris Bierly, Chul-Joon Park and Graham Elton, "Private Equity's Road Map to Profits," Bain & Company, November 2006.

6 For a full discourse on the private-equity approach, see Orit Gadiesh and Hugh MacArthur, *Memo to the CEO.*

7 See Stan Pace, Paul Rogers, and Chris Harrop, "Making Change Stick," Bain & Company, 2002.

8 Jack Welch and Suzy Welch, "Ideas—The Welch Way: Keeping Your People Pumped; Beyond the Obvious Incentives: Four Smart Ways to Light a Fire," *BusinessWeek*, March 27, 2006.

9 "Making Change Stick."

10 See Dianne Ledingham, Mark Kovac, and Heidi Locke Simon, "The New Science of Sales Force Productivity," *Harvard Business Review*, September 2006.

11 David N. Farr, "Epilogue," in Charles F. Knight with Davis Dyer, *Performance Without Compromise: How Emerson Consistently Achieves Winning Results* (Boston: Harvard Business School Press, 2005), 221–226.

12 Chris Zook, *Beyond the Core: Expand Your Market Without Abandoning Your Roots* (Boston: Harvard Business School Press, 2004), 136.

13 The 2006 figures are from the annual report; the 1992 figures are from HR Hambrecht's research report on Carter's (September 7, 2006).

14 Chuck Lucier, Steven Wheeler, and Rolf Habbel, "The Era of the Inclusive Leader," *Strategy + Business*, Summer 2007.

15 Kenneth W. Freeman, "The CEO's Real Legacy," *Harvard Business Review*, November 2004.

16 Ram Charan, "Ending the CEO Succession Crisis," *Harvard Business Review*, February 2005.

17 Melvin Sorcher and James Brant, "Are You Picking the Right Leaders?" *Harvard Business Review*, February 2002.

18 "Ending the CEO Succession Crisis."

19 Citigroup analyst Bonnie Herzog, quoted in "CBC—If You Ask Me . . . PepsiCo Succession," Chris Brook-Carter, http://www.just-drinks.com/article.aspx?id=87628, accessed September 4, 2006.

APPENDIX 1: RESEARCH METHODOLOGY

1 Data on total CEO departures in 2006 comes from the Challenger, Gray & Christmas report, "CEO Departures Surge 22% in April," May 7, 2007. The full dataset of departed CEO names is not publicly available and was provided to us by Challenger, Gray & Christmas specifically for the purposes of this research.

2 "CEO Turnover Remains High at World's Largest Companies, Booz Allen Study Finds," http://www.boozallen.com/publications/article/36608085, accessed May 22, 2007.

APPENDIX 2: EXPERIENCE CURVES

1 Richard E. Caves, Michael D. Whinston, and Mark A. Hurwitz, "Patent Expiration, Entry, and Competition in the U.S. Pharmaceutical Industry," *Brookings Papers on Economic Activity, Microeconomics*, 1991, 1–66.

Index